The Trials, Crucifixion, and Burial of Jesus of Nazareth

CRUCIFIXION:
A Multidisciplinary Investigation of the Death of Jesus of Nazareth

Many fine books on the subject of crucifixion are available today, but no in-depth, multi-volume investigation of Roman crucifixion and Jesus' death has been available, until now. CRUCIFIXION: A Multi-disciplinary Examination of the Crucifixion of Jesus of Nazareth consists of seven volumes, each dedicated to an integral subject related to Jesus' crucifixion. The Day Jesus Died identifies the year, date, day, and hour of Jesus' death. And there's From the Upper Room to Joseph's Tomb which examines each location on Jesus' journey to Calvary. Other titles include: Probing the Trials, Crucifixion, and Burial of Jesus of Nazareth, What Jesus' Crucifixion Accomplished for Us; Roman Crucifixion and the Death of Jesus, Watching Jesus Die, and Take Up the Cross. With the CRUCIFIXION series, every aspect of Roman crucifixion and the cross is explored with specific reference to the crucifixion of Jesus. The scholar will appreciate each book's depth of research, often reflected in each chapter's extensive endnotes. The nonprofessional reader will enjoy the thoughtful and readable style of each book in the series. Every reader will quickly find value in each volume of this seven-book series.

The Trials, Crucifixion, and Burial of Jesus of Nazareth

Grasping the Impact of Every Event the Day Jesus Died

WOODROW MICHAEL KROLL

Foreword by Edwin M. Yamauchi

RESOURCE *Publications* • Eugene, Oregon

THE TRIALS, CRUCIFIXION, AND BURIAL OF JESUS OF NAZARETH
Grasping the Impact of Every Event the Day Jesus Died

Copyright © 2024 Woodrow Michael Kroll. All rights reserved. Except for brief quotations in critical publications or reviews, no part of this book may be reproduced in any manner without prior written permission from the publisher. Write: Permissions, Wipf and Stock Publishers, 199 W. 8th Ave., Suite 3, Eugene, OR 97401.

Resource Publications
An Imprint of Wipf and Stock Publishers
199 W. 8th Ave., Suite 3
Eugene, OR 97401

www.wipfandstock.com

PAPERBACK ISBN: 979-8-3852-1504-1
HARDCOVER ISBN: 979-8-3852-1505-8
EBOOK ISBN: 979-8-3852-1506-5

VERSION NUMBER 03/11/25

Remember Him; Identify with Him; Die with Him

For you, O God, have tested us;
   you have tried us as silver is tried.
You brought us into the net;
   you laid a crushing burden on our backs;
you let men ride over our heads;
   we went through fire and through water;
yet you have brought us out to a place of abundance.

(Psalm 66:10–12)

Blessed are those who are persecuted for righteousness' sake, for theirs is the kingdom of heaven. Blessed are you when others revile you and persecute you and utter all kinds of evil against you falsely on my account. Rejoice and be glad, for your reward is great in heaven, for so they persecuted the prophets before you.

(Matthew 5:10–12)

He was despised and rejected by men,
    a man of sorrows and acquainted with grief;
and as one from whom men hide their faces
    he was despised, and we esteemed him not.

Surely he has borne our griefs
    and carried our sorrows;
yet we esteemed him stricken,
    smitten by God, and afflicted.

But he was pierced for our transgressions;
    he was crushed for our iniquities;
upon him was the chastisement that brought us peace,
    and with his wounds we are healed.
He was oppressed, and he was afflicted,
    yet he opened not his mouth;
like a lamb that is led to the slaughter,
    and like a sheep that before its shearers is silent,
    so he opened not his mouth.
Yet it was the will of the Lord to crush him;
    he has put him to grief;
when his soul makes an offering for guilt,
    he shall see his offspring; he shall prolong his days;
the will of the Lord shall prosper in his hand.

(ISAIAH 53:3–7, 10)

Contents

Foreword by Edwin M. Yamauchi	ix
Preface	xi
Acknowledgements	xv
List of Abbreviations	xvii
List of Tables	xxi
Introduction	xxiii
Chapter 1 Jesus' Trial Before Annas and Caiaphas	1
Chapter 2 The Constantly Changing Charges Against Jesus	18
Chapter 3 Jesus' Trial Before Pilate	33
Chapter 4 Was the Trial of Jesus Legal?	58
Chapter 5 The Essentials of Jesus' Crucifixion	93
Chapter 6 The Location of Jesus' Crucifixion	107
Chapter 7 Did Jesus Really Die on the Cross?	131
Chapter 8 The Burial of Jesus	163
Chapter 9 The Location of Jesus' Tomb	185
Chapter 10 An Inventory of Jesus' Suffering Between Gethsemane and Golgotha	237
Epilogue	250
Endnotes	253
Bibliography	265
Author/Person Index	271
Subject Index	275

Foreword

THE TRIALS, CRUCIFIXION, DEATH, and burial of Jesus form a large portion of the four Gospels (Matthew, Mark, Luke, and John). These events are the bedrock of the history of early Christianity. But many details in these narratives have been questioned by ancient pagan critics such as Celsus and Porphyry and by skeptical scholars since the Age of the Enlightenment (eighteenth century) and the rise of historical New Testament criticism.

How can differences between the four Gospels be reconciled? What non-biblical textual evidence can be cited in support of the New Testament? What archaeological finds buttress the biblical texts? How do we reconcile the New Testament accounts of the trials with the Jewish legal tradition found in the Mishnah and the Talmud? Is there not a contradiction between the portrait of a vacillating Pilate and the implacable enemy of the Jews portrayed in Jewish sources such as Philo and Josephus?

Where was Jesus tried before Pilate? Was it at the Fortress Antonia marked by the so-called "Ecce Homo" arch which begins the Via Dolorosa? Or was it at Herod's palace near the Citadel of Jerusalem? Where was Jesus crucified? Was it at Gordon's Calvary near the former Arab bus station or at the traditional site of the Holy Sepulchre? Where was Jesus buried? Was it in the Garden Tomb favored by Protestants or in the Holy Sepulchre favored by Catholics? What about other alternative sites for these events suggested by idiosyncratic scholars? What about the Muslim contention that Jesus did not die by crucifixion but another took his place?

Woodrow Kroll offers a comprehensive survey of these and many other details, examining many Roman, Jewish, and Christian texts and surveying archaeological and epigraphic evidence to support the historicity of the accounts in the Gospels and to reconcile alleged discrepancies. Kroll also examines the supernatural events that accompanied the crucifixion and goes into the excruciating details provided by medical studies of what may have been the physical cause of the death of Jesus. He answers with clarity what he considers to be the place of the trial of Jesus and the place of his burial.

He does this in a highly readable account, which is furnished with illuminating tabular lists and apposite quotations. His extensive bibliography indicates that he has surveyed a wide range of scholarship including studies by many Evangelical, Jewish, and Catholic scholars, as well as by liberal Protestant scholars.

As one who has also researched and written on these topics, I learned much from his excellent exposition. I can highly commend his book to all who have an interest in these vital subjects.

Edwin M. Yamauchi
Professor of History Emeritus
Miami University
Oxford, Ohio

Preface

WITHOUT A DOUBT, THE crucifixion of Jesus of Nazareth is the most famous, most talked about, most significant crucifixion in the history of humankind. That crucifixion was preceded by two trials, one Jewish and the other Roman. It was followed by a hurried burial in a borrowed tomb. The crucifixion, bookended by trials and burial, takes center stage. Those bookending events, however, contain much more than minor historical details. They are essential for Jesus' end-of-life narrative.

The Sanhedrin trial by Annas and Caiaphas, and the Roman trial by Pilate, were courtroom tragedies preparatory to Jesus' death. And the activities of Joseph of Arimathea and Nicodemus were preparatory to his resurrection. Probing these events and the people who figure in them aids us in better understanding the crucifixion itself.

Not only will we investigate the Jewish trial procedures and outcomes, but we will also focus on the irregularities of that three-stage trial. We will take note of the constantly changing charges against Jesus in the futile search for a charge that would stick. The question of legality will be explored as well.

This book will examine why Pilate was so hesitant to find Jesus guilty. Also, the much-debated issues of where Jesus' crucifixion took place, as well as the location of his tomb, will be investigated. Those questions deserve an entire volume by themselves. The book will conclude with a comprehensive inventory of Jesus' suffering from the beginning to the end of this Good Friday, the day the world turned dark.

As you read this book or any of my works, you will quickly notice that I appeal often to the four Gospels for accurate historical information. I believe these writings are the earliest, most accurate, and best documents we have to inform us of the life and times of Jesus of Nazareth. I accept the Bible at face value, and while I incorporate the valuable insights and research of other scholars into my own, I also come to common sense conclusions that are often not evident in much of modern liberal scholarship. As the final authority, I appeal to those "men [who] spoke from God as they were carried along by the Holy Spirit" (2 Pet 1:21).

> "The death of the Incarnate Son of God on a Roman cross . . . marks the central point in the history of mankind."
> —F. W. Mattox

Some decades ago many scholars adopted the designations of B.C.E. and C.E. to indicate dates on the calendar. I completely understand why this change was made. The B.C.E. and C.E. designations are more inclusive because they do not specifically relate to Christianity. However, most of the Western world is steeped in the use of BC and AD; even many highly influential scholars have chosen to retain these designations.[1] However, I use BC and AD for a different reason.

Greek scholar Vincent Taylor noted:

> We are bound to consider how we think of time, whether past events are only isolated points in a series, or whether God invades history with abiding consequences. This issue seriously engages the attention of theologians today. It is best considered by reflecting upon (1) events as points in the time-series; (2) events with permanent significance; and (3) events as divine invasions in time."[2]

I do not believe the advent of God's Son was a mere point-in-time series. I see the birth of the Messiah and Savior as an invasion of time by God himself. Thus, despite scholarly arguments to the contrary, I will use the designations BC and AD to reflect that incredible moment when God changed the world forever by invading time, not simply indicating a time-share for multiple religious communities.

Now some technical information. The Scripture references in this book are from the English Standard Version (ESV) of the Bible unless otherwise noted. The ESV is based on the Greek text in the 2014 editions of the Greek New Testament (5th corrected edition), published by the United Bible Societies (UBS), and *Novum Testamentum Graece* (28th edition, 2012), edited by Nestle and Aland. The Hebrew words in the text are from the Masoretic text of the Hebrew Bible, as found in *Biblia Hebraica Stuttgartensia* (2nd edition, 1983). Words in Greek are taken from the 1993 editions of the Greek New Testament (4ᵗʰ corrected edition) and *Novum Testamentum Graece* (27ᵗʰ ed).

Since multiple words in the Greek language may be used for the same word in English, wherever I have highlighted a Greek word, and there is more than one Scripture associated with it, I have always used the Greek of the first Scripture listed, as found in the 28ᵗʰ revised edition of the Nestle-Aland Novum Testamentum Graece.

> Upon the cross of Jesus
> my eye at times can see,
> the very dying form of One
> who suffered there for me:
> And from my stricken heart with tears,
> two wonders I confess,
> the wonders of redeeming love
> and my unworthiness!
> —Elizabeth Clephane

I have written with both the head and the heart in mind. Readers should be informed and enlightened in matters related to Jesus' crucifixion, but also have their hearts stirred by the magnificent love God displayed in sending his Son to die in our place. Our hearts should be softened to a Savior who would die for us, and I pray this will be true of you as you read the pages that follow.

WOODROW MICHAEL KROLL
Ashland, Nebraska

ENDNOTES

1. Witherington, Ben. "Biblical Views: The Turn of the Christian Era: The Tale of Dionysius Exiguus," *BAR* 43.6 (2017): 26.
2. Taylor, *The Cross*.

Acknowledgements

ACCORDING TO THE DICTIONARY, an acknowledgement is a "recognition or favorable notice of an act or achievement; the act of acknowledging something or someone." At this point in the near front of a book, is the place to recognize those individuals who have contributed to the creation of what you are about to read.

Publishing a book is a process. It begins in the mind of the author and ends in the mind of you, the reader. Along the way, however, many people are involved. Here are some of those people who deserve special recognition.

First, because he is infinitely worthy, I must acknowledge Jesus of Nazareth. After all, without him, *The Trials, Crucifixion, and Burial of Jesus of Nazareth* would have no historical foundation. Without him, there would be no trials before Caiaphas, the Sanhedrin, or Pilate worthy of our notice. Without him, there would be no crucifixion that still is impacting us today. Without him, there would be no Savior of the world. Thank you, Jesus, for all you've done.

Then, I want to acknowledge the silent contribution of my wife, Linda. She gave up a great deal of time with her husband so that I could research and write seven books in a series on crucifixion. This is book three, but there are more to come. Thank you, dear, for all you've done without.

Also, acknowledgement is due Tina Work, my faithful "sidekick," tech manager, project handler, and so much more. Tina is responsible for guiding me through the editorial process and keeping me from beating my computer with a hammer on occasion. Thank you, Tina, for all you've done.

As mentioned, publishing a book is a process and when the writing and editing are complete, the process is not. Someone must have the technology, the staff, and the desire to put into print—either electronically or on paper—what the author has written. For that, I acknowledge Managing Editor Matt Wimer and his leadership team at Wipf & Stock Publishers.

Emily Callihan, Assistant Managing Editor, George Callihan, Editorial Administrative Assistant, the Typesetter, and others, thank you, guys, for all you've done.

And I acknowledge you. Without you, there would be no one for me to share my heart and mind with. Without you, there is no one to read what I have written. So, thank you for reading this book.

I acknowledge you all and thank you all. Now, let's get this thing read.

List of Abbreviations

BIBLE TRANSLATION ABBREVIATIONS

CEV	Contemporary English Version
CSB	Christian Standard Bible
ESV	English Standard Version
GNT	Good News Translation
HCSB	Holman Christian Standard Bible
JBP	J. B. Phillips
KJV	King James Version
TLB	The Living Bible
NAR	New Bible translation for Native American readers
NASB	New American Standard Bible
NCB	New Catholic Bible
NIV	New International Version
NKJV	New King James Version
NLT	New Living Bible
NRSV	New Revised Standard Version
RSV	Revised Standard Version

SCHOLASTIC ABBREVIATIONS

AASOR	Annual of American Schools of Oriental Research
AHJ	American Heart Journal
AJA	American Journal of Archaeology
Ant.	Flavius Josephus, Antiquities of the Jews
BA	Biblical Archaeologist
BAR	Biblical Archaeology Review
BKBC	The Bible Knowledge Background Commentary
BibSac	Bibliotheca Sacra
BW	Biblical World
CBQ	Catholic Biblical Quarterly
CE	Catholic Encyclopedia
CT	Christianity Today
DSS	The Dead Sea Scrolls
EBib	Études Bibliques
EBL	Encyclopedia of Biblical Literature
EQ	Evangelical Quarterly
ExpTim	Expository Times
GosPet	Gospel of Peter
HSNTA	Hennecke and Schneemelcher, New Testament Apocrypha
HTR	Harvard Theological Review
HUCA	Hebrew Union College Annual
IEJ	Israel Exploration Journal
ISBE	International Standard Bible Encyclopedia
JBL	Journal of Biblical Literature
JETS	Journal of the Evangelical Theological Society
JRS	Journal of Roman Studies
JQR	Jewish Quarterly Review
JTS	Journal of Theological Studies
LXX	The Septuagint

NBD	New Bible Dictionary
NTS	New Testament Studies
NTG	Novum Testamentum Graece
OTP	The Old Testament Pseudepigrapha
PEQ	Palestine Exploration Quarterly
RevArch	Revue Archéologique
RB	Revue Biblique
RevQum	Revue de Qumran
SBLSP	Society of Biblical Literature Seminar Papers
SWJT	Southwestern Journal of Theology
TDNT	Theological Dictionary of the New Testament
VT	Vetus Testamentum
War	Flavius Josephus, Wars of the Jews
ZNW	Zeitschrift für die Neutestamentliche Wissenschaft

List of Tables

Seven Indications Jesus' Trial Was Hurried

Tearing One's Clothes in the Bible

The Events Beginning with Jesus' Arrest in Gethsemane to Caiaphas' Courtroom

The Contrasts Between Jerusalem and Rome

Accusations Made Against Jesus

Jesus is called the "Son of God"

Jesus: The King of the Jews

The Praetorium in Modern Translations

What the Roman Soldiers Did to Jesus

The Johannine Presentation of Jesus as the "I AM" God

Jesus' Encounters with Jerusalem's Religious Leaders

The Location of Jesus' Trial and Conviction

The History of Jerusalem's Walls

The Use of the Greek mégas in the New Testament

A Snapshot of Jesus' Suffering in Gethsemane

A Snapshot of Jesus' Suffering at the High Priest's Palace

A Snapshot of Jesus' Suffering at Pilate's Praetorium

A Snapshot of Jesus' Suffering at Golgotha

Parallels Between Jesus' Temptations at the Beginning and End of His Earthly Ministry

Introduction

The scope of inquiry into Jesus' trials, crucifixion, and burial began with Jesus' arrest and being schlepped directly to the residence of Annas. Here a charade began that defies all logic.

WITHOUT A DOUBT, THE crucifixion of Jesus of Nazareth is the most famous, most significant crucifixion in the history of humankind. That crucifixion was preceded by two trials, one Jewish and the other Roman. It was followed by a hurried burial in a borrowed tomb. The crucifixion itself, being bookended by trials and burial, takes center stage. Those bookending events, however, contain much more than minor historical details. They are essential for Jesus' end-of-life narrative.

The Sanhedrin trial by Annas and Caiaphas, and the Roman trial by Pilate, were courtroom tragedies preparatory to Jesus' death. And the activities of Joseph of Arimathea and Nicodemus were preparatory to his resurrection. Probing these events and the people who figure in them aids us in better understanding the crucifixion itself.

Not only will we investigate the Jewish trial procedures and outcomes, but we will focus on the irregularities of that three-stage trial. We'll take note of the constantly changing charges against Jesus in the futile search for a charge that might stick. The question of legality will be explored as well.

This book will explore why Pilate was so hesitant to find Jesus guilty. Also, the much-debated issues of where Jesus' crucifixion took place, as well as the location of his tomb, will be investigated. Those questions deserve an entire volume by themselves. The book will conclude with a comprehensive inventory of Jesus' suffering from the beginning to the end of this Good Friday, the day the world turned dark.

In one sense, the book's scope is exceptionally limited—from Jesus' arrest in the Garden of Gethsemane to his burial in Joseph's tomb. This was less than twenty hours, less than one day, about the same time it would take you to drive from Boston to Tampa, or London to Rome, using only superhighways. It all happened so quickly for something with such eternal consequences.

Beginning with Jesus' arrest and being schlepped directly to the residence of Annas, a charade began to take place that defies all logic. Annas was no longer the High Priest, having been deposed by Valerius Gratus, the Roman prefect in Judea from 15 to 26 AD, just before Pontius Pilate (*Ant.* 18.2.2). Annas was perhaps one of the most corrupt religious leaders in Jewish history. Josephus comments: "This man, Annas, by bribing the Roman governor, had obtained the dignity of the High Priest in the sixth year after the birth of Christ" (*Ant.* 1.20.9 notes 1, 2).

Annas' role was that of an investigator questioning Jesus at a preliminary hearing to the trial conducted by Caiaphas and the Sanhedrin. But make no mistake, it was in this inquisition by Annas the charges that might stick in the Sanhedrin trial were determined.

Caiaphas was not the son of Annas but rather a son-in-law. Even the lack of bloodline, however, couldn't keep these two birds from the same nest. Caiaphas was cunning and a man who sought power his entire life. He was cunning enough, however, not to cross his father-in-law, but to allow him significant influence in how the business of the priesthood was run.

Because Annas and Caiaphas were the Jewish leads in this tragedy, we'll begin by probing their lives and roles in crucifying the Lord of Glory. We want to discover why they took such an interest in Jesus, why they hated him so, and why they were hellbent on having him crucified.

Of the many irregularities of Jesus' Jewish trial, one that clearly stands out is how frequently the charges against Jesus changed. With each new role of the dice, a new charge was invented when these religious leaders recognized the previous one would not be sufficient for a Jewish trial, let alone a Roman one. We should question the validity of any trial where the charges against the plaintiff change so frequently during the trial.

Chapter 4 is dedicated to unpacking the irregularities in the Sanhedrin trial and assessing their impact on the trial of Jesus. When the Jews sent Jesus to Pilate for quick sentencing, they must have been shocked when Pilate decided to question Jesus himself rather than rubber-stamp the Sanhedrin's decision. Shock soon gave way to fear. What if Pilate found no fault in Jesus? What then? The religious leaders had a quick meeting of the minds about how to force Pilate into siding with them.

The Roman trial followed Roman jurisprudence and practice much more closely than the Jewish trial followed their courtroom protocols. Of course, it was much easier to go by the book when the Roman judicial system made the Prefect Pilate a one-man prosecutor/defense attorney/judge/jury. Still, Pilate attempted to be fair, to give Jesus a chance to respond to the charges against him. Ultimately, he wanted nothing to do with Jesus. In washing his hands, the prefect was saying to the Jewish religious leaders: "You want to kill this man so badly, you kill him. Do with him as you wish. I want no part in your injustice."

The crucifixion of the Nazarene gives rise to several very difficult questions. Two of those questions are addressed in chapters 5 and 8. The location of Jesus' crucifixion has been debated ever since 1883 when British General Charles Gordon identified a site he thought resembled Golgotha's hill.

Since the first days of the early church, the location of the Church of the Holy Sepulchre has been identified as the place where Jesus died. Pilgrims to the Holy Land need to know which of the two sites has the best evidence and should be visited on their pilgrimage. Thus, we will probe the evidence for both sites along with the difficulties each encounters in proving its case for validity.

Closely associated with that question is another. Where is the location of Jesus' tomb? There are several contenders and in the pages that follow we will investigate each, with special emphasis on the two major sites vying for this honor—the Church of the Holy Sepulchre and the Garden Tomb. Does proof for one eliminate proof for the other? And this question. Is it necessary for us to choose?

A third question that has kept the Internet buzzing is did Jesus actually die on the cross or did he somehow survive this horror? The four Gospel narratives plainly say Jesus died at about 3:00 pm on that dark Friday afternoon. But those who dismiss the Gospel accounts as myth have devised all kinds of crazy theories about what happened to Jesus' body. Was he placed alive in the tomb, dazed, and swooning near death, only to be refreshed and revived in the cool, dark tomb, so his disciples could sneak him out and claim Jesus had come back to life? We must examine these theories and present the facts that illuminate their absurdity.

Finally, the book closes with a comprehensive inventory of Jesus' suffering. As human beings, we cannot possibly fathom the suffering Jesus endured during those twenty hours. But there is good evidence that most people, even followers of Jesus, have not even tried to understand it. Chapter 9 will trace the physical, psychological, and spiritual suffering Jesus endured in a way that should cause us to tremble until we have a greater understanding of the price Jesus' paid to redeem us from our sins.

Prepare your mind to read what follows by absorbing the words of the Old Testament prophet Isaiah. Speaking prophetically of Jesus' suffering and death, with tears Isaiah wrote:

> He was despised and rejected by men,
> a man of sorrows and acquainted with grief;
> Surely he has borne our griefs
> and carried our sorrows;
> But he was pierced for our transgressions;
> he was crushed for our iniquities;
> He was oppressed, and he was afflicted,
> like a lamb that is led to the slaughter,
> so he opened not his mouth.
> Yet it was the will of the Lord to crush him;
> because he poured out his soul to death
> yet he bore the sin of many,
> and makes intercession for the transgressors.
> —Isaiah 53:3–12

Let these words pierce your conscience and burrow deeply into your heart as you probe the trials, crucifixion, death, and burial of Jesus of Nazareth, "who for the joy that was set before him endured the cross, despising the shame."

Chapter 1

Jesus' Trial Before Annas and Caiaphas

It was now almost midnight. The day of Preparation for the Passover would begin shortly. While Annas was interrogating Jesus, Caiaphas was busy rounding up as many of the Sanhedrin as he could for a hurried trial.

YOU COULD ARGUE THE suffering of Jesus related to his crucifixion and death began long before Passover Week. He announced his pending death to his disciples on multiple occasions (cf. Matt 16:21; 17:22–23; 20:17–19; 26:1; Mark 8:31; 9:30–31; 10:33–34; Luke 9:21–22; 18:31–34). They never fully grasped the meaning of his words.

In the Garden of Gethsemane, his humanity struggled with the will of the Father that sent him to the cross. Nevertheless, Jesus committed himself to obey the divine plan for our salvation. His pores secreted sweat mingled with blood because of his agony and the stress of wrestling with the thought of being crucified. Jesus was manhandled in the Garden and shuffled through the night to the palace of the High Priest. All of this occurred before any trial began.

The real suffering began with his Jewish trials and ended with his Roman death. Jesus' inquisition before Annas and the trial conducted by his son-in-law Caiaphas was anything but typical. In fact, almost everything about it was atypical.

It began with a preliminary interrogation by Annas around 11:00 pm, just before the day of Preparation for the Passover was about to begin. While the High Priest Caiaphas was the head of the Sanhedrin that would decide Jesus' guilt or innocence, Jesus was first sent to Annas for interrogation. The trial itself lacked many of the features of standard Jewish judiciary procedure.

In this chapter, we concentrate only on the elements that exemplify Jesus' trial before Annas and Caiaphas. We begin with a "bird's eye" view of the proceedings that night.

A HURRIED AND UNCOORDINATED TRIAL

The Gospel accounts give us the impression that the events leading to Jesus' crucifixion were hurried and lacked coordination. The Jewish leaders had planned to kill Jesus for some time (John 5; 7:1–2). Matthew 26:3–5 informs us that just days before the Passover, "The chief priests and the elders of the people gathered in the palace of the high priest, whose name was Caiaphas, and plotted together to arrest Jesus by stealth and kill him. But they said, 'Not during the feast, lest there be an uproar among the people'" (see Mark 14:1–2; Luke 22:1–2). John 11:47–48 also notes, "So the chief priests and the Pharisees gathered the council and said, 'What are we to do? For this man performs many signs. If we let him go on like this, everyone will believe in him, and the Romans will come and take away both our place and our nation.'"

While these religious leaders believed Jesus was a phony and a dangerous false messiah, they had to tolerate him because he was so popular with many Galileans. However, now things had gotten serious. The Galilean crowds had come to Jerusalem for Passover. They sang Jesus' praises as he entered the Holy City. Things had gotten out of hand.

The popularity of Jesus now clearly worried Jerusalem's religious elite. It was at this point Caiaphas uttered his famous statement about it being better for one man to die for the people than for the whole nation to perish (John 11:49–50). "So from that day on, they made plans to put him to death" (v. 53). The hatred for Jesus was tangible. The threat to his life was genuine. The commitment to kill Jesus was absolute. These religious leaders needed only a plan and a suitable opportunity. The fact they ruled out killing Jesus during the Passover but did so nonetheless indicates how hurried and uncoordinated the crucifixion was.

One of the more forceful and popular objections to the veracity of the Gospel accounts of Jesus' crucifixion is that it occurred through the morning hours of the day of Preparation for the annual Passover. Surely the religious authorities could have waited a few more days, waited until the pilgrims left Jerusalem. It does not seem logical. But then again, almost nothing about Jesus' trial before Caiaphas seems reasonable or logical.

Table 1: Seven Indications Jesus' Trial Was Hurried

Indicator	Scripture
Judas surprised the chief priests as a betrayer of Jesus	Matt 26:14–16; Mark 14:10–11; Luke 22:3–6
The way Judas was revealed as Jesus' betrayer	Matt 26:20–25; Mark. 14:17–20; Luke 22:22–23; John 13:21–28
Jesus was seized at night in a peaceful garden	Matt 26:47–50; Mark 14:44–46; Luke 22:47–48; John 18:4–6
Jesus was not arrested in the Temple or a public place	Matt 26:55; Mark 14:48–49; Luke 22:52–53; John 18:19–21
Only a few Sanhedrin members were present at the night trial	Matt 26:57; Mark 14:53
No witnesses were previously secured for the trial	Matt 26:59–60; Mark 14:55–56
Caiaphas was forced to wait until morning to convict Jesus	Matt 27:1; Mark 15:1; Luke 22:66

So why did they proceed to kill Jesus within hours of the most treasured celebration of the Jewish calendar? The Bible does not provide any details regarding the thinking of these Jewish religious leaders and scholarly opinion varies widely. Could it be that all of Jerusalem was abuzz about the tumultuous entrance of Jesus into Jerusalem just days earlier? Could it be that everyone was talking about how Jesus dared to disrupt the merchants and money changers in the Temple area? Everyone knew this disturbed the enormous income stream flowing into the Temple coffers and ultimately lined the pockets of Annas and Caiaphas. Within the first eighteen hours after Jesus was arrested, he faced both the judicial system of the Jews and the Romans. Each trial appears to have transpired in three separate segments.

The Roman trial consisted of a preliminary examination by Pilate, another hollow examination by Herod Antipas, and a final more serious examination again by Pilate. Similarly, the Jewish trial consisted of a preliminary examination by Annas, a night-time tribunal at the house of Caiaphas, and a morning gathering of the full Sanhedrin at the Chamber of Hewn Stone to ratify the night-time verdict.

Nothing about the hurried crucifixion of the Savior was a surprise to God. On multiple occasions, Jesus announced that he would go to Jerusalem and there be killed. He even gave details that only a true prophet of God would know. Read Mark 10:32–34 and Luke 18:33. While Jesus' trials before Caiaphas, and subsequently before Pilate, appear to be rushed affairs, clearly the religious leaders of Jerusalem wanted it that way.

JESUS' LATE-NIGHT INTERROGATION BY ANNAS

"So the band of soldiers and their captain and the officers of the Jews arrested Jesus and bound him. First, they led him to Annas, for he was the father-in-law of Caiaphas, who was high priest that year" (John 18:12–13). "It is not for allegorical reasons that John makes a distinction between Annas and Caiaphas, but because he has actual historical reminiscences at his disposal; this is the way things must have happened."[1]

The separation between the interrogation of Annas and the late-night tribunal of Caiaphas is evident in the Gospels. Table 2 presents the different events that transpired late on that Thursday evening and into Friday morning. Take note of the distinction between the events that occurred at the house of Annas and those at the house of Caiaphas.

"The interrogation by Annas was not a Sanhedrin trial. Indeed, John calls attention twice (18:21, 23) to the fact there were no witnesses, an essential in a Sanhedrin trial."[2] Some scholars insist, "None of the appearances before the Sanhedrin were necessarily formal trials, but rather they were preliminary questionings to establish the feasibility of bringing Jesus to trial and obtaining a conviction."[3] This may not hold for the trial by Caiaphas, but it was undoubtedly true for his appearance before Annas.

Annas's inquiry was not a Jewish trial; it was more of a hearing to establish the facts, gather evidence against Jesus, and determine how best to advise the High Priest and council to proceed. The interrogation by Annas was to elicit the facts that led to the arrest of Jesus of Nazareth. The arrest came first; checking the facts to legitimize the arrest followed. Was this justice? Annas wanted to know about Jesus' teaching. What had he said about the Law? He also wanted to know about Jesus' disciples. Why were they followers of his? Undoubtedly Annas questioned Jesus on his claim to messiahship. How dare he make such a claim. What evidence could he produce to corroborate this claim? Unlike a formal trial, the session with Annas was more of a hearing.

Jesus suggested that instead of him answering questions, for which the answers were already evident, Annas should have just called witnesses who heard Jesus teaching in the Temple. One of those present interpreted this as insolence and struck Jesus in his face. "For a Jew, it is a shattering insult. It is a violation, and it is cowardly. Strike a bound man? Again, it signals what is coming. This is the first of many blows Jesus will receive, and not one of them will be justified under the law."[4]

When Jesus pressed Annas to question the many who had heard him speak publicly, he was emphasizing a crucial legal point. Under Jewish law, a man was considered innocent, and could not be put on trial, until witnesses had provided substantial evidence of guilt.[5] Only then could a trial take place. Only then, as Israel Abrahams has shown, could Annas begin interrogating Jesus.[6] However, there is no record that Annas did this. Having gathered all the facts he deemed necessary, Annas sent Jesus across the courtyard of the High Priest's compound to the apartment of Caiaphas (John 18:13).

THE LATE-NIGHT MEETING OF THE SANHEDRIN

It was now almost midnight. The day of Preparation for the Passover would begin shortly. While Annas was interrogating Jesus, Caiaphas was busy rounding up as many of the Sanhedrin as he could for a hurried trial. "According to Mishnah *Sanhedrin* 4:1, capital cases had to be tried by twenty-three judges."[7]

> "Passover in the occupied Jewish homeland was a tinderbox situation because they were celebrating freedom from imperial oppression in Egypt, while they were under imperial oppression from Rome."
> —John Dominic Crossan

As we have just seen, some of the events associated with Jesus' trial before Caiaphas occurred during the hearing before Annas. When John mentioned that the High Priest inquired about Jesus' teaching, his disciples, and his public appearances, he was talking about Annas. When Jesus suggested the court call witnesses who heard what he taught in the Temple, it was one of Annas' officers who struck Jesus in the face. Most of the time when Jesus was questioned in those late-night sessions, it was Annas doing the questioning. Finally, after extensive interrogation, Annas sent Jesus to his son-in-law, Caiaphas (John 18:24).

From this point on, the Jewish trial of Jesus took place in Caiaphas' court. It was before Caiaphas that the chief priests, elders, and scribes of the Sanhedrin gathered to hear the case against Jesus. It was here that false witnesses were summoned but failed miserably to implicate Jesus. It was Caiaphas who asked Jesus if he was the Christ, the Son of God. It was Caiaphas who demanded the small group of Sanhedrin members present find Jesus guilty, which they did. All of this took place shortly after midnight as Thursday folded into Friday.

THE TEARING OF THE HIGH PRIEST'S CLOTHES

After the false witnesses testified against Jesus and the Savior remained silent refusing to dignify their claims, Caiaphas demanded Jesus answer the most significant issue of the tribunal: "Tell us if you are the Christ, the Son of God" (Matt 26:63; Mark 14:61). When Jesus admitted that he was both Messiah and Son of God and that he soon would be sitting next to the Father's throne in heaven, Caiaphas exploded. He tore his robes and exclaimed, "He has uttered blasphemy. What further witnesses do we need? You have now heard his blasphemy" (Matt 26:65; Mark 14:63–64).

In the ancient Middle East, tearing your clothes was an expression of extreme grief and shock. This practice went back to the earliest biblical times (cf. Gen 37:29, Num 14:6, Josh7:6,2 Sam 1:1–12; Job 1:20; Isa 36:22). As Table 2 indicates, tearing your clothes at a tragedy or unfortunate circumstance was a Middle Eastern custom for centuries. Caiaphas employed that custom to show his exasperation at Jesus' refusal to answer the loaded questions put to him.

It is not clear if the clothes the High Priest tore were his priestly vestments or his ordinary clothes. Matthew 26:65 uses a non-specific word (Greek: ἱμάτια; English: *himatia*) for "clothes." Eckhard J. Schnabel says, "Since the High Priest was forbidden to tear his priestly vestments, he was either wearing regular clothes when he presided over a session of the Sanhedrin, or he tore the inner tunics that he was wearing under his liturgical garments."[8] Regardless of what Caiaphas tore, he did it as a sign of severe malefaction. According to Leviticus 24:10–16, death is the penalty for blasphemy (see also M. *Sanhedrin* 7:4–5).

PHYSICAL ABUSE IN THE COURT OF CAIAPHAS

Not only did Jesus' trial not produce justice, but it also fabricated some complete injustices. This was in the house of the High Priest. This was a meeting of some members of the highest court of the Jews. These were lawmakers, future casters, influencers, and the elite of Jerusalem. That is what makes the physical abuse they inflicted on Jesus both shocking and significant. What kind of abuse did Jesus receive? It was diverse and reflected the hatred of the Jews toward Jesus.

Table 2: Tearing One's Clothes in the Bible

Person	Reason	Scripture
Reuben and Jacob	Upon hearing Joseph had been killed	Gen 37:29–34
Joseph's Brothers	Upon finding the silver cup in Benjamin's bag	Gen 44:13
Joshua and Caleb	When Israel murmured about entering the Holy Land	Num 14:6
Jephthah	When his hasty words came true for his daughter	Judg 11:35
David's Soldiers	When they learned of King Saul's death	2 Sam 1:11
David	Learning Abner died, he told Joab to tear his clothes	2 Sam 3:31
Tamar	After being raped by her brother Amnon	2 Sam 13:19
Hushai the Archite	When he met David, Hushai tore his clothes	2 Sam 15:32
Elisha	When Elijah was taken up into heaven	2 Kgs 2:12
King Joram	When Naaman was sent to him to cure his leprosy	2 Kgs 5:7
King Jehoram	Hearing women quarreling about eating their son	2 Kgs 6:3
Athaliah	When Jehoiada removed her from being queen	2 Kgs 11:14
King Hezekiah	As Rabshakeh denounced YHWH before the people	2 Kgs 19:1
King Josiah	Discovering and reading the Book of the Law	2 Kgs 22:11, 19
Ezra	Learning of Israel's mixed marriages with pagans	Ezra 9:3, 5
Job	Learning of the destruction and death of all he had	Job 1:20
Job's Three Friends	When they saw Job's disgusting condition	Job 2:12
Eighty Men	Upon coming to the House of the Lord	Jer 41:5
High Priest Caiaphas	When he condemned Jesus for blasphemy	Matt 26:65
Barnabas and Paul	When the people of Lystra worshipped them as gods	Acts 14:14

Members of the Sanhedrin spit in Jesus' face.

There is not much more humiliating or degrading than to have someone spit at you. These religious leaders despised Jesus so much that they did what most well-bred people are taught not to do—to spit into someone's face. Mark 14:65 documents, "And some began to spit on him and to cover his face and to strike him, saying to him, 'Prophesy!' And the guards received him with blows" (see Mark 15:19).

In antiquity, spitting was often used as an apotropaic rite. From the Greek *apotrepein* meaning "to ward off" (*apo* "away" and *trepein* "to turn"), apotropaic spitting was a type of magic intended to turn away harm or ward off evil. It was done to avert the evil eye.

Was the rationale for spitting on Jesus to ward off evil? It does not appear so. The Gospel narratives make it clear that on the two occasions where people spit in Jesus' face—those in Caiaphas' presence in Matthew 26 and those among the Roman soldiers in Matthew 27—it was done because they despised Jesus and who he claimed to be.

For any faithful follower of Jesus, it is difficult to picture Jesus' face, his eyes, his nose, and his cheeks dripping with the spittle of profane men. It was running down his beard, and because he was bound, he could not even wipe it away from his eyes. The Creator (John 1:2-4; Col 11:14-17; Heb 1:2-3) was covered with the spittle of those whom he had created. Indeed, "He was despised and rejected by men, a man of sorrows and acquainted with grief" (Isa 53:3).

Members of the Sanhedrin beat Jesus with their fists.

There was more abuse beyond spitting. Those in the room with Caiaphas were "the chief priests and the elders and the scribes," a skeleton crew that barely made up a quorum for the Sanhedrin (Matt 26:57). These jurists were angry because Jesus had not answered their questions. So they tossed propriety to the wind and took turns beating Jesus in the face with their fists, just as they had taken turns spitting on him.

The word (Greek: κολαφίζειν; English: *kolaphízein*) that both Matthew and Mark use to describe the Sanhedrin striking Jesus in the face means to pummel with the closed fist. These were not soft blows delivered to Jesus' face. They were severe blows designed to humiliate him and badly hurt him. "The Mishnah (*Baba Qamma*, VII, 6) imposes a fine on a man who administers a slap with the palm of his hand; this fine is doubled if the slap is administered with the back of the hand."[9]

Members of the Sanhedrin slap Jesus in the face and mock Him.

These men enjoyed beating on Jesus so much they began to make a game of it. They sent for a cloth to use as a hood to blindfold Jesus. Once he could not see any of them, these high-class men, men of esteem, took turns stepping up to the Savior, smacking him in the face and taunting him, "Prophesy to us, you Christ! Who is it that struck you?" (Matt 26:68). They thought it was all great fun.[10]

What followed was more spitting, beating, slapping, and mocking.

Matthew definitively established these combatants as "the chief priests and the whole council" (Matt 26:59; see also verses 65–68 and Mark 14:55, 63–65).

Let there be no confusion here. These were not Roman soldiers. These were not the lowly servants of the High Priest. These were the distinguished members of the Sanhedrin, the Supreme Court of ancient Israel. These were the religious shepherds of Israel acting more like out-of-control ravenous wolves.

THE EARLY-MORNING MEETING OF THE SANHEDRIN

In the initial years of the previous century, a French scholar named Jean Juster argued that the Sanhedrin in Jerusalem possessed the legal right both to indict Jews of capital criminal offenses and to execute capital punishment on the Jews.[11] This same point had been argued by Emil Schürer a few years earlier.[12]

The conclusions of Juster and Schürer were the basis for Hans Lietzmann's argument that if the Sanhedrin had tried Jesus on capital charges, he would have been stoned, not crucified. From that, Lietzmann extrapolated his belief that Mark's account of Jesus' trial before the Sanhedrin (Mark 14:55–65) cannot be accepted as historical because if the Sanhedrin had been involved, the Savior would not have been crucified, but rather stoned.[13]

Nevertheless, the evidence for the Sanhedrin's involvement is strong, and the majority of scholars today accept as valid the historical accounts of the Gospels depicting the Sanhedrin's role in the trial and condemnation of Jesus.

Table 3: The Events Beginning with Jesus' Arrest in Gethsemane to Caiaphas' Courtroom

Activity Surrounding Jesus	Scripture
Temple police seize Jesus, lead him to Caiaphas	Matt 26:57; John 18:12
The chief priests, elders, and scribes came together	Mark 14:53
The "scribes and the elders" were gathered there	Matt 26:5
The "chief priests and the whole council" were present	Matt 26:59
They all sought false testimony to put Jesus to death	Matt 26:59; Mark 14:55
No credible witnesses could be found	Matt 26:60; Mark 14:56
Witnesses heard Jesus claim to rebuild Temple in 3 days	Matt 26:61; Mark 14:58
Even about this, their testimony did not agree	Mark 14:59
Caiaphas demanded Jesus respond to the charges	Matt 26:62; Mark 14:60
Jesus remained silent	Matt 26:63; Mark 14:61
Caiaphas asked, "Are you the Christ, the Son of the Blessed?"	Mark 14:61
Jesus said, "You have said so" then speaks of being "seated at the right hand of Power and coming on the clouds."	Matt 26:64; Luke 22:69
They demanded Jesus say if he is Christ	Luke 22:67
Jesus: "If I told them, you would not believe me"	Luke 22:68
They then ask, "Are you the Son of God?"	Luke 22:70
Jesus responds, "You say that I am."	Luke 22:70
Caiaphas tore his robes claiming Jesus had uttered blasphemy	Matt 26:65; Mark 14:63
Caiaphas asks the council for a judgment	Matt 26:66; Luke 22:71
In lock-step, they respond, "He deserves death."	Matt 26:66; Mark 14:64
The Sanhedrin spit in Jesus' face	Matt 26:67; Mark 14:65
They cover his head and strike Jesus	Mark 14:63; Luke 22:63
They strike Jesus and some slap him	Matt 26:67
They mock him: "Prophesy... Who is it that struck you?"	Matt 26:68; Luke 22:64
The Jewish guards receive Jesus by beating him	Mark 14:65
Many other things they did to Jesus, blaspheming him	Luke 22:65
At daylight, they led Jesus to the Council chambers	Luke 22:66
No judgment is recorded by any of the gospels	

Jesus' interrogation by Annas took place at his house, and Jesus' late-night arraignment before Caiaphas took place at Caiaphas' house. It may have been that these two houses were at opposite ends of the High Priest's compound. They may have been connected but with a courtyard between them. While others suppose these two houses were at different locations, to date, any real placement of them is only speculation.

Mark also distinguished between the late-night meeting of the Sanhedrin and an early-morning meeting. He said, "And as soon as it was morning, the chief priests held a consultation with the elders and scribes and the whole council. And they bound Jesus and led him away and delivered him over to Pilate" (Mark 15:1; Matt 27:1–2).

Jesus' trial before Caiaphas was a two-stage event. The "real" trial was the one held in the late-night hours when Jesus was both interrogated by Annas and then shuffled across the High Priest's compound to the house of Caiaphas. The "legal" trial was held the next morning at the Temple's Chamber of Hewn Stone.

David W. Chapman and Eckhard J. Schnabel maintain about the "real" trial that, "Recent investigations of the legal situation in Roman provinces, in particular in Judea, have suggested that an interrogation of Jesus by the Sanhedrin, convened *ad hoc* by the High Priest, is historically plausible."[14] Josef Blinzler, Raymond Brown, Erika Heusler, and other scholars also contend this late-night convening was an *ad hoc* trial conducted by Caiaphas the High Priest, and a quorum of the Sanhedrin.

Edwin M. Yamauchi points out, "It was only legal to pronounce the actual death sentence in the Chamber of Hewn Stone, in the innermost court of the Temple."[15] For these reasons, a nighttime trial and daytime hearing seem impossible. One prominent Catholic theologian wrote:

> The fundamental decision to take action against Jesus, reached during that meeting of the Sanhedrin, was put into effect on the night leading from Thursday to Friday with his arrest on the Mount of Olives . . . It now seems reasonable to assume that what took place when Jesus was brought before the Sanhedrin was not a proper trial, but more of a cross-examination that led to the decision to hand him over to the Roman Governor for sentencing.[16]

One prominent Evangelical theologian, one of my respected seminary professors, wrote:

> The purpose of the night meeting was to find a valid reason to sentence Jesus to death. Matthew states specifically that the council was seeking false witness against Jesus (Matt 26:59). Many came forward, but no two of them agreed with each other

in every detail, as was required by law. Bear in mind that in Jewish legal practice witnesses were not allowed to hear each other's evidence and that in capital cases, the unanimous testimony of two was required for conviction. (Num 35:30; Deut 17:6; 19:15; Ant. 4.8.115).[17]

So, where did this early morning meeting of the Sanhedrin take place? Was it also in the house of Caiaphas or somewhere else? Luke 22:66–67 provides a detail that the other Synoptics and John do not. The physician says, "When day came, the assembly of the elders of the people gathered together, both chief priests and scribes. And they led him away to their council, and they said, 'If you are the Christ, tell us.'"

THE CHAMBER OF HEWN STONE

As a result of their late-night interrogation, the Jewish authorities condemned Jesus of Nazareth to death. They then ratified their judgment a few hours later when the full Sanhedrin gathered at the Chamber of Hewn Stone and from there sent the Nazarene to the Roman prefect Pontius Pilate for execution, just as the Gospels record.

The Mishnah indicates the Great Sanhedrin met in the Chamber of the Hewn Stone (*Lishkat Hagazit*), which was their usual meeting place during the Second Temple Period (sixth century BC to first century AD). It was built into the north wall of Jerusalem's Temple with the northern half built outside in the Temple courtyard and thus left unconsecrated, while the southern half was built inside the courtyard (*Sanhedrin* 11:2).

Doors would permit the Sanhedrin to enter from the outside and pass into the Temple without returning outside. The chamber was approximately 11 meters (36 feet) by 12 meters (40 feet), large enough to hold all seventy-one members of the Sanhedrin. That this chamber was designed as a special place is indicated by its name "the Chamber of the Hewn Stone," as opposed to being constructed with untooled stones.

The term for "hewn stone" in the LXX is translated as ξυστός (English: *Xystos*, 1 Chr 22:2; Amos 5:11) meaning a "covered garden walk" or "portico lined with trees." Some have translated this word as "the Hall beside the Xystos," meaning a large hall adjacent to a portico. The Temple Mount and the Xystos were connected by a bridge. What we know as Wilson's Arch was part of the bridge over the Tyropoean Valley.

As the home of the Sanhedrin, the Chamber of Hewn Stone functioned as the seat of Israel's Supreme Court, often with life or death decisions being made inside. Mishnah *Sanhedrin* 11 speaks of "the great court of the Chamber of Hewn Stone from whence instruction issued to all Israel." John Wilkinson writes, "This was the formal session of the Sanhedrin (Luke 22:66), sitting under the presidency of Caiaphas (John 18:24 . . . the result of this purely formal meeting is to ratify the charge formulated by the night committee (court), and make their proposal into an official act of the Sanhedrin so that Jesus can be taken as a condemned man to Pilate."[18]

WHY JESUS SO UPSET CAIAPHAS AND THE SANHEDRIN

The massive crowds at Jesus' Triumphal Entry were just the beginning. Caiaphas discovered that everywhere people were worshipping Jesus as God and treating him as the Messiah and King of the Jews. News quickly spread of every incident during Passion Week. One such example occurred just two days before Passover.

While Jesus and his disciples were in Bethany at the house of Simon, who had been a Leper, Mary, the sister of Martha and Lazarus, performed the ultimate act of worship toward Jesus. She took "an alabaster flask of ointment of pure nard, very costly, and she broke the flask and poured it over his head" (Mark 14:3). The ointment was valued at "more than three hundred denarii" (v. 5). In Jesus' day, a denarius was one day's wage for a laborer. This would make the value of this pure nard equal to nearly a year's salary.

When Judas Iscariot chastised Mary and said this was a waste of resources (John 12:4-6), Jesus said, "Leave her alone. Why do you trouble her? . . . She has done what she could; she has anointed my body beforehand for burial. And truly, I say to you, wherever the gospel is proclaimed in the whole world, what she has done will be told in memory of her" (Mark 14:6-9).

This kind of adoration for Jesus of Nazareth caused the sanctimonious hairs on the backs of the Sanhedrin's necks to stand on end. It could not be tolerated. Jesus had to be punished. Better still, he had to be executed, and the Sanhedrin would see that it was done. Eckhard J. Schnabel correctly observes:

> Jesus had never made messianic claims in public, nor had he explicitly claimed to be the Son of God. But his teaching and his actions raised the question of what authority he had or claimed to have—his claim to have the authority to forgive sins . . . his healings on the Sabbath . . . his public demonstration of unrestricted power over demons . . . his triumphal approach to Jerusalem . . . his action on the Temple Mount with the prediction that the Temple would be destroyed . . . and his claim to be the

Son of God implicit in the parable of the tenants (Mark 2:5–6; 3:1–6, 22; 11:17; 12:1–12).[19]

For the Jewish elite, that was enough.

JESUS' MESSIANIC CLAIM WAS THE LAST STRAW

An overt claim to messiahship from Jesus was not necessary. It was not just implied; it was demonstrated with so many incidents that pointed to Jesus as the Messiah of Israel, such as those indicated next.

NINE NEW TESTAMENT EPISODES THAT IDENTIFY JESUS AS MESSIAH

#1. John 4:25–26. Jesus' first messianic inference was made where you would least expect it—not to the Jewish people, not in Jerusalem, but in Samaria, to a lone woman, and perhaps most astonishing of all, to a Samaria woman who was the epitome of sin and shame.

#2. Matthew 10:42. Jesus' next reference to messiahship was incidental. John told Jesus that he and the others had forbidden a man to cast out devils in the name of Jesus because he was not one of his disciples. Jesus rebuked them saying those who were not against him were for him, and then gave his estimate of the dignity of the title Christ; "And whoever gives one of these little ones even a cup of cold water because he is a disciple, truly, I say to you, he will by no means lose his reward."

#3. Matt 16:16–20. The next claim of messiahship came at Caesarea Philippi, not from Jesus, but from Peter. Jesus questioned his disciples concerning what people were saying about him. Peter's affirming answer, "You are the Christ, the Son of the living God." Jesus commanded them to tell no one that he was the Christ.

#4. John 10:24–25. After speaking about the sheepfold, the sheep, and the Good Shepherd, the people said, 'If you are the Christ, tell us plainly" and he replied, "I told you, and you do not believe. The works that I do in my Father's name bear witness about me." Jesus implied his messiahship and declared that the truth of his claim was demonstrated by his works.

#5. Matt 22:41–46. When Jesus challenged the rulers about the meaning of messiahship, "What do you think about the Christ?" his question did not mean, "What do you think of me?" but rather "What was their religious concept of the Messiah? Whose son is he?" They said, "The Son of David." Jesus asked another question, "How is it then that David, in the Spirit, calls him Lord?" The problem as Jesus presented it to them revealed his own concept of the meaning of the title; Christ is Son of David, born a descendant of David, yet Lord of David, and somehow superior to him. Without saying he was the Messiah, they got the message.

#6. Matthew 23:10. Immediately after the conflict with the religious rulers, Jesus said to his disciples, "Neither be called instructors, for you have one instructor, the Christ." You will need guidance and direction; Jesus will be your one Master, one Guide, and one Director. Later, he warned them, saying, "There shall arise false Christs . . . For many shall come in my name, saying, I am the Christ: and shall lead man astray" (Matt 24:5; see also vv. 4, 11, 24; Mark 13:5, 6, 22; Luke 21:8; Gal 2:13; 2 Tim 3:6; and 2 Pet 2:15). Contrast the truth of the Christ with the lies of the false Christs.

#7. John 17:3. With the crucifixion fast approaching, Jesus prayed to the Father asking him to glorify the Son even as the Son, throughout his life, has glorified the Father. Then Jesus spoke of himself as the "sent one" praying, "And this is eternal life, that they know you, the only true God, and Jesus Christ whom you have sent." Jesus' self-understanding that he was sent by God identifies him as the Messiah sent from God.

#8. Matt 26:63–64; Mark 14;62; Luke 22:67–68. Finally, the High Priest challenged him, "I adjure you by the living God, tell us if you are the Christ, the Son of God." The three Evangelists gave different answers, each one filled with truth. Matthew's answer records Jesus' reply, "You have said so." Mark simply says, "I am." Luke tells us Jesus rebuked them saying, "If I tell you, you will not believe, and if I ask you, you will not answer." He did not outright claim to be the Christ, the Son of God, but neither did he deny it.

#9. Luke 24:26, 46–47. Finally, on the resurrection side of the cross, Jesus used the title Christ for himself. "Was it not necessary that the Christ should suffer these things and enter into his glory. . . Thus it is written that the Christ should suffer and on the third day rise from the dead, and that repentance for the forgiveness of sins should be proclaimed in his name to all nations, beginning from Jerusalem."

While it may have been the hatred of the Jewish religious leaders that precipitated the trial of Jesus before Caiaphas, it was the sovereignty of God that put him there. The actions of the Jewish council, of Caiaphas the High Priest, and even of the Roman prefect Pontius Pilate, were all orchestrated by the supreme God to place Jesus on Golgotha's Cross as an atonement for our sin. Nothing would speed this process; nothing would retard it.

The Greek form of the Hebrew word "Messiah" (Greek: Μεσσίας; **English:** *Messías*) is found only twice in the New Testament. In John 1:41 Andrew located his brother Simon Peter and said, "We have found the Messiah" (which means Christ)." In John 4:25, the woman at the well of Samaria said to Jesus, "I know that Messiah is coming (he who is called Christ). When he comes, he will tell us all things." On both occasions, John felt the need to mention the Hebrew word and the more familiar word "Christ" (Greek: Χριστὸς; English: *Christos*) for Messiah. The New Testament uses the title "Christ" fifty-eight times, as opposed to Messiah just twice.

In Jewish thought, "The Messiah" (Hebrew: המשיח; English *Ha Mashiach*) means "the anointed one." Down through the centuries since King David's time, the Jewish people anticipated and eagerly looked for their Messiah to come. They believed when he did, the Messiah would be descended from the line of King David through Solomon. He would unify the tribes of Israel, gather the Jews from the four corners of the earth to the land of Israel (*Eretz Israel*), rebuild the Temple in Jerusalem, and usher in the Messianic Age, a glorious period of universal peace.

> "The main reason Jesus was crucified is that he was an ultimate challenge to every authority in Jerusalem."
> —Michael Peppard

With expectations so high, you can see why the elite of Jerusalem both scorned and spurned the claim that this Nazarene could be the Messiah. Still, Jesus' anointing reflected those similarly anointed in the Old Testament: the prophet (Deut 18:18; Heb 1:1–2); the High Priest (Ps 110:4; Heb 5:5–6); and the king (2 Sam 7:10–16; Isa 9:6–7; Luke 1:31–32). Regarding the identity of the true Messiah of Israel, Jesus checked all the boxes.

Thus, Jesus was a clear and present danger to the Jewish religious leaders of Jerusalem. He was a threat to the corrupt practices of the Temple. He was a spiritual threat to Annas and Caiaphas. He was a political threat to Pilate. Only to the Jewish people was the Suffering Savior not a threat. He healed them. He taught them. He loved them. And for them, he died.

FROM JERUSALEM TO ROME

When Caiaphas and the Sanhedrin condemned Jesus to death and hustled him from the Chamber of Hewn Stone to Pilate's praetorium, the Savior was not just being transferred from one building to another. He was being sent from the Jewish legal system to the Roman legal system. He was being sent from a court that hated him to a court that could not care one way or the other. Jesus was being sent from Jerusalem to Rome.

The relationship between Pilate and Caiaphas was tenuous at best. Neither liked the other very much, but both were politicians. Pilate was sent to Judea to keep the peace. Caiaphas benefitted financially and personally from peace. It was in the best interest of both to get along, even though a lack of respect and a lack of trust lingered just below the surface of their relationship.

Table 4: The Contrasts between Jerusalem and Rome

Jerusalem Caiaphas and the Sanhedrin	Rome Pilate and the Roman Soldiers
Allegiance to God	Allegiance to Rome
Religious, but secular	Secular, but frequently not religious
Religious authority	Civil authority
Power of the Temple	Power of the State
Could condemn, convict, but not crucify	Could condemn, convict, and crucify
Wanted to kill Jesus	Wanted to spare Jesus
Preferred a murderer to a teacher	Puzzled by the Jews' preference

The difference between Jesus' trial before Caiaphas and his trial before Pilate was like night and day. Neither of them produced justice, but Pilate at least appeared to be more interested in justice. The Sanhedrin were offended by Jesus' blasphemy, as they saw it. The Roman court was offended by Jesus' creation of instability in Judea. Both Jews and Romans saw themselves as better off without Jesus. The solution was simple. Jesus had to die.

Chapter 2

The Constantly Changing Charges Against Jesus

Justice would prevail on this Passover weekend, but not in the human courtroom. There was no justice in either the courts of Caiaphas or Pilate. The only justice was divine justice, when the Son of God died on the cross, paying the penalty for our sins. That satisfied divine justice, and ultimately, that's all that matters.

BACK IN THE DAY, a cooking technique involved throwing pasta against the wall to determine if it was sufficiently cooked. If it stuck, it was done. When it comes to the charges made against Jesus, it appears with each charge Caiaphas and crew said to themselves, "Let's throw it against the wall and see if it sticks!" They would present a charge testing the reaction of those present to see if that charge would gain any traction. That is apparently why the charges against the Holy One of God were continually changing.

THE LIST OF ACCUSATIONS AGAINST JESUS

In criminal proceedings, there are multiple reasons why charges are not filed against a person suspected of criminal activity. In some cases, the offense is considered trivial or of low priority. Other times nonviolent cases go to mediation and are settled out of court. Occasionally the arresting police officer fails to protect the chain of evidence and the charge has to be dropped.

Jesus' crimes, as viewed by the religious establishment of Jerusalem, were not trivial, nor were they of low priority. You do not pursue a criminal case the day before the most significant celebration of the year if you view the case as trivial. The Gospels document that Jesus' trial was hurried and uncoordinated. Witnesses against him were unreliable at best, and felonious at worst. Nevertheless, charges were leveled against Jesus, and an infamous trial was held.

However, Caiaphas and the Sanhedrin faced the "pasta on the wall" problem. They could not make any of the false charges stick. While the accusations brought against Jesus were many, they often changed because even Caiaphas knew these trumped-up charges were bogus. Nothing Jesus did corresponded with what he was accused of doing. Thus, let's begin this chapter by investigating the crimes of which the Jewish authorities accused Jesus, as detailed in Table 1.

Table 1: Accusations Made Against Jesus

Jesus was accused of claiming to rebuild the Temple in three days (Matt 26:61; Mark 14:58)
Jesus was accused of claiming to be Israel's Messiah (Matt 26:63; Mark 14:61; Luke 22:67)
Jesus was accused of claiming to be God's Son (Matt 26:63; Mark 14:61; Luke 22:70; John 19:7)
Jesus was accused of claiming to be King of the Jews (Matt 27:11; Luke 23:2, 3; John 18:33, 37)
Jesus was accused of many things by the Jewish religious leaders (Mark 15:3–4; Luke 22:64)
Jesus was accused of misleading the Jewish nation (Luke 23:2,14)
Jesus was accused of forbidding the Jews to give tribute to Caesar (Luke 23:2)
Jesus was accused of stirring up the Jewish people (Luke 23:5)
Jesus was accused of false teaching throughout all of Galilee and Judea (Luke 23:5; John 18:19)
Jesus was accused of doing evil (John 18:30)

Listed in Table 1 are ten accusations leveled against Jesus of Nazareth at the time of his trial and crucifixion.[20] Some are weightier than others, but none had the facts to back them up. We should take special note of the background of each charge as we investigate them.

CHARGE #1: ARROGANCE

When Jesus commanded the Temple pigeon sellers, "Do not make my Father's house a house of trade," the Jews demanded a sign from him that would prove his authority. "Jesus answered them, 'Destroy this temple, and in three days I will raise it up.' The Jews then said, 'It has taken forty-six years to build this temple, and will you raise it up in three days?' But he was speaking about the temple of his body" (John 2:19–21).

Those present did not understand what Jesus was saying. He was not claiming to be able to tear down the Jerusalem Temple block by block and rebuild the whole building in just three days. He was speaking metaphorically of his crucifixion and resurrection. John verifies this completely by saying, "But he was speaking about the temple of his body" (vs. 21). He continued, "When therefore he was raised from the dead, his disciples remembered that he had said this, and they believed the Scripture and the word that Jesus had spoken" (v. 22). Jesus was saying that when they crucified his body at Golgotha, it would be "rebuilt" three days later when he was raised from the dead.

The Temple indeed was a magnificent building, glittering in the Palestinian sun. Craig Evans and N. T. Wright note:

> According to Josephus, Herod prepared a thousand wagons to carry the stones for the Temple and employed "ten thousand of the most skilled workmen," training "some as masons, others as carpenters" (*Ant.* 15.390). The Temple Mount was enormous (and still is) and included a series of buildings and colonnades, with the sanctuary itself the most impressive of all of the structures.[21]

When the Jews said, "It has taken forty-six years to build this temple," they did not mean the task was finished. Work on the Temple Mount continued until the year 64 AD under the direction of Herod's descendants. When work on the Temple Mount finally was completed, a massive workforce had to find other employment. Josephus tells us, "And now it was that the Temple was finished ... The people saw that the workmen were unemployed, who were above eighteen thousand and that they, receiving no wages, were in want because they had earned their bread by their labors about the Temple" (*Ant.* 20.9.7).

Evans and Wright comment, "This massive layoff contributed to the growing social and political instability that just two years later exploded into open rebellion. Some of the laid-off stone-cutters would later employ their tools and skills in building secret passageways for the rebels (*Wars* 7.26–27)."[22]

Given the size, intricacy, and beauty of the Second Temple, for Jesus to say he could rebuild it in just three days was viewed by the Jews as unmitigated arrogance. They hated him for it. However, arrogance is not a crime and you cannot kill a man for it, so they quickly moved on to another charge.

The first accusation against Jesus resulted from a misunderstanding about his third-day resurrection. However, after Jesus was dead, the members of the council went to Pilate and requested a guard be placed at the tomb of Joseph of Arimathea. Their reason? "Sir, we remember how that impostor said, while he was still alive, 'After three days I will rise'" (Matt 27:63).

Early nineteenth-century British Bible commentator Adam Clarke explained: "This they probably took from his saying, 'Destroy this temple, and in three days I will build it up.' If so, they destroyed, by their own words, the false accusation they brought against him to put him to death: then they perverted the meaning, now they declare it."[23]

CHARGE #2: MISREPRESENTATION

Jesus was accused of misrepresenting himself as the Messiah of Israel (Matt 26:63; Mark 14:61; Luke 22:67; 23:2). There are two problems with this accusation. First, during his public ministry, Jesus did not make an open claim about being the Messiah of Israel. Only once did he use the term Messiah of himself (Mark 9:41) and that was in private with his disciples. The disciples understood he was the Messiah, but Jesus had instructed them not to make a public pronouncement of it (Mark 8:29–30). The accusation that during his earthly ministry, Jesus claimed to be the Messiah is not supported in Scripture.

However, this did not stop the Sanhedrin from making the charge. They had seen plenty to verify Jesus acting like the Messiah. Their witnesses/spies had watched Jesus heal on the Sabbath and felt no remorse as if he were breaking the Law. They heard him claim to have the authority to forgive sin as well as to heal. Witnesses told tales of Jesus exerting power over demons that no human could exercise.

Perhaps some of the elder Sanhedrin were still alive from the group of teachers among whom Jesus sat asking and answering questions when he was only twelve years old. They would only be twenty-one years older now and continued to be "amazed at his understanding and his answers" (Luke 2:47).

With all this evidence to the contrary, the Sanhedrin nevertheless charged Jesus with falsely claiming to be the Messiah of Israel. It's tragic. These religious leaders falsely claimed Jesus made a claim he never made.

He did just the opposite, asking his disciples and others not to make that very claim. Unquestionably, this accusation would not stand up in court.

CHARGE #3: BLASPHEMY

When Jesus made no reply, the High Priest said to him, "I adjure you by the living God, tell us if you are the Christ, the Son of God." Jesus said to him, "You have said so" (Matt 26:63–64). While not coming right out and saying that he was the long-awaited Messiah of Israel, Jesus confirmed the fact by indicating that Caiaphas had spoken correctly. He is the Messiah of Israel. He is the Christ of God. Nevertheless, the second half of this accusation is new: "tell us if you are the Christ, the Son of God."

The expression "Son of God" was understood by the Jews of Jesus' day to mean someone equal to the Heavenly Father. When Jesus healed the man at the Pool of Bethesda (John 5), the Jews accosted Jesus because it was a Sabbath day and they accused him of breaking the laws of the Sabbath. John 5:17–18 records, "But Jesus answered them, 'My Father is working until now, and I am working.' This was why the Jews were seeking all the more to kill him, because not only was he breaking the Sabbath, but he was calling God his own Father, making himself equal with God." Without question, the Jews of the first century understood Jesus' claim to be the Son of God as a claim to be God in the form of flesh.

> "Blasphemy is seen as among the worst of sins, which is why it is worthy of death."
> —Darrell L. Bock

Caiaphas and the council were frustrated with Jesus. His answers had not been direct, and they needed a clear admission of guilt for a charge that would be punishable by death. With this interaction, Caiaphas thought he had it. He was convinced Jesus was guilty of blasphemy.

In what way was this statement considered blasphemous? In Jewish literature, there is an evolution of the meaning of blasphemy. Initially, blasphemy was speaking the Tetragrammaton. (The *Tetragrammaton*, from the Greek Τετραγράμματον meaning *tetra* "four" plus γράμμα (English: *gramma*) "letter," thus, "consisting of four letters." In Hebrew יהוה is the four-letter biblical name of the God of Israel—YHWH. In Western languages, with vowels added, this name often appears as Yahweh or Jehovah. But as Darrell L. Bock points out, there is "a kind of fluidity in the approach taken to blasphemy. Technically it requires the pronunciation of the Name, but practically it can involve actions that reflect total unfaithfulness."[24]

Table 2: Jesus is Called the "Son of God"

Those Who Called Jesus "Son of God" Proclaiming Him God	
Person	Scripture
Jesus	John 3:18; 3:36; 5:25; 10:36; 11:4
Demons	Matt 8:29; Mark 3:11; 5:7; Luke 4:41; 8:28
Angels	Luke 1:35
Disciples	Matt 14:33
John	John 1:34; 20:31
Peter	Matt 16:16
Nathaniel`	John 1:49
Mark	Mark 1:1`
Martha	John 11:27
Centurion	Matt 27:54; Mark 15:39
Paul	Acts 9:20; Rom 1:4,9; 5:10; 8:3; 1 Cor 1:9; 2 Cor 1:19; Gal 2:20; 4:4, 6; Eph 4:13
Hebrews	Heb 1:5, 8; 4:14; 6:6; 7:3; 10:29
1 John	1 John 3:8; 4:9, 15; 5:5, 9, 10, 12, 13, 20
2 John	2 John 1:9
Revelation	Rev 2:18

Those Who Called Jesus "Son of God" Questioning Him	
Satan	Matt 4:3; 6; Luke 4:3, 9
High Priest	Matt 26:63
Mockers	Matt 27:40, 43

According to Jewish law, blasphemy was "evil or profane speaking of God. The essence of the crime consists in the impious purpose in using the words, and does not necessarily include the performance of any desecrating act."[25]

However, Raymond Brown points out:

> Blasphemy does at times refer to cursing God, making fun of God, or belittling God. That, too, can be dropped from the discussion because nothing in the tradition suggests a deliberately irreverent attitude toward God by Jesus. From the

attested meanings of the word blasphemy, the only likely historical charge would have been that Jesus arrogantly claimed for Himself status or privileges that belonged properly to the God of Israel alone and in that sense implicitly demeaned God.[26]

Morna D. Hooker is right. "To claim for oneself a seat at the right hand of power, however, is to claim a share in the authority of God; to appropriate to oneself such authority and to bestow on oneself this unique status in the sight of God and man would almost certainly have been regarded as blasphemy."[27]

In the eyes of the religious leaders of Jerusalem, Jesus had committed the sin of blasphemy against God. Again, Darrell L. Bock writes:

> Jesus' bold affirmation of his presence at the side of God and coming authority . . . is what they found offensive . . . It is the juxtaposition of seating and coming on the clouds that makes clear the transcendent function that Jesus gives himself here, with the reference to clouds making it apparent that more than a purely human and earthly messianic claim is present.[28]

What Jesus was saying was titanic. He was telling the disrespectful High Priest that when he looked into the face of Jesus, Caiaphas was staring into the face of God. Jesus' words, "I and the Father are one," (John 10:30; see 17:11, 22) were being played out right before the sanctimonious Caiaphas. To him, this was blasphemy.

According to Leviticus 24:10-16, death is the penalty for blasphemy (see M. Sanhedrin 7:4-5). The Jewish court finally had an accusation against Jesus that had some teeth, an accusation they thought would stick. Blasphemy. The people of Jerusalem could get behind this charge.

Bock sums up the incident. "They [The Jewish religious leadership] saw in Jesus' claim of exaltation an affront to God's unique honor and to their position as representatives of God's people. Jesus saw in his anticipated exaltation a vindication of his calling, ministry, and claims, so that one day he would be seen by all as Son of Man seated at God's right hand."[29]

CHARGE #4: KINGSHIP

Jesus was accused of claiming to be the King of the Jews (Matt 27:11; Mark 15:2; Luke 22:67; Luke 23:2, 3; John 18:33, 37). This accusation is a classic case of wishful thinking gone wrong. The Jews so wanted a king who could rid the Holy Land of the Roman invaders that any potential candidate caught their attention.

The expression "king of the Jews" occurs eighteen times in the Bible. In Table 3, notice who it is who refers to Jesus as "King of the Jews."

Table 3: Jesus: The King of the Jews

Scripture	Speaker	Question or Statement
Matt 2:2	The Magi to Herod	"Where is he who has been born king of the Jews?"
Matt 27:11	Pilate to Jesus	"Are you the King of the Jews?"
Mark 15:2	Pilate to Jesus	"Are you the King of the Jews?"
Luke 23:3	Pilate to Jesus	"Are you the King of the Jews?"
John 18:33	Pilate to Jesus	"Are you the King of the Jews?"
Matt 27:29	Soldiers to Jesus	"Hail, King of the Jews!"
Mark 15:18	Soldiers to Jesus	"Hail, King of the Jews!"
John 19:3	Soldiers to Jesus	"Hail, King of the Jews!"
Matt 27:37	The *Titulus*	"This is Jesus, the King of the Jews."
Mark 15:26	The *Titulus*	"The King of the Jews."
Luke 23:38	The *Titulus*	"This is the King of the Jews."
John 19:19	The *Titulus*	"Jesus of Nazareth, the King of the Jews."
Mark 15:9	Pilate to the Mob	"Do you want me to release . . . the King of the Jews?"
Mark 15:12	Pilate to the Mob	"What shall I do with . . . the King of the Jews?"
John 18:38	Pilate to the Mob	"Do you want me to release . . . the King of the Jews?"
Luke 23:37	Roman Soldiers	"If you are the King of the Jews, save yourself!"
John 19:21	Chief Priests	"Do not write, 'the King of the Jews' . . . but rather . . . 'This man said, "I am King of the Jews."'"

Except for the Magi, who came from the East looking for the "king of the Jews," all the references to the "king of the Jews" occur in the Passion story. Also, ironically, these references all come from the lips of Jesus' antagonists. However, what is missing is more important than what is present, for there is no reference to him being the "king of the Jews" from the lips of Jesus. That is because Jesus never publicly claimed to be the Jewish king. This was another false charge the Jewish authorities could not make stick.

All four Gospel authors record Pilate asking Jesus this question: "Are you the king of the Jews?" (Matt 27:11; Mark 15:2; Luke 23:3; John 18:33).

Jesus was facing imminent death. His followers were now gone. One of his disciples had betrayed him. The chief priests and scribes, the Pharisees and Sadducees, were all out for blood. Surely Jesus would be ready to admit he misrepresented himself as the future king of Israel.

Instead, in each of the Synoptics, Jesus answered tersely, "You have said so." He would say nothing to this pagan governor about being a king, but he would enlighten Pilate on the kind of kingdom of which he would be king. "My kingdom is not of this world. If my kingdom were of this world, my servants would have been fighting, that I might not be delivered over to the Jews. But my kingdom is not from the world" (John 18:36). This prompted Pilate to say, "So you are a king?" to which Jesus replied, "You say that I am a king" (John 18:37).

The kingdom of Jesus Christ was entirely different from the concept of a kingdom understood by either the Romans or the Jews. But make no mistake. Jesus refused the line of questioning that identified him as a king, nonetheless, he is destined to be King of Kings. One of my favorite New Testament verses is found in Revelation 11:15. It claims, "The kingdom of the world has become the kingdom of our Lord and of his Christ, and he shall reign forever and ever."

CHARGE #5: MULTIPLE TRANSGRESSIONS

Jesus was accused of many other things by the Jewish religious leaders (Mark 15:3-4; Luke 22:64; Luke 23:10). When they cannot prove anything specific, people often make general accusations that are even more difficult to prove. That is apparently what the Sanhedrin did in the case of Jesus. They were not making any headway on charging Jesus with verifiable charges, so they accused him of "many other things," hoping that something, anything, might become legitimate.

What are some of the "other things" of which the Jews had accused Jesus? Here is a sampling; this is not meant to be a complete list.

- Jesus was accused of falsely claiming to have the ability to forgive sins (Matt 9:2-3; Mark 2:7; Luke 5:21).
- Jesus was accused of eating with tax collectors and sinners (Matt 9:11; Mark 2:16; Luke 15:1-2; 19:7).
- Jesus was accused of permitting work on the Sabbath (Matt 12:2; Mark 2:24; Luke 6:2).

- Jesus was accused of healing on the Sabbath (Matt 12:10; Mark 3:2; Luke 6:7; 13:14; John 5:15–18).
- Jesus was accused of performing miracles by the power of Beelzebub (Matt 12:24; Mark 3:22; Luke 11:15).
- Jesus was accused of permitting a break with Jewish tradition (Matt 15:1–2; Mark 7:1–5; Luke 11:38).
- Jesus was accused of being a false prophet (Luke 7:39).
- Jesus was accused of being demon-possessed (John 10:19–20).

Like the formal and specific charges the Sanhedrin leveled against Jesus, these unspecific charges had no validity. Most of them related, not to the Mosaic Law, but to the traditions devised by the Pharisees over the years. Traditions can be useful, but if they run counter to God's will and His Word, they must be abandoned, and quickly.

CHARGE #6: SEDUCTION

Unbelievably, Jesus was accused of seducing the Jewish nation (Luke 23:2, 14). In the eyes of the Jews, this seduction was an attempt to get the Jewish people to turn from YHWH to another god, Jesus himself. After Jesus was crucified and buried, "The next day, that is, after the day of Preparation, the chief priests and the Pharisees gathered before Pilate and said, 'Sir, we remember how that impostor (Greek: πλάνος; English: *planos*) said, while he was still alive, "After three days I will rise"'" (Matt 27:62–63).

Perspective matters. From the perspective of the Jewish religious leaders, Jesus was seducing the Jewish nation. From the perspective of the followers of Jesus, he was saving the Jewish nation, as well as the rest of humanity.

The members of the Sanhedrin, the chief priests, the elders, the scribes, and especially Annas and Caiaphas, saw Jesus of Nazareth as a threat to their religion and their way of life. Steeped in religious tradition as they were, for anyone to challenge that tradition was immediately deemed to be misleading fellow Jews.

Nevertheless, Jesus was very clear about his mission here on Earth. He did not leave heaven to deceive a whole nation. His words in Luke 19:10 record the clarity of his mission: "For the Son of Man came to seek and to save the lost." Jesus came to save the lost (Greek: ἀπολωλός; English: *apolōlos*), a word meaning to perish or be destroyed, a perfect description of Caiaphas and company.

Ironically, the Jews wanted Jesus crucified by the Romans because they genuinely believed he was leading Jews away from the faith of Abraham, Isaac, and Jacob. The religious leaders saw him as a charlatan, an Elmer Gantry, or a Jim Jones. However, while they sent Jesus to the cross to foil his purpose, unwittingly, they helped him accomplish it. He came to die so we might live. Without the cross, that could not have happened.

Charge after charge was leveled against Jesus, but the religious leaders of Jerusalem themselves perceived they were having no success in finding one that would stick. They didn't give up, however, and continued to charge Jesus with different crimes they knew he had never committed.

> "Success is going from failure to failure without a loss of enthusiasm."
> —Winston Churchill

The religious charade continued.

CHARGE #7: SEDITION

Sedition is the act of inciting others to resist lawful authority. Jesus was accused of forbidding the Jews to give tribute to Caesar (Luke 23:2). This accusation leaves you scratching your head. While the other allegations have no proof to back up their claims, this charge has proof demonstrating this claim to be both ludicrous and false.

All three of the Synoptic Gospels record this event. Luke 20:19–26 provides the details.

> The scribes and the chief priests sought to lay hands on him at that very hour . . . So they watched him and sent spies (Greek: ἐγκαθέτους; English: *enkathetous*), who pretended to be sincere, that they might catch him in something he said, so as to deliver him up to the authority and jurisdiction of the governor. So they asked him, "Teacher . . . Is it lawful for us to give tribute to Caesar, or not?" But he perceived their craftiness, and said to them, "Show me a denarius. Whose likeness and inscription does it have?" They said, "Caesar's." He said to them, "Then render to Caesar the things that are Caesar's, and to God the things that are God's." And they were not able in the presence of the people to catch him in what he said, but marveling at his answer they became silent.

Not only do Matthew 22:15-21 and Mark 12:13-17 record this account as well, but it is impossible to believe that the religious leaders of Jerusalem were unaware of it. After all, the spies were sent by the scribes and chief priests to attempt to trap Jesus in what he taught so they could hand him over to Pilate for trial and crucifixion. This was their plot; they had to know about it.

Still, Luke records, "Then the whole company of them [meaning the Sanhedrin] arose and brought him [Jesus] before Pilate. And they began to accuse him, saying, 'We found this man misleading our nation and forbidding us to give tribute to Caesar, and saying that he himself is Christ, a king'" (Luke 23:1-2).

These were the actions of Israel's highest body, led by the High Priest himself. In this case, the accusation was not only false, but it was foolish. Everyone knew Jesus did not forbid the Jews from paying taxes to the emperor. Just the opposite.

CHARGE #8: AGITATION

Jesus was accused of stirring up the Jewish people (Luke 23:5). Generalizations are all the religious leaders had left. They were losing the battle and they didn't even know it, or perhaps they didn't care.

What could they be talking about? The Jewish religious leaders were accusing Jesus of "rocking the boat." That is not just an expression; that is the essence of the word chosen to describe their accusation against Jesus. Only Luke records this accusation, and the word he used for "stirring up" (Greek: ἀνασείει; English: *anaseiei*) means to "excite" or to "move." The root of this word (Greek: σείω; English: *seíō*) signifies "to rock." This word is found only twice in the New Testament. Here Jesus is being accused of "inciting" or "stirring up" the Jews with his false teaching.

The only other occasion where this word is used is when the chief priests have juiced up the crowd against Jesus. Mark 15:11 says, "But the chief priests stirred up (Greek: ἀνέσεισαν; English: *aneseisan*) the crowd to have him [Pilate] release for them Barabbas instead." What the chief priests had accused Jesus of doing, they were doing themselves. It was a classic case of cruel hypocrisy.

In contemporary society, the word *anaseío* can mean being stirred up in spirit or stirred up to action. When you attend a symphony, and you hear a piece that is very powerful and filled with much meaning, you may say that you were "moved" by that work. What you mean is your spirit was stirred.

On the other hand, when the self-proclaimed leader challenges the members of his terrorist cell that it's time for action and they should place as many bombs in public places as possible, to kill as many civilians as possible, his fellow terrorists are "stirred up" and moved to action to kill innocent people.

Each of these is a valid example of being stirred up, but in the case of the symphony, you were pleasantly moved; in the case of the terrorist cell, you were violently motivated. There is an immense difference. The Jewish officials accused Jesus of stirring up the people to shed blood. However, Jesus stirred up people's spirits to do good works. This may be an accusation of convenience, but it is also one of fabrication.

CHARGE #9: FALSE TEACHING

Jesus was accused of false teaching throughout all of Galilee and Judea (Luke 23:5; John 18:19). It is said that beauty is in the eye of the beholder. In most cases, that is accurate for truth as well. Truth to an individual is what that person is convinced is truth. For the Jews of Jerusalem, the keepers of the traditions of Judaism, they believed what Jesus was teaching was not true. For Jesus and those who followed him, his words were the highest truth.

While the Jewish religious leaders did not have a good track record for telling the truth, Jesus had an excellent track record for honesty and truth-telling. Take note of the witnesses to Jesus' truthfulness from the Apostle John, his closest disciple, and the person who knew Jesus the best.

- "The Word [Jesus] became flesh and dwelt among us, and we have seen his glory, glory as of the only Son from the Father, full of grace and truth" (John 1:14).
- For the law was given through Moses; grace and truth came through Jesus Christ" (John 1:17).
- "Jesus said to the Jews who had believed him, 'If you abide in my word, you are truly my disciples, and you will know the truth, and the truth will set you free'" (John 8:31–32).
- "Now you seek to kill me, a man who has told you the truth" (John 8:40).
- "Because I tell the truth, you do not believe me" (John 8:45–46).
- "Jesus said to him [Thomas], 'I am the way, and the truth, and the life. No one comes to the Father except through me'" (John 14:6).
- [Jesus said], "I tell you the truth" (John 16:7).

- [Jesus said to Pilate], "For this purpose I was born and for this purpose I have come into the world—to bear witness to the truth" (John 18:37).

The religious leaders of Jerusalem accused Jesus of telling lies. However, teaching can only be determined to be false if you know what true teaching is, and from Jesus' perspective, these leaders of the Temple had become blinded to the truth. They didn't know lying because they didn't know the truth.

CHARGE #10: UNSPECIFIED EVIL

Jesus was also accused of doing unspecified evil (John 18:30). You certainly cannot get less specific than this accusation. No definition of "evil" is given; no examples of "evil" are given. The charge is simply leveled against Jesus because it appears the council has run out of ideas, options, or both.

This tenth accusation is recorded in John 18:30. When the Jewish leaders brought Jesus to Pilate's praetorium, John 18:29–30 notes, "So Pilate went outside to them and said, 'What accusation do you bring against this man?' They answered him, 'If this man were not doing evil, we would not have delivered him over to you.'" This is not exactly hard evidence against Jesus, certainly not enough to have him killed.

Can you imagine this scenario in a courtroom today? You haul your enemy before a judge. The judge asks, "What is the charge?" You respond, "Oh, I don't know. He does bad things." The judge comes back, "What bad things?" You respond, "Oh, you know. Bad things." "Can you be more specific?" asks the judge. "No, just things in general." At this point, the frustrated judge asks you, "Do you have any evidence?" You respond, "Well, not really, I just don't like him. He's a threat. He does bad things." How much longer do you think a judge would tolerate this ineptitude and foolishness? The trial of Jesus, however, was no better than this.

Just a few hours later, Jesus was put to death, not because he was a scoundrel, but because he was a Savior. The truth sucked the air out of each accusation against Jesus. Still, while the allegations fell flat, the Savior was lifted up (John 3:14–18).

THE UNDERLYING CAUSE OF THE CHARGES

When Pilate gave the Jerusalem mob a choice between Barabbas and Jesus and the crowd shouted for Barabbas, even Pilate could discern how jealous and envious these Jewish leaders were. "For he perceived that it was out of envy that the chief priests had delivered him up" (Mark 15:10).

The Jewish high court was not too concerned about proving the accusations against Jesus. They had already decided he was guilty before the court convened. The trials were just a formality. In the minds of the Sanhedrin, it was a done deal. It is intuitively perceptible that the Jewish council had difficulty finding a charge against Jesus of Nazareth that would pass the "pasta on the wall" test. It also had to pass the test of Roman justice. With sedition (Charge #7), Caiaphas and his cronies thought they had finally found that charge.

This constant changing of charges against Jesus would not be permitted in a court of law today. It would be evident to any judge that the prosecution did not have an accusation of merit and was only fishing for a charge, any charge, that would accomplish their obvious intention. In the case of Jesus, that was his crucifixion.

> "When you look at the exchange between Caiaphas and Pilate you end up despising them both. There are no winners here, there's only losers."
> —Ben Witherington III

Justice would prevail on this Passover weekend, but not in the human courtroom. There was no justice in either the courts of Caiaphas or Pilate. The only justice was divine justice, when the Son of God died on the cross, paying the penalty for our sins. That satisfied divine justice, and ultimately, that's all that matters.

Chapter 3

Jesus' Trial Before Pilate

Pilate never issued a guilty verdict. He released Jesus to be crucified after the Savior was acquitted of all charges. In essence, the prefect said, "He is not guilty of any crime. I'll just beat him up a little and release him." What kind of justice is that?

PONTIUS PILATE WAS THE fifth Roman prefect of Judea, governing from 26 to 36 AD. Had he served as the Roman governor during any other decade in history, we would not even know his name. However, he was the man given the task of trying the guilt or innocence of Jesus of Nazareth. This one fact places Pilate squarely in the crosshairs of first-century AD history.

To fully appreciate Jesus' trial before Pilate, we must first become somewhat familiar with Roman law and trial procedure in the courtrooms of the Roman Empire. It is these and other issues that now grab our attention.

PILATE AND ROMAN LAW

The emperor himself appointed the governor or prefect of a Roman province. Thus, he was "invested with full authority to administer his territory, exercise judicial functions, give orders for the defense of the province, and maintain internal law and order."[30] As prefect, Pilate possessed the full *imperium*, which included criminal and political jurisdiction,[31] permanent military occupations, and the power to levy taxes.[32]

These three authorizations are the real powers of the provincial administrator.[33] Since his jurisdiction was personally endowed by the emperor, the decision in capital sentences could not be delegated.[34] "There is no question but that he had the power of capital punishment over noncitizens and he could also 'execute humbler citizens or send them to the mines.'"[35,36]

> "[Pilate] traveled around his domain accompanied by no less than a cohort of troops—perhaps five hundred men—who, at his wish, beat and killed protesting crowds of Jews."
> —Jim Bishop

Pilate had the power to adopt the Sanhedrin's conviction of Jesus or reject it outright. The prefect could confer with others, as Pilate did in the case of Herod Antipas. He could defer to another, allowing the ethnic leaders of the province he governed to determine a person's innocence or guilt according to their own laws. He could also decide the case himself. "The Romans did . . . reserve the right to impose capital punishment, as in the case of Christ, but the day-to-day administration was none of their concern."[37]

"The governor had the power to impose the death sentence on all provincials except for the aristocracy, who had been specifically exempted. This power was the *ius gladii* . . . available to all governors from the Julio-Claudian Period at least."[38] This made the prefect an extremely formidable person. Pilate had the full weight of Roman law on his side. It gave him significant discretion in the implementation of the law. Nevertheless, it did not give him full dictatorial powers because he was always answerable to the emperor for his decisions and actions.

The particulars of Jesus' trial before Pilate

While Christians tend to focus on the injustice of Jesus' trial before Caiaphas and the anemic trial of Pilate, we must remember that Pilate's concern was not so much justice as it was to maintain Roman law. Central to Jesus' trial before Caiaphas was his claim of messiahship. This would not matter to the Romans. Central to Jesus' more political trial before Pilate was the charge that Jesus claimed to be King of the Jews.

The Jewish religious leaders never were concerned about Jesus' claim to be their king. They did not believe it, and that was that. Nevertheless, they did use the title King of the Jews to taunt Jesus while he hung on the cross (Matt 27:42; see also Mark 15:32 and Luke 23:35). "That Jews were interested in knowing whether Jesus thought he was the Messiah and that Romans were interested in knowing whether he thought he was the King of the Jews is attested in all four Gospels."[39]

Ernst Bammel rightly comments, "While the title 'King of the Jews' receives short shrift from most writings on Christology, it is very important to the writers of the Gospels as a clue to the explanation of the trial."[40] "Under Roman law, a claim to be king of a province under Roman rule was tantamount to insurrection and high treason: it was, by the *Lex Julia maiestatis* originally enacted by Caesar in 46 BC and re-enacted by Augustus in 8 BC, a capital offense known as *crimen laesae maiestatis* the crime of causing injury to the majesty of the emperor."[41]

"This injury comprised not only treason proper but also all insurrections and uprisings against Roman rule, desertion from Roman forces, usurpation of powers reserved to the emperor or his nominees, and all acts calculated to prejudice the security of Rome or of the emperor or of Roman governments in the provinces."[42] Clearly Caiaphas and Pilate were not on the same page when it came to the legal grounds upon which Jesus should be crucified.

ROMAN TRIAL PROCEDURE

The legal procedure in Roman courts later formed the basis for the modern legal practice in civil-law countries. The development of Roman trial procedure came in three overlapping stages: the *legis actiones* (fifth century BC) law code known as the Twelve Tablets was in force until the late second century BC.

The Twelve Tablets represent the earliest attempt by the Romans to create a code of law. In the struggle for legal protection and civil rights between the privileged class (patricians) and the common people (plebeians), in about 455 BC, a commission of ten men (*Decemviri*) was appointed to create a code of law that would be binding on both parties. This code the magistrates would then enforce impartially.

However, because the plebeians felt this attempt was unsatisfactory, in about 450 BC, the second commission of ten drew up two additional tablets making the Twelve Tablets.

Unlike many justice systems today, a jury of one's peers was not a part of Roman trials. The Roman system of justice was more vertical and less horizontal. "When a man stands trial on a charge of that kind (claiming to be king while living under Roman rule), three ways are open to the governor; (1) he can find him guilty and sentence him (*condemnatio*); (2) he can find him not guilty and acquit him (*absolutio*); (3) or he can find the case not proven and ask that further evidence be adduced (*ampliato*)."[43]

Historian Sherwin-White says, "The judgment could be handed down in chambers. The designated alternative, *pro tibunali* (a raised platform), is reflected in the Gospel account of Jesus' appearance before Pilate. This public situation is described by 'on the judgment seat' of Matthew 27:19, *bēma* being the common technical term for an official's raised platform or judicial bench."[44]

Many societies today use a four-stage judicial procedure based in large part on Roman law.

First, there was the public accusation. Another person would accuse the defendant of committing a crime. Without such allegations, there could be no trial.

Second, the civil authorities would provide an indictment. An indictment was a formal written charge of a crime. In some societies, like the United States, there would be one or more "counts" to the indictment, that is, one or more specific incidents or examples where the accused had broken the law.

The third stage of the Roman trial procedure was the opportunity for the defendant to present a defense on his behalf or be assisted by a counselor. This would be followed by interrogation, examination, and cross-examination by the judge and others on the council. "As far as the procedure which a governor would follow is concerned, it is documented that he could 'deal with crime inquisitorially, i.e., by investigating on his own initiative and by any means at his disposal."[45]

Finally, the judge would make his pronouncement and announce a verdict, and the accused would either be set free or face the full wrath of Roman law. When a person was found guilty, the Roman ritual of condemnation went like this. The judge would say, *Illum duci ad crucem placet,* meaning "this man should be taken to a cross." Then, he would turn to the centurion or guard and say, *I miles expedi crucem,* which means "Go, soldier, prepare the cross."[46] While the cross was being prepared, Jesus was turned over to the Roman soldiers for their malicious, tasteless, and barbaric amusement.

This procedure has remained intact throughout history and is practiced by many societies today, especially in the Western world. The Roman judicial procedure can also be extrapolated from Egyptian court documents. Numerous papyri documents of trials in Roman Egypt have surfaced which indicate trial protocol was composed of something like this: introductory formulae, the trial itself, the judgment, and the conclusion.[47]

The Oxyrhynchus Papyri demonstrates how recording the names, dates, and places of a Roman trial was important.[48] These papyri are a group

Jesus' Trial Before Pilate   37

of manuscripts discovered in the late nineteenth and early twentieth century at an ancient rubbish heap in Oxyrhynchus, near modern el-Bahnasa, Egypt. Papyrologists Bernard Pyne Grenfell and Arthur Surridge Hunt were responsible for their discovery. Since dates and places were important in Roman *juris prudence*, we now must examine two of the places that were significant in the trial and crucifixion of Jesus.

Because the Jews were governed by Roman law, and thus did not have the power to execute Jesus, we are told by the Gospels that early in the morning, the Temple officials took Jesus to Pontius Pilate's praetorium. "And the soldiers led him away inside the palace (that is, the governor's headquarters), and they called together the whole battalion" (Greek: σπεῖραν; English: *speiran*) [a Roman army cohort, 480 men or a tenth of a Roman legion] (Mark 15:16).

PILATE'S PRAETORIUM

The praetorium was the name of the governor's residence.[49] Like the emperor in Rome, governors in the provinces held court in the palaces where they lived.[50] The word praetorium (Greek: πραιτώριον; English: *praitōrion*) is a loanword from the Latin *praetor*, a word that came to mean the official seat of a provincial governor.[51]

A *praetorium* originally described the general's tent within a Roman encampment.[52] The name comes from one of the chief Roman magistrates, the *praetor* (Latin for "leader"). When an army general gathered his council together in the field, they would meet in his tent (the *praetorium*), and thus the word adopted the meaning of an administrative site. Eventually, the general's security officers came to be known as the *cohors praetoriae*, from which developed the elite forces of the Praetorian Guard.

The praetorium became not so much a place or a building as it was a presence. In some respects, the praetorium was wherever the prefect held court. From Josephus (*Wars, 11.14.8*) we learn that the Roman procurators "resided in Herod's palace and took their seat in front of that palace on a raised pavement to pronounce judgment."[53]

The *praefecti* of Roman Judea was in the seaside city of Caesarea Maritima. This was the seat of Roman power in Judea. Here the prefect lived with his family and many attendants, plus his military guard. The living quarters in the palace were built by Herod the Great. It was here that Festus, then the Roman prefect, "took his seat on the tribunal (Greek: βήματος; English: *bēmatos*) and ordered Paul to be brought" for a hearing (Acts 25:6).

The word praetorium had multiple uses, but in the New Testament, it always referred to Pilate's administrative site. Even then, translators have used a variety of words for the Greek word *praitōrion*, as seen in Table 1.

Table 1: The Praetorium in Modern Translations

Scripture	ESV	KJV	NIV	CSB
Matt 27:27	governor's headquarters	common hall	praetorium	Governor's Residence
Mark 15:16	governor's headquarters	the hall, praetorium	palace, the praetorium	Governor's Residence
John 18:28	governor's headquarters	judgment hall	the palace	Governor's Headquarters
John 18:33	headquarters	judgment hall	the palace	Headquarters
John 19:9	headquarters	judgment hall	the palace	Headquarters
Acts 23:35	Herod's praetorium	Herod's judgment hall	Herod's palace	Herod's Palace
Phil 1:13	imperial guard	palace guard	palace guard	Imperial Guard

As mentioned, in Caesarea, where he spent most of his time, Pilate maintained his administrative headquarters in the palace of Herod the Great. When he needed to ascend the mountain to Jerusalem, he set up his headquarters at Herod the Great's magnificent palace on the western hill of Jerusalem. The praetorium, then, was both the residence of the governor and his administrative headquarters wherever he happened to be, in this case at Herod the Great's Jerusalem palace.

THE LITHOSTROTOS

Outside of, but adjacent to, the praetorium was the Lithostrotos. This was a raised pavement, a platform, an elevated spot that was exceptionally well adorned. Everywhere a Roman official or person of high civilian rank went, his attendants carried with them a portable floor or pavement, composed of little colored cubes or tesselae (tesserae).

> "Wherever the Roman's feet went, there went the tessellated pavement for them to stand on."
> —Arthur Quiller-Couch

The Roman general on foreign service carried the tesserae on muleback. This was an outward and visible sign of his status. At each camping place, they were laid down, to be taken up again when the regiment or army moved forward. It was to such a "Pavement' that Jesus was brought as 'prisoner at the Bar."[54]

Eckhard J. Schnabel says the Lithostrotos was adjacent to the south side of the praetorium.[55] Perhaps "Pilate chose this location for its historic grandeur (procurators traditionally delivered speeches here), the larger size of the courtyard surrounding it, and the proximity to the scourging post."[56]

On this elevated platform, the Roman governor would sit on a portable seat known as the *bema*. This was a chair, often more of a throne, placed outside the palace on the raised dais or platform. Here, on his ivory *sella curulis* (the magistrate's official chair), the governor would hear disputes or other matters that came to his attention and pronounce his judgments.

It should be noted that just outside the Basilica of St. John Lateran is a Catholic relic known as the *Scala Sancta*, the "Holy Stairs." This has become a pilgrimage destination for Catholics from all over the world. Consisting of twenty-eight white marble steps, according to Catholic tradition, during her pilgrimage to the Holy Land, Constantine's mother, Helena, had dismantled and taken to Rome the staircase that Jesus climbed leading to the praetorium of Pilate, The *Scala Sancta* may only be ascended on your knees. For everyday use, the staircase is flanked by four additional staircases, two on each side, constructed circa 1589 AD.

The *Scala Sancta*, Rome

On the top of the Holy Stairs, a window protected by very thick glass and by a grating allows pilgrims a peek inside the *Holy of Holies*. It's the pope's private chapel, considered by Catholics one of the most sacred places in the world. Under one of the main frescos is this expression: *"Non est in toto sanctior orbe locus,"* «*There is not a more holy place in the world.*» Understandably, non-Catholics remain skeptical.

Gabbatha

Gabbatha (Greek: γαββαθά; English: *gabbathá*) is the Aramaic name for the Greek Lithostrotos. They identify the same place. John 19:13 tells us, "So when Pilate heard these words, he brought Jesus out and sat down on the judgment seat at a place called The Stone Pavement, and in Aramaic Gabbatha."

The area originally thought to be the Lithostrotos beneath the Convent of the Sisters of Zion.

Since Aramaic was the language spoken most commonly in Judea at the time, as it had been since the return of the Babylonian exiles, likely the Jews were more familiar with the name Gabbatha. At the same time, the Romans would be more familiar with the Greek name Lithostrotos. Gabbatha is not a translation of Lithostrotos as the two names do not derive from the same root word. Gabbatha comes from the root word meaning "elevation," whereas Lithostrotos derives from a root word describing the cube-like construction of the Gabbatha. The Aramaic term relates to the height of the artificial flooring; the Greek term refers to the construction of the floor.

THE LOCATION OF PILATE'S PRAETORIUM

As with most issues related to the accounts presented by the Gospels, the location of Pilate's Jerusalem headquarters has been the subject of tenacious and sometimes abrasive debate. There are but two options for the Jerusalem praetorium; we will examine both.

Some say that when Pilate would visit Jerusalem he would make both his headquarters and his living quarters in the Fortress of Antonio. Others understand Herod the Great's palace to be more suitable for the governor. Here are the arguments for both locations.

THE FORTRESS OF ANTONIO

Emil Schürer has ably laid out the scholastic case for Pilate setting up shop in the Antonia Fortress when he was in Jerusalem. His strongest argument relates to the Roman soldiers who were stationed in Jerusalem. Schürer holds that "in Jerusalem, there was stationed only one cohort."[57] He explains, "This is the *tagma* spoken of by Josephus in his *Jewish Wars* 5.5.8 as always stationed in the Antonia." Schürer believes this permanent deployment of Roman troops cannot mean a legion. He also quotes Josephus's *Antiquities* 20:6, 8 in support of the meaning of "cohort."

The Gospel authors record that when Jesus was crowned with thorns, Pilate's soldiers gathered together the whole cohort (Greek: σπεῖραν; English: *speiran*—Matthew 27:27; Mark 15:16). Schürer argues that this gathering would have been impossible unless Pilate was living where the troops were already stationed. This assumption leads to the inevitable conclusion that all the events of Jesus' trial before Pilate took place in the army barracks of Jerusalem.

Schürer reasoned that Herod the Great's palace in Jerusalem, the alternative site, could hardly be garrisoned effectively if the cohort was in the Antonia Fortress, which it was. However, even Schürer admitted that Herod's palace "was not only a princely dwelling but at the same time a strong castle, in which at times (during the rebellion in BC 4 and again AD 66) large detachments of troops could maintain their position against the assaults of the whole mass of the people."[58]

Model of the Fortress of Antonio

In 1879, huge stone slabs were unearthed in Jerusalem's East Hill just north of the Temple precincts. This led some to think this was confirmation of the twelfth-century tradition that Pilate's judgment hall was in this vicinity. Famous archaeologist Père L. H. Vincent excavated the site in the 1930s.[59] It is located under the convent of *Les Dames de Sion* on the Via Dolorosa and for hundreds of years has been understood as the first two pilgrim stops on the Via Dolorosa.[60] However, archaeological opinion has shifted over the years.

HEROD'S PALACE

The critical question for this site is whether or not a cohort of Roman soldiers (approximately 480 men) could assemble in Herod's Palace, then hassle, rough-up, mock, and beat Jesus of Nazareth before he was led to Golgotha.

Mounting evidence now favors Herod's Palace as the Jerusalem residence of the prefects. Their palace stood in the western part of the upper city, today just inside the Jaffa Gate. It served as a luxurious residence and a military fortress. There seems hardly any comparison between the Antonia Fortress and Herod's palace when it comes to the desirability of the Roman governors of Judea (and their wives). Antonia was a military fortress in which one of the five cohorts commanded by the prefect of Judea was garrisoned. Its comforts and conveniences may have been quite spartan.

On the other hand, the palace constructed by Herod the Great in Jerusalem rivaled in luxury the famed southern Italian city of Sybaris. Two of the palace wings–the Caesareum and Agrippium–were large enough to accommodate the prefect and his entourage as well as a military escort traveling with him. The archaeological evidence for Herod's palace is strong

Literary evidence for Herod's palace

In his *Wars of the Jews*, Josephus described the size and grandeur of Herod's Palace in Jerusalem. "Herod rebuilt the Temple and encompassed a piece of land about it with a wall, which land was twice as large as that before enclosed. The expenses he laid out upon it were vastly large also, and the riches about it were unspeakable"[61] (*Wars* 1.21.1). As Josephus continues to depict Herod's Palace, the impression you get is that this was a massive complex. Archaeologist Shimon Gibson says, "Herod's palace was not a building—it was a compound. The compound was ideal for Roman governors."[62]

Josephus says that within the palace, there were...

> Rooms of great magnificence, and over them upper rooms, and cisterns to receive rain-water. They were many in number, and the steps by which you ascended up to them were every one broad: of these towers then the third wall had ninety, and the spaces between them were each two hundred cubits [1,200 feet]; but in the middle wall were forty towers, and the old wall was parted into sixty, while the whole compass of the city was thirty-three furlongs [2,420 feet].[63]

In *Antiquities*, the historian described the amenities of Herod's palace. "He built himself a palace in the upper city, raising the rooms to a very great height, and adorning them with the most costly furniture of gold, marble scats, and beds; and these were so large that they could contain very many companies of men. These apartments were also of distinct magnitudes."[64] Without question, the Jerusalem palace of Herod the Great was massive and well-fortified.

In his *Legation to Gaius*, Philo of Alexandria (c. 2 BC–c. 5 AD) said, "To annoy the Jews, Pilate erected in Herod's palace in the Holy City gilt shields with his own name and that of the Roman emperor, Tiberius. When the Jews protested, the emperor ordered the shields to be moved to the Temple of Augustus in Caesarea."[65]

Also, Gessius Florus, a successor of Pilate who served as prefect of Judea from 64–66 AD, "Took up his quarters at the palace; and on the next day, he had his tribunal set before it." This site sounds remarkably like John's description of Pilate's Lithostrotos. Josephus also recorded that prefect Cumanus (48–52 AD) sent reinforcements from this palace to the Antonia Fortress (*Wars* 2.12.1; 2.14.8–15; *Ant.* 20.5.3), demonstrating that soldiers could be easily and adequately housed in Herod's palace.

Grammatical evidence for Herod's palace

There is also grammatical evidence that favors the palace of Herod the Great for the site of Jesus' trial. Secular literature uses the word *aulē* (Greek: αὐλή; English: *aulē*) when it speaks of Herod's Jerusalem palace (Josephus uses this term often), but never is *aulē* used for the Antonia Fortress.[66]

The Gospel reference that speaks most strongly to this identification is Mark 15:16, which says, "And the soldiers led him away inside the palace (that is, the governor's headquarters), and they called together the whole battalion." For "palace," Mark used the word αὐλή. For the "governor's headquarters," he chose the word πραιτώριον (praetorium). And for "battalion," Mark went with σπεῖραν (military cohort).[67] Each of these choices by Mark indicates that a formidable force of Roman soldiers could be housed in the residence of Jerusalem's prefect, along with his praetorium.

Archaeological evidence for Herod's palace

Excavations in 1999–2000 underneath the Kishle, an abandoned Ottoman-Period prison enclosed within the so-called Tower of David, added archaeological proof that Pontius Pilate's praetorium was located in Herod the Great's Jerusalem palace. Israel Antiquities Authority archaeologist Amit Re'em uncovered the foundation walls of the palace and the sewage system that serviced it.

This was not the first time the archaeologist's work had pinpointed this location as the site of Herod's palace, as pointed out by the University of North Carolina at Chapel Hill archaeologist Jodi Magness.[68] As a result of these and subsequent excavations, the site has opened to the public so all may view the foundations of this most critical New Testament site.

David's Tower

Senior Associate Fellow at the Albright Institute, Shimon Gibson, articulates the majority academic opinion that Pilate's praetorium was located in Herod's palace complex.

> [T]here can be no doubt that on the occasions when [Pilate] stayed in Jerusalem, particularly during the Jewish festivities, he took up residence at Herod's old palace situated on the west side of the city, also known as the praetorium. The word praetorium might refer to a palace or a judicial, or military seat, but it is likely that in Jerusalem, it referred to the entire palace compound, which on the north included palatial buildings used for residential purposes and on the south, military barracks.[69]

If the question of the location where Jesus was condemned to be crucified, beaten by the Roman soldiers, and released to the Jewish mob has not been settled, it has now been nearly established for good.

Domestic evidence for Herod's palace

This is not empirical evidence, but I refer to it as "domestic" evidence because it reflects a common-sense approach to Pilate's home life. My wife and I were married in 1965. Over those many years, I've learned some things. I've learned certain, shall we say, "domestic priorities." Since, as Theodor Mommsen noted, emperors and governors held court where they lived, it is unlikely Procula, Pilate's wife who accompanied him to Jerusalem on his official visits, would have been subjected to living in a military barracks when a glorious palace was available to her.[70]

Pontius Pilate may have been a hard-nosed politician when holding court on the Lithostrotos, but in his private residence, things may have been much different. At home, there were certain domestic priorities he may have had to adhere to. When in Caesarea, Pilate and Procula made their home in the opulence of Herod the Great's seaside palace. It would make no sense to expose Procula to the hardships of an army barracks when an equally ornate palace to that of Caesarea was available in Jerusalem. The prefect no doubt observed those domestic priorities in choosing a Jerusalem residence for Procula. Pilate may have been tough, but he wasn't stupid!

The New Testament says only that Jesus' trial before Pilate occurred at Pilate's praetorium, which was anywhere a Roman magistrate decided to hold court.[71] "That the actual chamber or hall in the palace or praetorium where trials were held was called *secretarium* confirms the secrecy of the proceedings."[72]

This area appears to be isolated from the other parts of the building by a wall or curtain, called *vellum*, which could be opened for someone to enter the courtroom, but otherwise had to be closed during court proceedings. The expression *"lifting the velum"* meant giving entrance to the litigants in a trial (*Codex Theodosius* 1.16.7).

From the literary, grammatical, and archaeological evidence, plus just plain common sense, we are obliged to conclude the judgment hall in which Jesus stood before Pilate was not along the northeastern corridor of Old Jerusalem, but rather on the southwestern hill, the upper city, the residential area for the wealthiest Jews of Jesus' day.

Tradition does not change quickly or easily. Today, pilgrims to the Holy Land still make that pilgrimage along the Via Dolorosa, many singing and carrying crosses. Will this sacred walk be adjusted to begin at the more likely place, Herod's palace? It will take time.

THE PROCEEDINGS AT JESUS' TRIAL

Even though the Jewish leaders of Jerusalem had a significant degree of local self-government and were permitted by the Romans to regulate the internal matters of their people, they lacked jurisdiction to impose the death sentence on anyone they found guilty. This is precisely the sentence they wanted for Jesus of Nazareth. Thus, the Jewish leaders were dependent on the Roman governor also finding Jesus guilty of a crime worthy of death and imposing the death penalty on him.

Whereas the Jews had an established procedure that required witnesses, sworn testimony, laws, and regulations attendant to their justice system, Pilate was empowered to be the judge, jury, and executioner for Rome's interests. Jesus' trial before Pilate would have been very different from his trial before Caiaphas.

> Three courses of action are open to the Procurator—to impose the death penalty without any examination whatever—to review the evidence heard by the Sanhedrin and determine whether it warrants the verdict 'worthy of death,' and justifies him in delivering Jesus into the hands of the executioner—to try the Prisoner upon any charge submitted by his Priestly accusers regardless of what they already have heard or done.[73]

As mentioned earlier, one of the greatest innovations of the ancient Romans was their assiduous collection of governmental documents kept in archives. Public decrees, tax records, land transactions, and so many other documents were carefully recorded on papyrus, vellum, or parchment.

Today only a small percentage of Roman documents still exist. We can be certain, however, that an amanuensis created a detailed record of every judicial proceeding under the auspices of Pontius Pilate. An amanuensis (in Latin, the noun *manu*, meaning "hand" and gave us words such as *manuscript*, which initially meant a document written by hand) was essentially a scribe or a court reporter (see Rom 16:22). What makes Roman record-keeping unique is that it was nearly universal. Roman soldiers were required to be able to read and write if they wanted to become Roman citizens. It would not have been difficult to hire a court recorder to take down all the things that occurred in Pilate's courtroom.

Having already been "railroaded" in his trial before Caiaphas, Jesus' trial before Pilate was more thoughtful, more deliberate, and except for the unjust verdict, more moral.[74] There are two statements made by Pilate during Jesus' trial that deserve special attention. They are as follows.

What is truth?

From *Metaphysics*, Aristotle's definition of truth is: "To say of what is that it is not, or of what is not that it is, is false, while to say of what is that it is, and of what is not that it is not, is truth" (*Metaphysics* 1011b25). To state that in a less Aristotelian way, "Truth is the correspondence between story and reality."

This is what Pontius Pilate was wrestling with in the trial of Jesus. He'd heard the story about Jesus from the Jewish leaders, but did that reflect reality? Trying to pin down Jesus, Pilate asked directly if he was a king. Jesus spoke of a kingdom different from what Pilate knew. Pilate again asked him, "So you are a king?" Jesus answered, "You say that I am a king. For this purpose I was born and for this purpose I have come into the world—to bear witness to the truth. Everyone who is of the truth listens to my voice." In desperation, Pilate mumbled, "What is truth?"

Pilate was stymied and confused. He wanted to get to the truth, but this Nazarene spoke of himself as a witness to true truth. Still, the truth of Jesus was not the truth that Pilate knew.

In reality, Jesus did not just bear witness to the truth; he is the truth. John 14:6, "I am the way, and the truth, and the life. No one comes to the Father except through me." The most exclusive statement in any religion is the statement that Jesus is the only way anyone can come to God. This runs entirely counter to a world that is hell-bent on inclusivism. However, truth is not a value; it's a virtue. Values change; virtues never do.[75]

Pilate's second noteworthy statement at Jesus' trial was when Christ was presented to the mob outside Herod's Palace. Pilate said in Latin, *Ecce Homo* ("Behold the man.")

Ecce Homo

From the Gospel narratives, it seems that Pilate was uncomfortable with Jesus' trial. Likely he felt it was being forced upon him by the Jews, and he despised that. He also discovered through his interrogation that Jesus had done nothing that broke Roman law, and yet the Jews wanted Pilate to give the order to kill him.

Why present Jesus to the crowd with the words, "Behold the man" (Greek: ἰδοὺ ὁ ἄνθρωπος; English: *idou ho anthrōpos*)? To understand these words, we must read them in their context.

Caiaphas wanted Jesus dead, but could not crucify him. Pilate did not want Jesus dead but gave the order to crucify him. It was the cat-and-mouse game being played by the Jewish High Priest and the Roman prefect that precipitated this situation.

Once Pilate had questioned Jesus, he went out of the palace to the Jewish leaders and said, "You brought me this man as one who was misleading the people. And after examining him before you, behold, I did not find this man guilty of any of your charges against him. Neither did Herod, for he sent him back to us. Look, nothing deserving death has been done by him. I will therefore punish and release him" (Luke 23:14–17).

The Ecce Homo Arch in Jerusalem

Pilate thought if he had his soldiers flog Jesus with a whip (the Roman *flagrum*), and if the scourging was severe enough, cruel enough, he could present Jesus to them with flesh so marred he hardly appeared human. Surely the Jews would accept that as sufficient punishment and drop their demands that Jesus be crucified. Matthew describes that flogging in Matthew 27:28–30.

> "Behold the man. He added no more, concluding that the deplorable condition to which Jesus was reduced would plead sufficiently on his behalf, and extort compassion from the most obdurate."
> —Thomas Coke

It was then Pilate brought Jesus out to the Jews to show a man who was all but dead. Pilate said, "Behold the man" meaning something like this: "Look at him. He's pathetic, nearly dead. My soldiers have brutalized him, disgraced him, and robbed him of his human dignity. Look at him. Look at him! Surely what we Romans have done to him should satisfy your bloodthirsty hatred for this man. Take a look. What more could you want?"

The Jewish religious leaders responded; "We want him dead. Crucify him!"

The Jewish leaders "have no intention of letting the Roman slither out of the dilemma they have fashioned for him. 'We have a law, and according to that law he must die, because he claimed to be the Son of God.'"[76]

PILATE'S PREDICAMENT

In the 1974 American crime film *The Godfather Part II*, Michael Corleone used the famous quote: "Keep your friends close, and your enemies closer." [The origin of this quote is undetermined, but a likely origin is from Machiavelli in *The Prince*]. It is a phrase that Pontius Pilate might have used in his day.

The Jewish High Priest Caiaphas and the Roman prefect Pilate had a love/hate relationship, or more like a trust/mistrust relationship. They had to work together to govern the Jews who always seemed to be badgering the Romans about something. There was never any defined level of trust between them. They were both politicians who made promises they had no intention of keeping. They managed by manipulation, and in each other, they had met their match.

The Roman-Jewish Chess Game

Pilate and Caiaphas were not friends; they co-existed. Their terms of office overlapped, both ending in 36 AD within a few years of Jesus' crucifixion. They were like two pugilists, punching and counter-punching. Whatever they could do to embarrass, humiliate, or defeat the other, they would do.

It is clear from the Passion narratives that each leader attempted to pass off to the other the responsibility for killing Jesus. Caiaphas used the Jews' inability to crucify a prisoner to his advantage. On the other hand, Pilate sought opportunities to evade judging Jesus. He tried to send Jesus back to Caiaphas to be tried by Jewish law (John 18:31). He attempted to get Herod Antipas to try Jesus because he was a Galilean and out of Pilate's jurisdiction (Luke 23:6–7). When nothing was succeeding, he attempted to inflict cruel and unusual punishment on Jesus and hoped the Jews would accept that as sufficient justice (John 19:1–5). Nothing worked. Nothing assuaged the Jewish leaders' hatred for Jesus.

Moving Jesus from the courtroom of Caiaphas to the praetorium of Pilate placed the Roman prefect in a serious predicament. He appears to have been "played" by the crafty Caiaphas.

> "Set by the Eternal to do the right,
> he can think only of [the] expedient."
> —Cunningham Geike

In the Passion accounts, the Jews wanted Jesus dead (Matt 26:3–4). Herod wanted Jesus dead (Luke 13:31–32). However, there is no indication in any written record that Pilate wanted Jesus dead. Still, who is remembered as the villain in this story? It was Pilate. I am not defending Pilate in any way. He bears much of the blame for Jesus' crucifixion. He was a dark-hearted tyrant. Nevertheless, in this instance, the Roman prefect was cornered by the wily High Priest and left hung out to dry by Herod Antipas.

"NO FRIEND OF CAESAR"

One-third of the way through John 19, which describes Jesus' crucifixion, Pilate is portrayed as being unconvinced of Jesus' guilt and is ready to release him. This is where the Jews perform their endgame for Pilate.

"From then on Pilate sought to release him, but the Jews cried out, 'If you release this man, you are not Caesar's friend. Everyone who makes himself a king opposes Caesar.' So when Pilate heard these words, he brought Jesus out and sat down on the judgment seat at a place called The Stone Pavement, and in Aramaic Gabbatha" (John 19:12–13).

The Jews' endgame

Without this "not Caesar's friend" ploy, the trial of Jesus would have been over. Pilate knew the Nazarene was not guilty. Any sense of justice he had was often squelched by his need to "toe the line" for the Roman emperor. This was such a case, and the Jews used that against him.

This was the Jewish dagger in Pilate's Roman heart. "Pilate realized the affair was taking a serious turn; he was in danger of being denounced in Rome. The Jews are capable of bringing an accusation against him before

Tiberius; his career is at stake" (John 19:15).[77] "The phrase 'friend of Caesar' is a technical phrase which meant that such a one was among the elite in the Roman government who were loyal to the emperor.[78] "On his finger, Pilate wore a prized ring of gold given to him by Tiberius Caesar. Engraved on the ring were the Latin words *Amicus Caesaris*—'Caesar's Friend.' The ring marked him out as a man exceptionally honored by the emperor in Rome."[79]

In leveling the "no friend of Caesar" charge against Pilate, the Jews under Caiaphas' direction did two things. First, they knew it was time to play their trump card, to take their kill shot. With this charge, it was checkmate; game over. Secondly, while the Jews were ambushing Pilate, they were also blaspheming YHWH their God. "Most of the vast throng, which was composed of the priestly establishment as well as the staff, police, and servant corps of the Temple, had marched directly westward from the Temple to Herod's palace, and they were starting to get restless."[80]

The words "We have no king but Caesar" imply a formal rejection of the Old Covenant God had made with his chosen people. The God of Abraham, Isaac, and Jacob made a pact between the Israelites and himself. "I will walk among you and will be your God, and you shall be my people" (Lev 26:12). Yahweh said he would be their king, and they would be his people. He had confirmed this pact with astonishing miracles.

However, now Caiaphas and his corrupt priesthood led the call for Jesus to be crucified by denying the kingship of God over Israel. "Thus spoke the same Jews who a short time before, when the Redeemer promised them that the acceptance of his doctrine would give them freedom, had answered him by saying, 'We have never been slaves to any man: How sayest thou; You shall be free?' (John 8:33)."[81]

Caesar was considered a god in the Roman pantheon of deities. To paint Pilate into a corner, these Jewish leaders gave an unbelievable repudiation of the theocracy that God had created for them. They shamelessly disregarded at least one of God's Ten Commandments (Exod 20:1–17).

Nevertheless, what they did to Pilate was even worse, at least for Pilate. They accused him of not being a friend of the emperor, and the implied threat was they would send an envoy to Rome to tell Tiberius that his prefect in Judea was disloyal to him. For Pilate, this would undoubtedly have meant a recall to Rome and likely death.

Pilate knew that Tiberius was a most jealous, most suspicious despot. "During his reign, accusations of conspiracies flourished, founded on the silliest pretenses, and punished with excessive cruelty. The historian Suetonius said of Tiberius, '*Qui atrocissime exercebat leges majestatis*,' which loosely translated means, 'He tried all the laws atrociously.'"[82]

While everything else the Jewish leaders said or did to Pilate ran like water off a duck's back, this charge stopped him dead in his tracks. This changed the course of history. It is evident Pilate found no reason to crucify Jesus, nor would any sane person. However, to be accused of not being a friend of Caesar, and to lose the coveted status of *Amicus Caesaris,* was political suicide, and Pilate knew it.

"Pilate realized that he had overstepped himself in the shields episode and could not afford to get into more trouble with Tiberius. Moreover, if Pilate had just received the instructions from Tiberius to remove the shields, the Jews would have known all too well that he could not afford to quarrel with the emperor."[83]

PILATE WASHES HIS HANDS

At the Roman trial of Jesus, Pilate had a basin of water brought in, and in the presence of the people, both Jews and Romans, he washed his hands. "He is a man who by the pressure of a fate which he cannot circumvent has arrived at an impasse from which he cannot escape. Circumstances compel him to a deed of which he himself cannot approve. In the presence of the people, and looking out upon the open heavens, Pilate officially asks that they take note of his innocence."[84]

The phrase "washing one's hands" of something, means declaring your unwillingness to take responsibility for something or even share complicity in it. This is precisely what Pilate was doing. The practice of symbolically washing your hands to rid yourself of blame originated with the account in Matthew 27:24. It has been found that people, after having contemplated or recalled unethical acts, tend to wash their hands more often than others.[85,86]

> "Whether we believe in Jesus, whether we approve of his teaching, let alone whether we like the look of the movement that still claims to follow him, we are bound to see his crucifixion as one of the pivotal moments in human history."
> —N. T. Wright

The cat-and-mouse game continued right up to the end. In some respects, both Caiaphas and Pilate won; in other respects, both lost. At the end of the day, Caiaphas was back on his couch in the High Priest's mansion; Pilate was back on his judgment chair seeing to the affairs of state; and Jesus, the only one innocent in this tragedy, was dying on a cross at Golgotha.

The Tortures Inflicted by the Roman Soldiers

After the Jews rejected Pilate's attempts to present Jesus as innocent, Pilate's antepenult action was to have Jesus mercilessly beaten to placate the Jewish mob. Make no mistake. Roman soldiers were experts at torturing prisoners.[87,88]

When Pilate became tired of arguing with the Jewish leaders and representatives of Caiaphas, he gave a non-verdict in the case of Jesus. He did not pronounce him guilty; he simply allowed the Jews to have their way. Before Jesus was taken to Golgotha, however, the Roman soldiers took their turn mocking, ridiculing, and beating Jesus.

Some sources say it was Roman law that a criminal had to be flogged before he was crucified.[89] Others believe that Pilate had Jesus flogged in the hope of getting him off with a lighter punishment.[90] There is truth in both beliefs. It was the usual Roman practice to scourge a criminal before crucifying him. However, in the case of Jesus, it appears Pilate also wanted to shame the Jews into releasing Jesus without crucifying him.

Table 2: What the Roman Soldiers Did to Jesus

- Pilate had Jesus flogged (Greek: ἐμαστίγωσεν; English: *emastigōsen*) (John 19:1)
- Jesus was stripped (Greek: ἐκδύσαντες; English: *ekdysantes*) of his clothing (Matt 27:28)
- The soldiers put a scarlet (Greek: κοκκίνην; English: *kókkinēn*) robe on Jesus (Matt 27:28)
- The soldiers twisted (Greek: πλέξαντες; English: *plexantes*) or intertwined a crown of thorns and drove it into his head (Matt 27:29; Mark 15:17; John 19:2)
- Soldiers put a reed (Greek: κάλαμον; English: *kalamon*) in his right hand as a scepter (Matt 27:29)
- The soldiers knelt before Jesus and mocked (Greek: ἐνέπαιξαν; English:*enepaixan*) him saying, "Hail, King of the Jews!"(Matt 27:29; Mark 15:18; John 19:3)
- The soldiers struck (Greek: ἐδίδοσαν; English: *edídosan*) Jesus with their hands (John 19:3)
- The soldiers took turns spitting (Greek: ἐμπτύσαντες; English: *emptysantes*) on Jesus (Matt 27:30; Mark 15:19)
- The soldiers repeatedly pummeled (Greek: ἔτυπτον; English: *etypton*) Jesus on the head with the reed (Matt27:30; Mark 14:19)
- Having mocked Jesus, the soldiers stripped Jesus of the scarlet robe and put his own clothes (Greek: αὐτοῦ ἱμάτια; English: *autou himatia*) on him (Matt 27:31; Mark 15:20)
- Finally, the soldiers led (Greek: σταυρῶσαι; English: *staurōsai*) Jesus away to be crucified (Matt 27:31; Mark 15:19)

What the Roman soldiers did to Jesus before his Via Dolorosa walk to Golgotha was more than typical. The mocking, the spitting, the crown of thorns, the fraudulent kneeling, the crimson robe—all these things were done especially to mock the Suffering Savior. The Roman soldiers were left to their own impulses, and they were having a field day. Never was Roman brutality so unmistakably evident or profoundly blatant as when Pilate gave his soldiers leave to humiliate and pummel God's Suffering Servant in any way their sinister hearts could imagine.

JESUS APPEARS TO BE IN CONTROL

The crucifixion of Jesus Christ and the interaction of the players in this drama were always behaving in consort with the eternal plan of God. It often appears that Jesus is not the victim in the Passion narratives, but the co-director. God was working all things together for our good and his glory (Rom 8:28). John A. Hutton of Westminster Chapel in London noted, "We have the habit of saying, 'Christ before Pilate. What we ought to say is 'Pilate before Christ.'"[91]

Jesus stands up to the religious authorities

Jesus of Nazareth was subjected to a trial by Caiaphas and the Sanhedrin. Most Jews would fear the prospect, but Jesus displayed no fear or any deference to the Jewish court. John 18:19–21 demonstrates Jesus' lack of fear or esteem for Annas.

Jesus was not afraid of Annas. When questioned about his teaching, Jesus questioned Annas' intent and timing in even asking the question. In essence, Jesus said, "Look, I have taught in public places like synagogues and the Temple. Everyone knows what I have taught, and you should too. Instead of asking me, you should be asking those who heard me. You need to establish my teaching in the testimony of two or more witnesses, and you have not done it."

That Jesus' response to Annas was not deemed appropriate by the rank-and-file Jews of Annas' circle is verified by what happened next. "When he had said these things, one of the officers standing by struck Jesus with his hand, saying, 'Is that how you answer the high priest?' Jesus answered him, 'If what I said is wrong, bear witness about the wrong, but if what I said is right, why do you strike me?' Annas then sent him bound to Caiaphas, the high priest" (John 18:22–24). Jesus was not intimidated by the powerbroker Annas.

Jesus only spoke when he chose to speak

The only person in this courtroom who seemed sure of himself was Jesus. He was in complete control.

> "One of the most extraordinary features of the trial of Jesus is that nowhere in it does he seem to be on trial. In the whole collection of characters there, Jesus alone is in control of Himself and the situation."
> —William Barclay

Things were no different when Jesus was dragged to Pilate's praetorium. What was true in Caiaphas' chambers was also true at Pilate's judgment hall. Jesus answered his antagonists only when he chose to answer. Again, here is how Matthew records this incident.

> Now Jesus stood before the governor, and the governor asked him, "Are you the King of the Jews?" Jesus said, "You have said so." But when he was accused by the chief priests and elders, he gave no answer. Then Pilate said to him, "Do you not hear how many things they testify against you?" But he gave him no answer, not even to a single charge so that the governor was greatly amazed (Matt 27:11–14).

Jesus acted according to God's eternal plan

Jesus was completely aware that the religious leaders and Jews of Jerusalem wanted to kill him. That fact is established in all four Gospels. Matthew 26:3–4, "Then the chief priests and the elders of the people gathered in the palace of the high priest, whose name was Caiaphas, and plotted together in order to arrest Jesus by stealth and kill him" (see also Mark 14:1; Luke 22:1–2; John 5:18; 7:1, 19, 25; 8:37, 39–40).

Nevertheless, fully aware that his death at Calvary was the eternal plan of God for our salvation, Jesus both demonstrated prior knowledge of his crucifixion and acceptance of it. Luke 18:31–34:

> And taking the twelve, he said to them, "See, we are going up to Jerusalem, and everything that is written about the Son of Man by the prophets will be accomplished. For he will be delivered over to the Gentiles and will be mocked and shamefully treated and spit upon. And after flogging him, they will kill him,

and on the third day he will rise." But they understood none of these things (see also Matt 17:22–23; 26:2; Mark 8:31; 9:30–31; 10:33–34; Luke 9:21–22; 18:31–33).

This drives the notion that while Jesus was being tried and neither the Jews nor Pilate was certain of what the outcome would be, Jesus certainly knew and was moving everything and everyone forward to his date with destiny.

The scenes where Jesus was placed under the most pressure from others are the scenes where he demonstrated he was in charge of every situation. He was not intimidated by authority. He was not coerced by threats. He was standing before Caiaphas and Pilate to do Kingdom business, and nothing or no one would be able to deter or delay that. Jesus believed, "All authority in heaven and on earth has been given to me" (Matt 28:18), and his actions proved it.

Chapter 4

Was the Trial of Jesus Legal?

At Caiaphas' house, Jesus was judged by the church. At Pilate's palace, he was judged by the State. From those experiences, it appears he couldn't get a fair trial anywhere.

HISTORY IS FILLED WITH social and legal documents that have defined the laws, customs, and regulations of society. Whether they are ancient (The Cyrus Cylinder or Code of Hammurabi), theological (*Summa Theologica*), or foundational (The Magna Carta or The Declaration of Independence), law codes have formed the cornerstone of every well-ordered civilization. For most Jewish people, there was only one code of law—the Law of Moses.

Throughout generations, the Jews have bounced around from nation to nation, mostly living under harsh and cruel conditions (1 Chr 16:19–20).[92] In some situations, like living under the thumb of the Roman Empire, the Jewish people were able to continue to live by their law, as long as it did not conflict with Roman law. In other cases, like the ghettos of Poland during World War II, they were in near-total subjection to their Nazi overlords.

The Law of Moses, along with the specific Levitical laws, was quite specific about what a Jew could and could not do. The law was established, it was firm, and it was not to be broken.

However, many Jewish rabbis became quite skilled at teaching the law in ways that circumvented its restrictions. Jewish Levitical law may have been codified, but it was subject to a variety of interpretations. Many of those interpretations did not break the law; they just "clarified" it in ways that provided the most freedom from the law.

LEGAL REQUIREMENTS FOR JEWISH TRIALS

Convinced that Caiaphas' court could not have so flagrantly disregarded its own rules, some writers have concluded that the accounts in the Gospels are anti-Jewish inventions. This is a very unfortunate misunderstanding.

In 1967, the Israel Law Review Association, published in Hebrew Haim Cohn's book that offered a novel approach to explaining the objective of Jesus' trial. Numerous jurists, both Christians and Jews, as well as those who have no religious bent, have also published studies on the trial of Jesus before Caiaphas. It is not Associate Justice Cohn's interest in this matter, but rather his novel conclusion that distinguishes him from others.

Cohn believed that instead of being hell-bent on executing Jesus, the Sanhedrin was attempting to prevent his execution. He claimed the Jewish Council wanted Jesus acquitted of any criminal activity by persuading him not to plead guilty, or if he was convicted to have his sentence suspended.

Cohn suggested that the Sanhedrin wished Jesus not to make any claims that could be taken as seditious by the Romans.[93] Of course, Cohn's proposal is preposterous. The Gospels, the early Christian writers, plus almost all of history and tradition, assert just the opposite of Cohn's ideas. Sometimes nonsense is mistaken for novelty.

Cohn was once an Associate Justice on the Supreme Court of Israel. However, he was also profoundly biased against the narratives provided in the four Gospels, and almost everything he wrote was shaded by his jaded view of them.

Cohn admitted:

> To clear the way for our inquiry into those reasons [for asking the Romans to deliver Jesus to the Sanhedrin], we must first dispose of the theories that the Sanhedrin was convened either to try Jesus and sentence him to death, as the Gospel reports convey, or to hold a preliminary investigation into the charges to be leveled the next morning in the Roman governor's court.[94]

Cohn chose the easy way out. He simply dismissed the Gospel accounts as "theories." However, in doing so, he foolishly dismissed 2,000 years of history and tradition.[95]

Haim Cohn lists the seven statutes of Jewish law that bear on Jesus' trial before Caiaphas, statutes to which one had to adhere if a trial by the Sanhedrin was legal. In his book, Cohn then denies that the Jews broke any of these statutes in condemning Jesus. Those seven statutes are:

1. No Sanhedrin was allowed to sit in a criminal court and try criminal cases outside the Temple precincts, in any private house.

2. The Sanhedrin was not allowed to try criminal cases at night; criminal trials had to be commenced and completed during the daytime.

3. No person could be tried on a criminal charge on festival days or the eve of a festival.

4. No person may be convicted on his own testimony or the strength of his own confession.

5. A person may be convicted of a capital offense only upon the testimony of two lawfully qualified eyewitnesses.

6. No person may be convicted of a capital offense unless two lawfully qualified witnesses testify that they had first warned him of the criminality of the act and the penalty prescribed for it.

7. The capital offense of blasphemy consists of pronouncing the name of God, Yahweh, which may be uttered only once a year by the High Priest in the innermost sanctuary of the Temple, and it is irrelevant what "blasphemies" are spoken so long as the divine name is not enunciated.

You see the problem immediately. In claiming that no Jewish law was broken in the crucifixion of Jesus of Nazareth, Cohn completely rejects history and invents fantasy.

> "The impression, then, is not one of the favorable Roman and the hostile Jew—rather it is of a Jesus who had no support on any side."
> —Raymond E. Brown

There are, however, two very pertinent questions related to these seven statutes. They are: (1) did the Sanhedrin disregard these statutes in the course of finding Jesus guilty of blasphemy? and (2) were these statutes practiced during the first century or did they come into play only later with the advent of the Mishnah? For the trial of Jesus to be legal, the answer to both these questions must be no.

Was the Trial of Jesus Legal?   61

To be fair, it should be recognized that Cohn and his unidentifiable "overwhelming majority of modern scholars" hold that indeed the answer is no. Some offer a split decision on these two critical questions, while still others believe the answer is yes. My intention is not to defend one position and negate the other but to compare these Mishnah statutes against the record of the Gospels to see if they were assiduously followed or not.

Within the New Testament accounts of Jesus' arrest, trials, and crucifixion there are many details that skeptics over the years have questioned, such as the apparent violations of Jewish law concerning the trial and execution of a capital offender.[96] In this chapter, we examine only the seven legal issues Associate Justice Cohn proposed the Gospels misrepresent. Let us investigate them carefully.

Issue #1.

No Sanhedrin was allowed to sit in a criminal court and try criminal cases outside the Temple precincts, in any private house.

The Chamber of the Hewn Stone was the usual meeting place for the Sanhedrin during the Second Temple Period (sixth century BC to first century AD). The Mishnah indicates the Great Sanhedrin met at the Chamber of Hewn Stones functioning as a court with full judicial authority, including the power to impose criminal penalties.

The following very instructive passage from the Babylonian Talmud describes in some detail both the legal procedure and the importance of the Chamber of Hewn Stone in that procedure. *Sanhedrin* 88b reports that:

> It is taught in a *baraita* that Rabbi Yosei said: Initially, discord would not proliferate among Israel. Rather, the court of seventy-one judges would sit in the Chamber of Hewn Stone. And there were two additional courts, each consisting of twenty-three judges; one would convene at the entrance to the Temple Mount, and one would convene at the entrance to the Temple courtyard. And all the other courts consisting of twenty-three judges would convene in all cities inhabited by the Jewish people ... If the members of the court heard a clear halakhic ruling with regard to that matter, they sent it to them, and if not, these judges and those judges would come to the Chamber of Hewn Stone, where the Sanhedrin would be convened from the time that the daily morning offering is sacrificed until the time that the daily afternoon offering is sacrificed.

From *Sanhedrin* 88b it appears that the Sanhedrin kept regular office hours at the Chamber of Hewn Stone. They must have had a strong union because they only worked 9:00 am to 3:00 pm.

The progressive nature of the judicial procedure in *Sanhedrin* 11.2 is as follows:

- If any matter of the law (*halakha*) was uncertain in the minds of the elders in a particular city, they sent the matter to the elders of a neighboring city for clarification.
- If the elders of an adjacent city could not clarify the matter of halakhic law, it was sent to the twenty-three judges who held court at the entrance to the Temple Mount for clarification.
- If these twenty-three judges could not agree on the interpretation of a matter of halakhic law, it was sent to the twenty-three judges who held court at the entrance to the Temple courtyard.
- If all these avenues were exhausted and there was still no consensus on the interpretation of a matter of halakhic law, the matter was then taken by all forty-six judges to the Chamber of Hewn Stone where the Sanhedrin would be convened daily. The Sanhedrin then made the final interpretation of halakhic law.

At the preliminary hearing by Annas and the late-night trial by Caiaphas, no one adhered to this procedure. Instead, the examination by Annas was done at his house in the palatial High Priest's compound. The preliminary trial held by a quorum of the Sanhedrin was held in Caiaphas' private residence (see John 18:12–13; Matt 26:3–4, 57).

In neither the case of Annas nor his son-in-law Caiaphas was the preliminary hearing and trial of Jesus of Nazareth by the small group of the Sanhedrin held in the official location for the Sanhedrin to hear matters of halakha law—the Chamber of Hewn Stone. The law was violated in both cases.

Issue #2.

The Sanhedrin was not allowed to try criminal cases at night; criminal trials had to be commenced and completed during the daytime.

The tractate *Sanhedrin* is the document in which Jewish legal procedure is laid out in detail. Thus, it is in the Babylonian Talmud's *Sanhedrin* 4 that we chiefly look for answers regarding the legality of Jesus' trial. In non-capital cases, they held the trial during the daytime, and the verdict may be reached during the night. In capital cases, however, the Sanhedrin held trial during the daytime and the verdict must also be reached during the daytime.

Universal jurisprudence prefers daytime trials because juridical bodies that meet at night are often suspected of being kangaroo courts. What occurred during the daytime was generally perceived as being done right. What was done during the nighttime was generally perceived as being suspicious.

If Jewish law and the exercise of it were to be acceptable to a holy God, it had to be just, it had to be fair, and it had to be accomplished in the light of day. Thus, no Sanhedrin meeting was to occur at night, and no decision made during the night was deemed acceptable.

Nevertheless, Jesus was detained, interrogated, tried, and condemned all during the hours of darkness. Jesus referenced the darkness of night in warning his disciples that he would be taken captive in the Garden of Gethsemane, and they all would lose heart and flee for their lives (Matt 26:31).

> "At Calvary, God accepted His own unbreakable terms of justice."
> —Phillips Brooks

Having heard Jesus' words about the disciples' soon desertion, Peter audaciously announced, "Even though they all fall away, I will not" (Mark 14:29). "Jesus said to him, 'Truly, I tell you, this very night, before the rooster crows, you will deny me three times'" (Matt 26:34; Mark 14:30). Again, Peter denied his Lord "this very night" in the courtyard of Caiaphas while Annas and Caiaphas were interrogating Jesus.

Some scholars have attempted (unsuccessfully) to rectify the difference between the requirements for Jewish legal procedures and the accounts of the Gospels by adjusting the days upon which these events occurred.[97] Nevertheless, the Gospel record stands. The narratives indicate failure to abide by the statutes of Jewish halakha law. The only way to disallow this, as Cohn does, is to disregard the historical accounts of the Gospels.

Issue #3.

No person could be tried on a criminal charge on festival days or the eve of a festival.

Sanhedrin 4 is specific. "Trials may not be held on the eve of a Sabbath or the eve of a Festival." There is no question this provision was not kept. Jesus was tried and condemned by Caiaphas and a handful of

Sanhedrin during the nighttime hours of the eve of the principal festival in Judaism—Passover.

The eve of the Passover was the day Jews prepared for a celebration that lasted more than a week. Still, Jesus' trial was held both on the eve of the Sabbath as well as the eve of the Festival of the Passover, the most sacred and meaningful of the Feasts of the Jews. The Mosaic Law was ignored in the palace of Caiaphas the night Jesus was tried.

It's amazing, and somewhat amusing, that Associate Justice Cohn claims that no law of the Jewish code of laws was disregarded or disobeyed in the trials and death of Jesus. His claims are patently false.

Issue #4.

No person may be convicted on his own testimony or the strength of his own confession.

Jewish law would not permit a person to be condemned to death on his own statements alone. There had to be corroborating testimony. Perhaps this was done to keep someone from admitting to a crime they did not commit or someone who was not mentally capable of understanding the charges against him. Each of the Gospel writers presents the self-testimony of Jesus at the trial before Caiaphas. In John's record, Jesus does not respond when asked for testimony. Instead, he rebuffs the High Priest's questioning when everyone knew what Jesus had taught (John 18:20-21; see also Matt 26:59-61 and Mark 14:55-59).

Having not secured certain testimony from the so-called witnesses but seeking personal testimony with which to condemn Jesus, Caiaphas demanded, "'Have you no answer to make? What is it that these men testify against you?' But Jesus remained silent." Luke tells us when the Council led Jesus away to an overnight dungeon holding cell, they asked him one more time, "If you are the Christ, tell us." But he said to them, "If I tell you, you will not believe, and if I ask you, you will not answer" (Luke 22:67-68).[98]

However, suddenly, Jesus appears to change tactics. Much to the delight of the High Priest and the few gathered members of the Sanhedrin, when the High Priest said to Jesus, "'I adjure you by the living God, tell us if you are the Christ, the Son of God.'" Jesus said to him, "'You have said so. But I tell you, from now on you will see the Son of Man seated at the right hand of Power and coming on the clouds of heaven'" (Matt 26:63-64).

Mark couched Jesus' response in slightly different language. Whereas in response to Caiaphas' demand that Jesus admits he is the Christ, the Son of God, Matthew recorded, "You have said so." (Matt 26:64). Luke records

Jesus' response as, "You say that I am" (Luke 22:70). But Mark has Jesus' response to Caiaphas' demand, "I am, and you will see the Son of Man seated at the right hand of Power, and coming with the clouds of heaven" (Mark 14:62). This is one of those ἐγώ εἰμί (English: *egṓ eimí*) passages, the "I am" passages. These passages in the Gospel of John present "I am" as a declaration of Jesus defining who he is and claiming to be God.[99]

Table 1: The Johannine Presentation of Jesus as the "I AM" God

Scripture	Testimony ἐγώ εἰμι
John 6:20	"It is I; do not be afraid." (εἰμι ἐγώ)
John 6:35	"I am the bread of life."
John 6:41	"I am the bread . . . from heaven."
John 6:48	"I am the bread of life."
John 6:51	"I am the living bread."
John 8:12	"I am the light of the world."
John 8:18	"I am the one who bears witness about myself."
John 8:24	"Unless you believe that I am he . . ."
John 8:28	"The Son of Man . . . I am he."
John 8:58	"Before Abraham was, I am."
John 10:7	"I am the door of the sheep."
John 10:9	"I am the door."
John 10:11, 14	"I am the good shepherd."
John 11:25	"I am the resurrection and the life."
John 13:19	"You may believe that I am he"
John 14:6	"I am the way."
John 14:6	"I am the truth."
John 14:6	"I am the life."
John 15:1	"I am the true vine."
John 15:5	"I am the vine."
John 18:5, 6, 8	"Jesus of Nazareth . . . I am he."
John 18:37	"I am a king."

In the Gospels' record, Caiaphas' response to Jesus' claims was not one of recognition but of offense. He began to tear his clothes in horror, not to proceed to the logical conclusion of the trial. It is an indication, although not intended, that the High Priest wanted a quick ending to this trial with a predetermined verdict. Jesus must die.

Issue #5.

A person may be convicted of a capital offense only upon the testimony of two lawfully qualified eyewitnesses.

For Caiaphas, rounding up the false witnesses was like rounding up the usual suspects. It is almost as if they were "on call" to be deployed at a moment's notice when needed to provide Caiaphas' court with testimony. You get the impression the Sanhedrin had them on speed dial, and whenever a witness was required to say, a few shekels slipped into their hands would buy their testimony.

More than a score of them were on hand to testify against Jesus. However, their testimony was so contradictory and so unreliable that the Sanhedrinists themselves were very much ashamed of their performance. They had to be dismissed because their testimony would fall under the weight of its inherent incredulity.

The law of two or three witnesses is a bedrock principle of Jewish justice. It goes back to Moses and the giving of the Law (Deut 17:6; 19:15). The law of two or three witnesses is repeated by Jesus (Matt 18:16), as well as the Apostle Paul (2 Cor 13:1; I Tim 5:19) and the writer of Hebrews (Heb 10:28), all of whom were Jewish. *Sanhedrin* 5.1 describes how careful the Jews were to make sure the witnesses knew what they were talking about, especially in capital cases. They examined a witness's testimony by asking seven-pointed time questions:

1. In what week of years?
2. In what year?
3. In what month?
4. On what date in the month?
5. On what day?
6. At what hour?
7. In what place?

In capital cases, two or three witnesses and their testimonies were required to agree on every detail.[100] The Mishnah also describes how the court would interview one witness at a time. "They afterward bring in the second witness and examine him. If their words were found to agree together, they begin [to examine the evidence] in favor of acquittal (*Sanhedrin* 4).

There is even this stern warning in *Sanhedrin* 4.5:

> They brought them in and admonished them, [saying], "Perhaps you will say something that is only a supposition or hearsay

or secondhand, or even from a trustworthy man. Or perhaps you do not know that we shall check you with examination and inquiry? Know, moreover, that capital cases are not like non-capital cases: in non-capital cases, a man may pay money and so make atonement, but in capital cases, the witness is answerable for the blood of him [that is wrongfully condemned], and the blood of his descendants [that should have been born to him] to the end of the world."

While these procedures possibly were not recorded by any of the four Gospel authors, it is much more likely that none of them were followed and thus not recorded. Mark 14:55–59 clearly states the testimony given by the witnesses at Jesus' trial did not agree, even though they claimed to have heard Jesus from his own lips. But what had they heard? A confession? Not according to Luke 22:70–71. This critical requirement of the law was cast aside in their rush to judgment. Significantly, none of the Gospel narratives record witnesses with corroborating stories testifying against Jesus. It did not happen and was simply dispensed with. The long-standing law of Judaism had become an inconvenience. Apparently, Associate Justice Cohn missed this.

Issue #6.

No person may be convicted of a capital offense unless two lawfully qualified witnesses testify that they had first warned him of the criminality of the act and the penalty prescribed for it.

Jesus had frequent encounters with the Jewish religious leaders throughout his teaching ministry and at his trial and crucifixion. The record of Matthew is representative of all the Gospel narratives.

Not all these encounters were confrontations, but many were. The point in listing these encounters is to demonstrate that at no time, at least according to the Gospel accounts, was Jesus ever warned that he was criminally liable for his actions and his teaching. He was never told that if he did not cease, he would be crucified as punishment for his "crimes." This statute of Jewish law was completely neglected. Today, this would be grounds for a mistrial.

Table 2: Jesus' Encounters with Jerusalem's Religious Leaders

Pharisees	Matt 9:10	Jesus ate with tax collectors and sinners
Pharisees	Matt 12:1–2	Jesus' disciples ate grain on the Sabbath
Pharisees	Matt 12:24	They questioned Jesus' power to cast out demons
Pharisees	Matt 12:38	Scribes/Pharisees seek a sign from Jesus
Pharisees	Matt 15:1–2	Scribes/Pharisees ask why traditions not obeyed
Pharisees	Matt 15:12	Pharisees were offended by Jesus' sayings
Pharisees	Matt 16:1	Pharisees asked Jesus for a sign
Sadducees	Matt 16:1	Sadducees asked Jesus for a sign
Chief priests	Matt 21:15	They were indignant at the Triumphal Entry
Scribes	Matt 21:15	They were indignant at the Triumphal Entry
Chief priests	Matt 21:23	Jesus' ability to teach in Temple questioned
Scribes	Matt 21:23	Jesus' ability to teach in Temple questioned
Chief priests	Matt 21:45	They sought to arrest Jesus for his teaching
Pharisees	Matt 21:45	They sought to arrest Jesus for his teaching
Pharisees	Matt 22:15	They sought to entangle Jesus in his teaching
Herodians	Matt 22:15	They sought to entangle Jesus in his teaching
Sadducees	Matt 22:23	Jesus' teaching on resurrection questioned
Pharisees	Matt 22:34,35	Lawyer questioned greatest commandment
Pharisees	Matt 22:41	They question Jesus about who is the Christ
Chief priests	Matt 26:4	They plotted with the elders to arrest Jesus
Elders	Matt 26:4	Chief priests and they plotted Jesus' arrest
Chief priests	Matt 26:47	They enabled Jesus' arrest in Gethsemane
Elders	Matt 26:47	They enabled Jesus' arrest in Gethsemane
Chief priests	Matt 26:59	They sought false witnesses against Jesus
High Priest	Matt 26:66	The High Priest called for a guilty verdict
Council	Matt 26:66	The Sanhedrin condemned Jesus to death
Council	Matt 26:67,68	The Council members abused Jesus
Chief priests	Matt 27:1	They determined to put Jesus to death
Elders	Matt 27:1	They determined to put Jesus to death
Chief priests	Matt 27:12	They accused Jesus before Pilate
Chief priests	Matt 27:20	Persuaded the crowd to choose Barabbas
Elders	Matt 27:20	Persuaded the crowd to choose Barabbas
Chief priests	Matt 27:41	They mocked Jesus on the cross
Scribes	Matt 27:41	They mocked Jesus on the cross
Elders	Matt 27:41	They mocked Jesus on the cross
Chief priests	Matt 27:64	Asked Pilate for a Roman guard at the tomb
Pharisees	Matt 27:64	Asked Pilate for a Roman guard at the tomb

Issue #7.

The capital offense of blasphemy consists of pronouncing the name of God, YHWH or Yahweh. It is irrelevant what "blasphemies" are spoken so long as the divine name is not vocalized.

Associate Justice Cohn would have us believe that this highest requirement for any Jew—demonstrating reverence for the sacred name—was just one of many "blasphemies" for which a Jew could be charged and found guilty by the Sanhedrin. He is partially right, but that misses the point. Blasphemy and speaking the name of God had a special negative relationship. The Third Commandment warned: "You shall not take the name of the LORD your God in vain, for the LORD will not hold him guiltless who takes his name in vain" (Exod 20:7). For the breaking of no other commandment would God fail to hold someone guiltless.

The *Jewish Encyclopedia* says, "The essence of the crime consists in the impious purpose in using the words, and does not necessarily include the performance of any desecrating act."[101] That's where Cohn is partially right. One did not have to say the word Yahweh to blaspheme the name of God. The use of God's name in any irreverent way, the misuse of the name, or even using the name when there was no reason to invoke it, were all considered blasphemy.

The Third Commandment highlights the misuse or cavalier use of the name of God. The word "vain" (Hebrew: שָׁוְא; English: *shâveʾ*) in "You shall not take the name of the LORD your God in vain" is equivalent to an English adverb. It should be understood as "vainly," meaning without cause or reason, hence cavalierly.[102] It was the deep respect the Jews had for the personal name of God that prohibited them even from saying the name (Hebrew: יהוה; YHWH). Yahweh or Jehovah are just transliterations of the Tetragrammaton, the four Hebrew consonants YHWH that make up the name of the personal God of Israel.[103]

Beyond the Leviticus 24:10–23 reference to cursing, there is no other specific reference in the Bible to what would constitute the crime of blasphemy. The Bible does not say that to blaspheme you had to say the name of God. The Mishnah, on the other hand, has plenty to say about it.

Sanhedrin 7.5 notes, "The blasphemer is punished only if he utters [the divine] name." Rabbi Joshua ben Korcha said: 'The whole day [of the trial] the witnesses are examined utilizing a substitute for the divine name." But the Gemara, (rabbinical analysis and commentary on the Mishnah) goes further extending the crime of blasphemy to "any impious use of any words which indicate the sacred attributes of God, such as 'The Holy One' or 'The Merciful One.'"

As long as criminal jurisdiction was handled by Jewish courts, i.e., before the fall of Jerusalem in 70 AD, the death penalty may only be inflicted on the blasphemer who uttered the ineffable Name (see *Sanhedrin* 56a). Because Jesus did not blaspheme the Sacred Name, He could not receive the death penalty.

So in what way was Jesus guilty of blasphemy in the minds of the Jewish Sanhedrin? It was this. Although Jesus had not uttered the Name (*Sanhedrin* 7.5), he claimed special privilege with the One who bore the name. When Caiaphas demanded, "I adjure you by the living God, tell us if you are the Christ, the Son of God," Jesus' response was, "You have said so. But I tell you, from now on you will see the Son of Man seated at the right hand of Power and coming on the clouds of heaven" (Matt 26:63–64; Mark 14:61–64; Luke 22:67–71).

In essence, the Savior was saying, "You have identified me as the Messiah and Son of the Blessed, but hereafter you will identify me as the Son of Man who is seated next to the Father, on his right hand, and returning through the clouds as the Father's duly appointed Judge" (John 5:22). This is what set off the High Priest when he called for the Sanhedrin to vote in favor of executing Jesus.

The Son of Man was Jesus' favorite name for himself. It is used eighty-two times in the Gospels, mostly Jesus speaking of himself. The identification is clear here. Jesus was talking about himself when he said he would soon be sitting "at the right hand of power." In this case, "Power" (Greek: δυνάεως; English: *dynameōs*) is the ultimate Power, the Almighty God, the omnipotent ruler of heaven and earth. Jesus had just placed himself at the chief seat of honor, at God's right hand.[104]

When the Roman soldiers mocked Jesus, they stripped him of his clothing and put a scarlet robe on him in jest. They twisted together a crown made of thorns and shoved it into his head. And they put a reed in his right hand before kneeling and snorting, "Hail, King of the Jews!" (Matt 27:27–31). It was not by chance they put that reed in his right hand. That was the hand of power and authority.[105]

Psalm 110:1 is considered to be a messianic psalm, that is, a psalm that points to the future Messiah of Israel. It begins with this powerful statement: "The LORD (Hebrew: יְהוָה; English: Yᵉh ôv âh) says to my Lord (Hebrew: אָדוֹן; English: 'âdôwn), 'Sit at my right hand until I make your enemies your footstool'" (see Matt 22:41–46; Mark 10:35–40; 12:35–37; Acts 2:34–35; Heb 1:5, 13). David was saying that the LORD, YHWH to Most High God, said to David's Lord, the Messiah of Israel, Jesus himself, sit next to me and share my throne and authority.

The High Priest and Council were more than upset when Jesus claimed he would be "seated at the right hand of Power and coming on the clouds of heaven." It drove them into a blood-vessel-popping rage to condemn Jesus and require his execution.

After Jesus gave his disciples their marching orders, "Go into all the world and proclaim the gospel to the whole creation" (Mark 16:15), Mark records, "So then the Lord Jesus, after he had spoken to them, was taken up into heaven and sat down at the right hand of God" (verse 19; see Rom 8:34; Acts 2:33; 5:30–31). The theme of Jesus Christ seated at the right hand of the Almighty God is a prevalent one in the book of Hebrews 1:3; 8:1; 10:12–13; 12:2; see also 1 Peter 3:18, 22.

> "Archaeological, historical, and documentary evidence, scientific and medical evidence, evidence presented by the arts, evidence of statistical probabilities—all types of evidence exist to prove much more than a sufficient case that the testimony of the writers of the Gospels is true."
> —Pamela Binnings Ewen

In his book, *The Trial and Death of Jesus*, Associate Justice Cohn wrote 331 pages explaining why these alleged illegalities are not illegal at all. It is not difficult to see what most scholars and ordinary Bible readers would understand to be a very high degree of irregularity in Jesus' trial.

While the list given by Cohn is accurate even if his conclusions are not, it is not complete. There are additional irregularities in Jesus' trial before Caiaphas that Cohn does not mention. We now examine those additional irregularities.

TWENTY-FIVE ADDITIONAL IRREGULARITIES IN JESUS' TRIAL

Even if one would deem the trial of Jesus as legal, it was fraught with many irregularities. Associate Justice Cohn has addressed some of these; most he has not. Of the many irregularities, here are the most prominent ones. Each of these requirements is found in the Mishnah tractate *Sanhedrin* unless otherwise noted.

Annas' interrogation

Irregularity #1.

The Godfather of Israel, the former High Priest Annas, was a very powerful man in Jerusalem and Judea. Although he was no longer the High Priest and had no legal authority to question Jesus, nevertheless his influence over the High Priesthood allowed him to do so. Jesus was brought to Annas for interrogation before he was sent to Caiaphas. This is a legal irregularity.

Irregularity #2.

Mishnah *'Abot* 4.8 cites Rabbi Ishmael ben Jose's ruling against judging alone. "He used to say: judge not alone, for none may judge alone save one." This restriction forbids any judge to be the lone judicial authority at any Jewish court. Nevertheless, John 18:12–13 and 19–24 depict Annas interrogating Jesus with no other members of the Sanhedrin or Caiaphas' court present. This is a clear violation of mishnaic standards.

Irregularity #3.

John's Gospel informs us, "The high priest [Annas] then questioned Jesus about his disciples and his teaching." In effect, Jesus was being interrogated and arraigned even though he had not yet been indicted. When Jesus responded that his teaching was publicly and commonly known, "One of the officers standing by struck Jesus with his hand, saying, 'Is that how you answer the high priest?'" (John 18:22). Jesus' answer was neither impertinent nor out of line, which demonstrates the hatred the religious leaders felt for him. This interrogation before the indictment was certainly out of line.

Irregularity #4.

What could be the purpose of Jesus' interrogation by Annas? Undoubtedly it was to gain information by which to send the Savior to Caiaphas with specific charges. The game plan appears to have been that Annas would listen to Jesus rehearse his teaching and then would sift through that teaching to find something concrete by which to try Jesus legally. However, nothing was found to be criminal or blasphemous, and Annas knew he should have released Jesus. Instead, he sent the Savior to Caiaphas and to a trial that resembles reality TV. This was highly irregular.

Court procedure

Irregularity #5.

Jewish law, along with every other nation governed by laws, required that a formal document or warrant be issued by the governing authority for the arrest and detainment of any alleged criminal. This is reflected in the actions of Saul of Tarsus. "But Saul, still breathing threats and murder against the disciples of the Lord, went to the high priest and asked him for letters to the synagogues at Damascus so that if he found any belonging to the Way, men or women, he might bring them bound to Jerusalem" (Acts 9:1–2). However, where is a written warrant for the capture of Jesus? Why did Caiaphas not issue one? Because the High Priest had no grounds upon which to issue such a warrant. This was obviously irregular.

Irregularity #6.

The Mishnah states that judges in a trial were to be defenders of the accused. If the judge could not or would not defend the accused, he was to be given a court-appointed advocate, a *balil rib*. This would be like a public defender or solicitor today. In either event, judges could not serve as prosecutors. Caiaphas' neutrality is not evident. He was not a defender of the accused but rather an accuser himself. In none of the four Gospel accounts of Jesus' trial before Caiaphas was he provided a *balil rib* or even offered one. The judge also acting as the prosecutor is inappropriate in any system of justice.

> "The more a judge examines the evidence the more he is deserving of praise."
> —*Sanhedrin* 5.2

Irregularity #7.

Sanhedrin 4.1 asks then answers, "How do non-capital cases differ from capital cases? Non-capital cases [are decided] by three and capital cases by twenty-three. Non-capital cases may begin either with reasons for acquittal or conviction; capital cases begin with reasons for acquittal and do not begin with reasons for conviction." In none of the four Gospel narratives of Jesus' trial are any reasons for acquittal given as required by law. No one provided any positive information about Jesus' alleged offense. It appears that the Council was not interested in justice, only crucifixion. This is a significant irregularity.

Irregularity #8.

Sanhedrin 4 goes on to say, "In non-capital cases, all may argue either in favor of conviction or of acquittal; in capital cases, all may argue in favor of acquittal, but not all may argue in favor of conviction." In none of the four Gospel accounts of Jesus' trial before Caiaphas are any persons mentioned who argued for acquittal. This is manifestly a one-sided trial. All who were present argued in favor of conviction, contrary to mishnaic law—another significant irregularity.

Irregularity #9.

The Mishnah *Sanhedrin* 4.1 is explicit about daytime trials. "In capital cases, they hold the trial during the daytime and the verdict also must be reached during the daytime." In none of the four Gospel accounts of Jesus' trial was this the case. All of them report the trial of Jesus was in the darkness of night. Yet another significant irregularity.

Irregularity #10.

The law required trials to be held continuously with no breaks or recesses during the day. This was so unjust individuals could not collaborate during those breaks and "fix" the testimony, or so witnesses could not harmonize their stories. And yet there appear to be hours between the trial at Caiaphas' house just before midnight and the official trial at the Chamber of Hewn Stone the next morning. The legality of Jesus' trial is beginning to have more holes in it than Swiss cheese.

Irregularity #11.

"In non-capital cases, the verdict, whether of acquittal or conviction, may be reached the same day; in capital cases, a verdict of acquittal may be reached on the same day, but a verdict of conviction not until the following day" (*Sanhedrin* 4.1; 5.5). Simply, the call for a verdict in a capital case could not be made on the same day as the trial. This would give the men of the Sanhedrin the night to "sleep on it" and ensure that justice was done. The Mishnah *Capita Patrum* I.1 advises, "Be cautious and slow in judgment." In none of the four Gospel accounts of Jesus' trial was a verdict of guilty reached on the day after the trial. It was offered at the time of Caiaphas' trial. Clearly Caiaphas violated the Jewish law.

Irregularity #12.

Mishnah *Sanhedrin* 4.2 tells us that younger members, who sat in the back row, cast their votes before the older members to protect them from the influence of the votes of the older Sanhedrin members. This makes good sense, but at Jesus' trial, the ranking member, the High Priest Caiaphas himself shouted, "What further witnesses do we need? You have now heard his blasphemy. What is your judgment?" (Matt 26:65–66; Mark 14:63–64). Honestly, what could their judgment be after Caiaphas' inappropriate conduct? He wasn't calling for a disciplined or reasoned vote. He was calling on the handful of Sanhedrin present to ratify his vote and he voted to crucify Jesus. This was highly irregular.

Irregularity #13.

Each member of the Sanhedrin was to vote his conscience. They were to hear the reasons for acquittal, hear the charges, and examine the evidence carefully before making up their mind. This requirement is found both in the Mosaic Law, "You shall inquire and make search and ask diligently" (Deut 13:14), and in the mishnaic law, "He must judge them according to his best conscience" (*Sanhedrin* 4.5; ḤM 17:10). This did not happen in the trial of Jesus. The "fix" was in from the start.

Irregularity #14.

Mishnah *Sanhedrin* 7.5 mentions the blasphemy of speaking the Sacred Name, and even though Jesus had not done that, his claims were taken as evidence of blasphemy. Caiaphas bellowed, "What further testimony do we need? We have heard it ourselves from his own lips" (Luke 22:71). However, hearing this alleged blasphemy would make the Sanhedrin witnesses, and witnesses cannot be judges. This was totally unsuitable, irregular, and illegal, and Caiaphas knew it.

Irregularity #15.

Matthew records, "Now the chief priests and the whole council were seeking false testimony against Jesus that they might put him to death, but they found none, though many false witnesses came forward" (Matt 26:59–60). The Sanhedrin was to act in the capacity of impartial judges. By publicly soliciting testimony against Jesus, they were acting more like prosecuting attorneys. Historian Alfred Edersheim clarified saying, "The Sanhedrin did not and could not originate charges; it only investigated those brought before it."[106] Clearly the procedure for a Jewish court of law was not followed. According to Jewish law, a trial starts when witnesses come forward to testify. The Sanhedrin should not have gone out to look for witnesses. The witnesses come first, then the trial. The Sanhedrin got it backward.

Irregularity #16.

Sanhedrin 5.5 dictates, "If they find him not guilty, he is discharged; if not, it [the trial] is adjourned till the following day. During this time, they [the judges] go about in pairs, practice moderation in food, drink no wine the whole day, and discuss the case throughout the night. Early the next morning, they reassemble in court." The Sanhedrin members were to discuss the case in pairs before the court reassembled the next morning. It appears most of the Sanhedrin were not present the previous night during the trial at Caiaphas' house, and thus could not "discuss the case throughout the night." Another irregularity in Jewish jurisprudence.

Irregularity #17.

Sanhedrin 4.1 indicates, "In capital cases, all may argue in favor of acquittal but not all may argue in favor of conviction." As clear as this restriction is, in none of the four Gospel accounts is it recorded there was anything but unanimous consent for the conviction of Jesus of Nazareth. The Sanhedrin's unanimous verdict was to have Jesus executed. But Sanhedrin 4:1 excludes condemnation based on every Sanhedrin member pronouncing a person guilty. This irregularity seems to imply that Caiaphas and the Sanhedrin threw all the principles of Jewish jurisprudence to the wind to find Jesus guilty and kill Him.

Irregularity #18.

The Law of Moses speaks to the proper deportment of those involved in capital cases. One of the requirements of the court was that "you shall inquire diligently" into the details of the case, including both the testimony for and against the person charged (Deut 17:4). In none of the four Gospel accounts of Jesus' trial is there evidence that Caiaphas or anyone else "inquired diligently" into the circumstances that led to Jesus' appearance before the High Priest. The high court had only two things on its mind—conviction and execution.

The witnesses

Irregularity #19.

Mishnah *Sanhedrin* 4.1 indicates, "Both non-capital and capital cases require examination and inquiry [of the witnesses]." To ensure that witnesses were worthy and believable, so their testimony did not reflect poorly on the holiness of God (see Lev 24:22), witnesses were to be examined regarding their credibility. In none of the four Gospel accounts, was this examination done. Besides, everyone knew these witnesses were known to be fraudulent and unreliable. They could not possibly withstand an examination and inquiry. This is another severe irregularity in the trial process.

> "There should probably be an organization called 'Hearsay Anonymous' . . . the rule against hearsay ranks as one of the law's most celebrated nightmares."
> —Peter Murphy

Irregularity #20.

The law required witnesses to be sworn in and reminded that any false testimony they gave would mean the Council would mete out the same punishment they were seeking for the defendant. Although this could have occurred without being logged, in none of the four Gospel accounts of Jesus' trial are these requirements recorded as being completed. Had these false witnesses been sworn in, it would mean they perjured themselves when they gave their testimony. Likely for most, whatever they would be paid to testify against Jesus was not worth being found guilty of perjury.

Irregularity #21.

"In capital cases, the witness is answerable for the blood of him [that is wrongfully condemned] and the blood of his descendants [that should have been born to him] to the end of the world." Giving false testimony at a trial carried with it very severe and far-reaching consequences. In none of the four Gospel accounts of Jesus' Jewish trial does the High Priest or the Sanhedrin appear to be adequately concerned for the fate of their false witnesses. These religious leaders are so laser-focused on condemning Jesus they were willing to let the false witnesses jeopardize not only their own lives but the blood of all their descendants to the end of time—a terrible consequence of irregularity.

Irregularity #22.

One of the strongest elements of the Gospel testimony is that the false witnesses brought forward by the Sanhedrin could not agree on their testimony. Ben Zakkai asked, "What is the difference between inquiries and examinations?" He then replies, "With regards to inquiries, if one [of the two witnesses] says 'I do not know,' their evidence becomes invalid . . . Yet if they contradict each other, whether during the inquiries or examinations, their evidence becomes invalid." (*Sanhedrin* 5:2). By law, the testimony of the witnesses against Jesus should have been disallowed. The mishnaic law deemed such testimony invalid. Caiaphas couldn't care less. He just wanted Jesus out of his hair.

Irregularity #23.

Mishnaic law provided that witnesses were never interviewed together but were brought in for testimony one at a time, separately. "They brought them in and admonished them . . . They afterward bring in the second witness and examine him" (*Sanhedrin* 4.5; 5.4). Matthew 26 indicates credible witnesses were not found, but finally, "At last two came forward and said, 'This man said, "I am able to destroy the temple of God, and to rebuild it in three days"'" (Matt 26:60–61). This certainly implies that these witnesses appeared before Caiaphas and the Sanhedrin together, which was a violation of Jewish legal procedure and yet another legal irregularity in the trial of Jesus.

Irregularity #24.

Caiaphas still needed credible testimony to legally charge Jesus with a crime. But Mark 14:56–59 indicates clearly that the witnesses' testimony did not agree. Their testimony should have been excluded as hearsay. Still, by this point, even testimony that could not be corroborated or that was given by two witnesses who did not agree was all Caiaphas had, and he had to run with it.

Courts have four principal concerns with the reliability of witness statements: (1) the sincerity risk—the witness may be lying; (2) the narration risk—the witness may have misunderstood what he heard; (3) the memory risk—the witness's memory may be wrong; and (4) the perception risk—the witness' perception of what he heard may have been inaccurate. In Jesus' trial before Caiaphas, only the final of these criteria was met. In fact, the first two were not even attempted.

The litigant

Irregularity #25.

The mishnaic law stated that as long as a litigant could produce proof that contradicted the Sanhedrin's verdict, he was allowed to do so and overturn the verdict. If they had said to him, "Bring all of the proofs that you have within thirty days," and he brought them within thirty days, the court may overturn the verdict. But if he brought any proof after thirty days, the court cannot reverse the verdict." (*Sanhedrin* 3.8). All four Gospel accounts of Jesus' trial record no indication Jesus was allowed to gather and present proof of his innocence. Instead, he was merely judged guilty and whisked away to Pilate's praetorium for sentencing and execution.

Whether it was defined by the Mishnah or by the international standards of jurisprudence from time immemorial, there was little about this trial that could be called appropriate. If you add the issues raised by Associate Justice Haim Cohn to the 25 irregularities we have just examined, we are looking at 32 issues that throw suspicion on the legality of Jesus' trial before Caiaphas. In any just court, this case would have been jettisoned before a trial even got started.

> "Innocent men have been condemned to death whose accusers were unaware of their innocence. But Jesus was condemned to death when his accusers were fully aware of his innocence."
> —Woodrow Michael Kroll

There are, however, many scholars who argue that everything said above is irrelevant. They hold that you cannot apply the standards of the law written in the Mishnah, which was published near the end of the second century AD, to the Sanhedrin court procedures of the first century. That begs the question of when the statutes and practices codified in the Mishnah were first practiced in daily practice. If there is evidence that the mishnaic law had roots that go back to the first century, the argument that you cannot apply mishnaic law to the trial of Jesus is shattered. More investigation is needed.

WAS MISHNAIC LAW PRACTICED IN THE FIRST CENTURY AD?

Harvard professor George Foot Moore wrote, "The inquiry whether the trial of Jesus was 'legal,' i.e., whether it conformed to the rules in the Mishnah, is futile because it assumes that those rules represent the judicial procedure of the old Sanhedrin."[107] Herbert Danby, who was a translator of the Mishnah into English, stressed the legal provisions of the Mishnah largely reflect the views of the Pharisees. In contrast, it was the Sadducees who were in control in Jesus' day, and their views would be reflected in Caiaphas' trial.[108] The case for the trial of Jesus not adhering to mishnaic law because this law was not practiced in the first century is chiefly laid out by German Catholic historian Joseph Blinzler.[109]

However, August Strobel, German theologian and former Director of the German Evangelical Institute for Ancient Studies in Jerusalem and Amman, maintains that "in basic legal matters there is no fundamental difference between Sadducean law, which the Jerusalem Sanhedrin would have followed before AD 70, and mishnaic law." He continues, "the legal rules of the Mishnah and Tosefta, particularly regarding capital cases, reflect the legal situation during the first century AD."[110] Craig Blomberg, Distinguished Professor of New Testament at Denver Seminary, says, "There is no way to know if any or all of these laws on this topic were already in existence in Jesus' day, though many of the mishnaic laws probably were."[111]

Many scholars are aware of the Jewish legal procedure outlined in the Mishnah, but their conclusions are as dissimilar as possible.[112] Some understand the trial to be illegal because it does not meet the statutes of Mishnaic law. Others see the trial as legal because Jesus was being tried only as a blasphemer. Smaller numbers have other dissimilar opinions. "Biblical scholars are just as divided as the lawyers and have arrived at an even wider range of possibilities,"[113] notes Raymond Brown.

While it is true that the Mishnah was codified a century and a half after Jesus' trial, it is still very possible that what the Mishnah recorded about crucifixion germinated in the first century or even before. There are relevant facts that bear on whether or not the concepts of the Mishnah were already being practiced in the Sanhedrin court of Jesus' day. Consider two of these.

MANY ELEMENTS IN MISHNAIC LAW WERE ALREADY FOUND IN MOSAIC LAW

Many tenets of Mishnah law and procedures were already tenets in the Law of Moses. They had been practiced throughout the history of the Jewish people. These canons of Jewish faith and practice arose from the fairness principle of Leviticus 24:22, "You shall have the same rule for the sojourner and for the native, for I am the LORD your God."[114]

Josef Blinzler and others have insisted that nothing of the written Law found in the Pentateuch was violated in the trial of Jesus because Blinzler and others have denied the influence of the Mishnah on the trial of Jesus.[115] However, perhaps they did not look deep enough into the Mosaic Law. Here are some examples of quotes from the Mishnah along with the corresponding statute in the Law of Moses.

First, in some cases, the Mishnah uses a story or historical feature from the Old Testament upon which to build a statute. Examples from the tractate *Sanhedrin* are:

- 2.1—"The High Priest can judge and be judged; he can testify, and others can testify against him. He can perform *halitzah*[116] for another's wife, and others can perform *halitzah* for his wife or contract levirate marriage with his widow, but he cannot contract levirate marriage since he is forbidden to marry a widow" (see Deut 25:5–10; Gen 38:8).

- 6.2—"When he is about ten cubits away from the place of stoning, they say to him, 'confess,' for such is the practice of all who are executed, that they [first] confess, for he who confesses has a portion in the world to come. For so we find in the case of Achan" (Josh 7:19–20).

- 7.4—"The following are stoned: a blasphemer; an idolater; one who gives of his seed to Molech; a necromancer or a wizard; one who desecrates the Sabbath; he who curses his father or mother; he who commits adultery with a betrothed woman; one who incites [individuals to idolatry]; one who seduces [a whole town to idolatry]; a sorcerer . . ." (see Deut 18:10–12).

- 7.7—"He who gives of his seed to Molech is not liable unless he delivers it to Molech and causes it to pass through the fire" (see Lev 18:21; 20:1–5).

Second, in most cases, Mishnah's use of the Old Testament is just to quote a verse and apply it as a statute of the Mishnah. Examples from *Sanhedrin* are:

- 3.7—"Of such a one it says, 'Do not go about as a talebearer amongst your people' (Lev 19:16), and it also says, 'He that goes about as a talebearer reveals secrets'" (see Prov 11:13).

- 7.6—"He who engages in idol-worship [is executed]. This includes the one who serves it, sacrifices, offers incense, makes libations, bows to it, accepts it as a god, or says to it, 'You are my god'" (see Exod 32:1–8).

- 7.8—"He who desecrates the Sabbath [is stoned], providing that it is an offense punished by "*kareth*"[117] if deliberate, and by a sin-offering if unwitting" (see Exod 20:8).

- 7.10—"One who incites [individuals to idolatry]—this refers to an ordinary person who incites an individual who said, 'There is an idol in such and such a place; it eats thus, it drinks thus, it does good [to those who worship it] and harm [to those who do not]." For all who are liable for the death penalty according to the Torah" (see Exod 20:3-4).

7.11—"A sorcerer, if he actually performs magic, is liable [to death], but not if he merely creates illusions" (see Isa 19:3).

8.2—"This our son is stubborn and rebellious; he will not obey our voice; he is a glutton and a drunkard. (see Deut 21:20).

10.4—The inhabitants of a city seduced into worshipping idols have no portion in the world to come, as it says, 'Certain men, wicked persons, have gone out from among you and seduced the inhabitants of their town'" (see Deut 13:14).

10.5—"You shall surely smite the inhabitants of that city with the edge of the sword" (see Deut 13:16).

10.6—"And you shall gather all its spoil into the public square" (see Deut 13:16).

10.6—"A whole burnt offering for the Lord your God" (see Deut 13:16; 33:10).

11.1—"The following are strangled: one who strikes his father or mother; one who kidnaps a Jew; an elder who rebels against the ruling of the court; a false prophet" (see Jer 27:13; Ezek 13:9).

11.1—"If a man is found to have kidnapped a fellow Israelite, enslaving him or selling him" (see Deut 24:7).

11.4—"And all the people shall hear and fear, and do no more presumptuously" (see Deut 17:13).

11.5—"A false prophet; he who prophesies what he has not heard, or what was not told to him, is executed by man" (see Ezek 13:9).

11:5—"[And if anybody fails to heed the words he speaks in my name] I myself will call him to account" (see Deut 18:19).

Often it is the case that the Mishnah's use of the Old Testament is nothing more than to quote a verse and apply it as a mishnaic statute.

Third, the Mishnah also applies existing legal precedents from the Old Testament to its understanding of Jewish law at the beginning of the third century. Examples are:

11.2—"If there arise a matter too hard for you for judgment, you shall promptly repair to the place that the Lord your God will have chosen, and appear before the Levitical priests, or the magistrate in charge at the time, and present your problem" (see Deut 17:8-10).

- 11:2—"Should a man act presumptuously and disregard the priest charged with serving the Lord your God or the magistrate, that man shall die" (see Deut 17:8–13).

- 11.2—"They all proceed to the great court of the Chamber of Hewn Stone from whence instruction issued to all Israel, for it says, [you shall carry out the verdict that is announced to you] from that place that the Lord chose" (see Deut 17:10).

- 4.5—"And if perhaps you [witnesses] would say, 'Why should we be involved with this trouble,' was it not said, 'He, being a witness, whether he has seen or known,' [if he does not speak it, then he shall bear his iniquity]" (see Lev 5:1).

- 6.4—"For it is said: 'The hand of the witnesses shall be first upon him to put him to death, and afterward the hand of all the people'" (see Deut 17:7).

There's not much difference to be seen between Mosaic Law and mishnaic law.

> "It presented only the appearance of a court,
> in reality, it was an assault of robbers."
> —Chrysostom

Fourth, in several cases, the Mishnah only qualified an existing Mosaic statute by attaching a number to that statute. Examples are:

- 1.3—"The laying on of the elders' hands and the breaking of the heifer's neck [are decided upon] by three, according to Rabbi Shimon. But Rabbi Judah says: 'By five'" (see Deut 21).

- 1.3—"Things dedicated to the Temple [are redeemed] before three" (see 1 Chr 26:26–28; 2 Chr 31:6).

- 1.3—"Vows of evaluation to be redeemed with movable property, [are evaluated] before three" (see Num 30).

- 1.5—"And they may not proclaim [any city to be] an Apostate City (*ir ha-niddahat*) save by the decision of one and seventy. No city on the frontier may be proclaimed an Apostate City, nor three together, but only one or two" (see Deut 13:12–15).

- 2.4—"'And he shall not have many wives, eighteen only" (see Deut 17:17).

- 2.4—"'He shall not keep many horses, enough for his chariot only" (see Deut 17:16).

3.1—"Cases concerning property [are decided] by three [judges]" (see Lev 25).

Mishnah *Sanhedrin* 4:1 advises, "Both non-capital and capital cases require examination and inquiry [of the witnesses], as it says, "You shall have one manner of law." But this is not the first time this principle was applied to legal matters, as is evidenced by Leviticus 24:22. This was an established practice for 1,600–1,700 years before the Mishnah was written.

I know the list of examples is long, but it is necessary to show that each of these practices was in force long before the Mishnah mentioned them. Often the Mishnah added to them, such as placing time, number, or term limits on a practice, and more often, it listed the quasi-authoritative teachings of notable rabbis. Still, many of the basic principles for legality and life were already being practiced in the first century and before.

While it is true that we cannot force the teachings of the second-third-century Mishnah onto the first-century court of Caiaphas, neither can we force the daily practice of these teachings out of the lives of the contemporaries of Caiaphas and limit them to the Mishnah. If there is evidence these mishnaic laws were already in force before the Mishnah was written, the fact that they are reflected in the first century does not exclude them from inclusion in the Mishnah.

POLICIES AND PRACTICES EVOLVE OVER DECADES BEFORE BEING CODIFIED INTO LAW

There is a second consideration that must be accounted for concerning the codified statutes of the Mishnah. Codification of law and practice does not happen overnight. It took decades, even centuries, for a law that was being practiced to become a law that was written down as a code.

When Americans think of significant documents of their freedom, their minds often migrate to the United States Constitution. But in reality, the ideas and practices in the Constitution were being formed many years before it was codified on September 17, 1787. It took 168 years of daily dissatisfaction over heavy taxation by Great Britain for the official document of the United States, the U.S. Constitution, to be codified.

We do not know for certain the year the Mishnah was first written or the year Jesus was crucified, but if we use 200 AD as the year of the Mishnah's codification and 33 AD as the year of Jesus' death, the difference is 167 years. The two timespans between the codification of the U.S. Constitution and the span between Jesus' death and the codification of the Mishnah are virtually identical. It is reasonable to assume that many of the legal practices in Caiaphas' day were similar to those later written down in the Mishnah.

More than a hundred years ago, attorney Walter Chandler noted, "After the fall of Jerusalem, the additions and developments in Hebrew law were more a matter of commentary than of organic formation—more of Gemara than of Mosaic or mishnaic growth."[118] This insight is worth noting.

Eduard Lohse argued this must have taken place at a time when the Jews were under the *jus gladii*.[119] Josef Blinzler remained unconvinced that Mishnah *Sanhedrin* 6:2 and Talmud *Sanhedrin* 9:5 proved the mishnaic criminal law was in force at the time of Jesus.[120] Jacob Neusner dated the requirements of the Mishnah to the Usha Period (125–70 AD).[121]

> "Virtually every single aspect of the trial of the Lord Jesus Christ contravened these safeguards and made the whole affair a mockery."
> —Frank J. Powell

August Strobel, on the other hand, argued that the requirements of the Mishnah were a part of Jewish law in the first century and were in play during the days of Jesus.[122]

Among the Dead Sea Scrolls, the Temple Scroll verifies that the requirements of mishnaic law against seducers were practiced before the first century (11QTemple LIV, 8-LV, 10).[123] The requirements of the mishnaic law concerning the seducer (*mesit*) are commensurate both with the requirements of Deuteronomy 13 and 11QTemple LIV-LV. Israelite law has always treated those accused of seducing the people of God severely. This did not begin with the Mishnah; it was in force during the days of Jesus.

"The *Mishnah* was the more or less codified 'Bill of Rights,'" says Frank J. Powell, "protecting the individual in various life situations. Its instructions had been developed out of experience over the preceding centuries and virtually had the status of civil law. It was compiled in its final form by Rabbi Judah Ha-Nasi (c.135–220 AD) but had already been in effect for a long time."[124]

It is fair to argue that the tenets of the codified Mishnah of 200 AD were evolving for centuries before that. It is also fair to argue that the Mosaic Law played an essential role in the justice systems of the first century as it had for centuries before that.

THE LOCATION OF JESUS' TRIAL AND CONVICTION

If the hearing at the house of Annas and the arraignment at the house of Caiaphas on Thursday night as it turned into Friday were not official trials, were they held in the proper location for a Jewish trial? The pre-midnight meeting of Caiaphas and whatever Sanhedrin he could rouse to attend was held at the private dwelling of Caiaphas in the palace of the High Priest. However, if the entire body of the Sanhedrin was not in attendance at what was essentially an arraignment with a full-blown trial the next morning, for multiple reasons anything done at this midnight meeting should have been inadmissible in a Jewish court. Besides the full Sanhedrin not being present, it was the wrong time of day and the wrong place for a trial.

"When day came" (Luke 22:66) marks the dawning of the day of Preparation. It is the morning after the nighttime meeting at Caiaphas' house. Since the usual meeting place of the Sanhedrin was the Chamber of Hewn Stone in the Temple complex, and they were at Caiaphas' residence, when Luke says, "they led him away to the council" it implies Jesus was shuttled from Caiaphas' private quarters to the Chamber of Hewn Stone for the final judgment on Friday morning (Luke 22:66). It also suggests a full complement of the Council [Sanhedrin] was gathered at the Chamber of Hewn Stone, awaiting Jesus' arrival. Mark 15:1, "And as soon as it was morning, the chief priests held a consultation with the elders and scribes and the whole council." For a Jewish trial, this was the correct location, it was the correct time, and the full complement of the Sanhedrin was in attendance.

Table 3: The Location of Jesus' Trial and Conviction

The Gospels' Testimony to the Location of Jesus' Trial and Conviction
John 18:19-21: Location—Annas' private quarters in the High Priest's palace. "The high priest then questioned Jesus about his disciples and his teaching." (v. 19) "I have always taught in synagogues and in the temple." (v. 20) "I have said nothing in secret." (v. 20) "Ask those who have heard me what I said to them; they know what I said." (v. 21)
Matthew 26:59-68: Location—Caiaphas' private quarters in the High Priest's palace. "Were seeking false testimony against Jesus." (v. 59) "This man said I am able to destroy the temple of God, and rebuild it in three days.'" (v. 61) "Jesus remained silent." (v. 63) "Tell us if you are the Christ, the Son of God." (v. 63) "The Son of Man seated at the right hand of Power." (v. 64) "Then the high priest tore his robes." (v. 65) "He has uttered blasphemy. " (v. 65) "What further witnesses do we need?" (v. 65) "What is your judgment?" (v. 66) "They answered, 'He deserves death.'" (v. 66)
Mark 14:55-65: Location—Caiaphas' private quarters in the High Priest's palace. "Were seeking testimony against Jesus to put him to death." (v. 55) "We heard him say, 'I will destroy this temple that is made with hands, and in three days I will build another, not made with hands.'" (v. 58) "He remained silent and made no answer." (v. 61) "Are you the Christ, the Son of the Blessed?" (v. 61) "The Son of Man seated at the right hand of Power." (v. 62) "Coming with the clouds of heaven." (v. 62) "And the high priest tore his garments." (v. 63) "What further witnesses do we need?" (v. 63) "You have heard his blasphemy." (v. 64) "What is your decision?" (v. 64) "They all condemned him as deserving death." (v. 64)
Luke 22:66-71: Location-the Chamber of Hewn Stone. "When day came... they led him away to their council." (v. 66) "If you are the Christ, tell us." (v. 67) "If I tell you, you will not believe. (v. 67) "The Son of Man shall be seated at the right hand of the power of God." (v. 69) "Are you the Son of God, then?" (v. 70) "You say that I am." (v. 70) "What further testimony do we need?" (v. 71)

Given these differences, how are we to understand the appropriate arrangement of the events at Caiaphas' house and the Temple of Hewn Stone?

Eckhard J. Schnabel is correct when he says, "The Sanhedrin session held at daybreak is not meant to evaluate the evidence for or against him—it has been convened to ratify and formalize the verdict that was rendered in the night session."[125] The night session heard the evidence but did not have a full complement of Sanhedrin members, so they could not pass judgment and issue a verdict. They had to wait until morning when the full session could ratify the decision of Caiaphas and his colleagues the night before.

This means the full body of the Sanhedrin never heard the evidence that was presented at the trial the night before. They were asked to "rubber stamp" the decision of a minority of their members, likely at the insistence of Caiaphas, the High Priest. Marcellus in Shakespeare's *Hamlet* could have been describing the Jewish trial of Jesus when he said, "Something is rotten in the state of Denmark."

Caiaphas' timetable for that Friday morning was discomfited. Having arrested Jesus at night, he could take no official action against him for perhaps six hours until the next morning. But Caiaphas had another problem. The longer the desired execution of Jesus was delayed, the more opportunity there would be for Jesus' followers to hear of the bogus trial and respond violently, which Caiaphas wanted to avoid.

John Wilkinson writes, "Caiaphas had to collect a quorum of the Sanhedrin by daybreak (first light at 4:30 am or sunrise at 5:30 am). This meeting had to condemn Jesus on charges which Pilate could recognize as deserving the death penalty."[126] The pre-midnight meeting was at the private residence of Caiaphas. The formal meeting the next morning was held at the Chamber of Hewn Stone in the Temple. For these reasons, a nighttime hearing with false evidence presented and a daytime trial where the verdict was decided and handed down seems to be the most likely configuration for Jesus' trial before Caiaphas.

CONCLUSIONS

At Caiaphas' house, Jesus was judged by the synagogue. At Pilate's palace, he was judged by the State. From those experiences, it appears he couldn't get a fair trial anywhere!

As Craig Blomberg concludes, "Leaders desperate to do away with someone they perceive as a serious threat will often violate even what existing laws they may otherwise follow. With all these variables, it is difficult to see how one could mount a convincing case that the Sanhedrin could not have acted as the Gospels claim they did."[127] That leaves us with two possible conclusions.

First, some conclude that since claims of illegality stem from Jesus' trial not adhering to the mishnaic laws, and given that the Mishnah was not codified for approximately seventeen decades after Jesus' trial, the assertion that the trial of Jesus was illegal, as presented in the Gospel narratives, is not reliable.

Josef Blinzler argued that, before 70 AD, the Sanhedrin followed a Sadducean code and not the Pharisaic code as recorded in the Mishnah.[128] He believed not a single Pharisaic and, more notably, humane regulation of the Mishnah was observed in the trial of Jesus, and that proves that only Sadducean rules were observed.[129] Blinzler concluded: "Thus the thesis that the Tractate Sanhedrin did not yet apply in Jewish penal law in the period before A.D. 70 which is so important for a correct assessment of the trial of Jesus, can be regarded as unshaken."[130]

Unshaken for Blinzler, perhaps, but there is a genuine alternative to rejecting the Gospel accounts of the trial and death of Jesus as historically accurate. It is a possibility many liberal scholars do not wish to consider.

Perhaps the Sanhedrin and Caiaphas the High Priest followed neither the Pharisaic code nor the Sadducean code at Jesus' trial. Blinzler believed that the trial of Jesus had to be legal because of the absence of proof of any Pharisaic elements in the trial (i.e., mishnaic law). Nevertheless, the absence of proof that Pharisaic rules were used does not qualify as the presence of proof that Sadducean rules were. It could just as easily prove that no rules were observed by the Pharisees or the Sadducees at all. The evidence from the Gospels raises the possibility that at the trial of Jesus, the High Priest, the Sanhedrin, the court proceedings, and everyone involved went rogue.

The legality of the trial of Jesus does not depend on the Mishnah. This second view sees the trial in Caiaphas' private quarters that night as nothing more than a bold attempt by the religious leaders of Jerusalem to rid themselves of a growing threat to their authority. Exasperated by the purity and popularity of the Savior, the religious leaders threw caution to the wind and engaged in what was nothing less than a kangaroo court.

Even if the Mishnah's guidelines were not followed in the trial of Jesus, that does not mean the trial was legal. There are broader considerations here than just the measuring stick of the Mishnah. There is also a measuring stick of international law, i.e., "the basic notion is that a general principle of international law is some proposition of law so fundamental that it will be found in virtually every legal system."[131]

Although it was not until the fifteenth century that a confluence of factors contributed to the accelerated development of international law, throughout history this law, the law of society, universally recognizes the following principles, in addition to others, as representative of serving human justice:

- Only those qualified and unbiased should be considered lawful judges.
- No one may be punished except for a distinct breach of an existing law established in the ordinary legal manner before ordinary legal courts.
- No person should be judged for whom accusations or charges were not made.
- All individuals are "innocent until proven otherwise."
- Every human being should be treated equally by the same courts and should have the same rights.
- Every accused person must be given the opportunity for an adequate defense.
- No person should be found guilty based on self-incrimination.
- A conviction for offenses should be based solely on the evidence. Ideally, evidence should include personal testimony from two or more witnesses.
- To ensure there is no false testimony, witnesses should be sworn in by an oath.
- Witnesses accusing a defendant should be vigorously cross-examined.
- Both judge and jury must bring no presumption of guilt or innocence to the trial.
- There must be no collusion between witnesses, judge, jury, or court officials.
- To avoid even the appearance of injustice, trials should be held at a time and a place available to observers for public scrutiny[132]

If the Gospel narratives are to be believed and considered an accurate history, almost nothing of Jesus' trial before Caiaphas and the Sanhedrin will meet these minimum standards of universally accepted justice. One does not need the Mishnah to detect that. All the irregularities in the trial of Jesus are not just irregularities concerning the code of the Mishnah; there are irregularities of natural justice as well.

Nearly all those principles were openly flouted in the trial of Christ. His trial was unjust and illegal by virtually every principle of jurisprudence that was known at the time. Caiaphas and the Sanhedrin turned their own Council into a kangaroo court with the predetermined purpose of killing

Jesus. The trial they imposed on him was one extended act of deliberate inhumanity, the greatest miscarriage of justice in the history of the world.[133]

Was the trial of Jesus legal? Some say yes; some say no; some say partially. Nevertheless, the One who was being tried did not seem to be concerned about legality. For him, the trial was painful, unfair, unjust, and necessary. It was all part of the eternal plan of the Triune God to send Jesus to Golgotha's Cross to be "the propitiation for our sins and not for ours only but also for the sins of the whole world" (1 John 2:2).

The prospects are enormous.

Chapter 5

The Essentials of Jesus' Crucifixion

Jesus was not unfamiliar with "the place of the skull." He had passed it dozens of times, arrayed each time with criminals being crucified. He looked at Golgotha with eyes of passion, awaiting his day, his turn, his date with destiny.

THE FIRST-CENTURY ROMAN EDUCATOR and rhetorician Quintilian wrote:

> Whenever we crucify the guilty, the most crowded roads are chosen, where the most people can see and be moved by this fear. For penalties relate not so much to retribution as to their exemplary effect" (Quintilian, *Declamations* 274).

Roman law decreed that crucifixions must occur in the most public places so the highest number of passersby could view their indecency. This would have the most significant possible impact on the citizens of occupied territories, such as Judea. In the case of Jesus, this was Passover week when the largest number of Jews would be in the Holy City and able to witness his crucifixion at Calvary.

Nevertheless, how was it determined where the killing fields would be? Who decided where those to be crucified were crucified? We must investigate.

THREE LOCATIONS FOR A TRIAL

Since in the provinces Roman justice was entirely up to the governor or those appointed by him, there was little chance for any standardization in judicial procedure. The Roman prefect would consider the facts and make his judgment. There was, of course, Roman law that he had to be aware of and follow, but laws passed by the Senate in Rome could not possibly address all the nuances of criminal activity in distant provinces. Here the locals had their own laws. As a result, the prefect had a great deal of discretion in how and where justice was applied.

The twentieth-century Dutch Neo-Calvinist theologian and professor, Klaas Schilder, wrote a trilogy about Jesus' death (*Christ in His Suffering, Christ on Trial*, and *Christ Crucified*). In *Christ on Trial*, addressing the appropriateness of Pilate sending Jesus to Herod Antipas for trial because Jesus was from Galilee, Schilder reports:

> As it happened, there was a regulation at the time which had it that an accused person might be tried in any of three places: 1) at the place of his birth; 2) at the place where he established his residence, or 3) at the place in which he had committed his crime. According to this regulation, more than one basis could be named to justify calling the tetrarch of Galilee into the trial of Jesus.[134]

This regulation generated a real problem for Pilate and the Romans. The site of Jesus' birth was Bethlehem in Judea (Matt 2:1; Luke 2:4, 15; John 7:42; Mic 5:2). However, very little of Jesus' life is associated with Bethlehem after his birth. Though he was raised in Nazareth, Jesus made Capernaum his residential home (Matt 4:13; 9:1; 17:24; Mark 1:21; 2:1; 9:33; Luke 4:23; 4:31;7:1; John 2:12; 4:46; 6:17, 24, 59).

It was also the common Roman practice to execute a lawbreaker where he committed a crime (*Forum Deliciti*). But how does one determine where Jesus committed a crime if his crime was healing the sick, raising the dead, and teaching the people about God? Jesus was an itinerant teacher. Where does one begin? Would you hold his execution in Galilee (Mark 1:14); by the Sea of Galilee (Matt 14:14); in Cana (John 2:1); Gennesaret (Matt 14:34); Sychar of Samaria (John 4:5); Caesarea Philippi (Matt 16:13); Capernaum (Matt 17:24); Jericho (Matt 20:29); the land of the Gerasenes (Mark 5:1); Bethsaida (Mark 8:22); beyond the Jordan (Mark 10:1); Tyre and Sidon (Matt 15:21), just to name a few sites where Jesus worked the works of his Heavenly Father?

Holding trial and executing punishment at the location of the crime seems to be a Jewish practice as well. The Jewish Talmudist Rabbi Samuel bar Naḥmani (c. 270–330 AD) lived in Babylonia and is known throughout the Talmud only as Rabbah. Rabbah said, "In the place where the brigand robs, there they crucify him." The rabbi demonstrates the common practice of holding court wherever a crime was committed.

> "Jesus was not crucified in a Cathedral between two candles, but on a cross between two thieves; on the town garbage heap . . . at the kind of place where cynics talk smut, and thieves curse, and soldiers gamble."
> —George F. Macleod

It was determined that since most of his "crime" was committed in Jerusalem, it was appropriate to crucify Jesus there. This was likely more for expedience's sake rather than for adherence to any regulation.

A PLACE OUTSIDE THE CITY

Hebrews 13:11–12, "For the bodies of those animals whose blood is brought into the holy places by the high priest as a sacrifice for sin are burned outside the camp. So Jesus also suffered outside the gate in order to sanctify the people through his own blood." In the Pentateuch, the expression "outside the camp" occurs twenty-two times. More than a quarter of those times, it refers to making the sin offering "outside the camp" (Exod 29:14; Lev 4:12, 21; 8:17; 9:11; 16:27). The writer of Hebrews is crystal clear that Jesus would become our sin offering "outside the camp" as well. Thus, the most certain facet of the location of Jesus' crucifixion is that it had to occur outside Jerusalem's city walls.

Literary affirmation

There is evidence in the sources that certain cities in the Roman Empire had places of execution permanently established outside the city walls. In *Miles Gloriosus* 2.4.6–7, the Roman playwright Plautus specifies that the person who carried the crossbeam of his cross would be crucified outside the gate.[135]

The Roman historian Tacitus records there was such a place in Rome on the Campus Esqulinus. It was called *Sessorium* and was the place slaves were crucified, their execution being accomplished by the *carnifex servorum* or executioner.[136] Later this disgraceful location became known as the "forest of crosses," where the bodies of many executed victims became the prey of vultures and other predatory birds.[137] Justus Lipsius says their bodies were eaten while the slaves were still alive and hanging on their crosses.[138] Charles Duane Johnson confirms, "The crucified body was sometimes left to rot on the cross and serve as a disgrace, a convincing warning and deterrent to passersby."[139]

In Jerusalem, those deemed worthy of execution by the Roman prefect were crucified at Golgotha, the place of the skull, outside the city. This established killing field is mentioned by all four Gospel writers as the site where Jesus of Nazareth was crucified. (Matt 27:33; Mark 15:22; Luke 23:33; John 19:17). Golgotha was Jerusalem's equivalent of Rome's *Sessorium*.

Jesus was not unfamiliar with "the place of the skull." He had passed it dozens of times going in and out of the city, each time arrayed with criminals being crucified. He looked at Golgotha with eyes of passion, awaiting his day, his turn, his date with destiny.

Biblical affirmation

Leviticus 24:13-14 specifies that the blasphemer was to be taken outside the camp and stoned by the entire community of Israel. Similarly, Numbers 15:35-36 indicates the Sabbath-breaker was to be stoned outside the camp. Raymond Brown remarks:

> [In Greek,] both passages use *exagein*, the verb employed here only by Mark 15:20b. When Israel settled in the Promised Land, that directive was understood in terms of outside the city, that is where Naboth was led to be stoned for cursing God and king (I Kgs 21:13), and where Stephen was dragged to be stoned for blasphemy against Moses and God (Acts 7:58; see 6:1).[140]

Another reason executions took place outside the city was the strict Jewish laws regarding the proximity of dead bodies to the living. Coming into contact with a dead body meant a period of ritual cleansing for uncleanness (Num 19:11-22). The Pharisees especially took this very seriously. As a result, those few tombs that happened to be within the city were often whitewashed, so no Jew could accidentally come into direct contact with death. Besides this restriction, there was a curse upon anyone who was hanged on a tree (Deut 21:22-23; see also Gal 3:13). Therefore, to avoid a curse from God within the Holy City, all crucifixions had to occur outside the gates.

> "Jesus doesn't want us whitewashed; He wants to wash us white."
> —J. Clay Stevens

Grammatical affirmation

The grammar used by the four Gospel writers is not only quite similar, but it is also quite telling. In each of the Gospel accounts of Jesus being led by Roman soldiers to Golgotha, the verbs confirm Jesus was led outside of Jerusalem to be crucified.

Matthew 27:32-33 says, "As they went out, they found a man of Cyrene, Simon by name. They compelled this man to carry his cross. And they came to a place called Golgotha (which means Place of a Skull)." The words "they went out" (Greek: Ἐξερχόμενοι; English: *Exerchomenoi*, are a combination of ἐκ "out of" and ἔρχομαι "to bring, come, or pass") and therefore mean "to pass out of."

Mark 15:20-22 indicates, "And they led him out to crucify him." The phrase "led him out" (Greek: ἐξάγουσιν; English: *exagousin*), is a combination of ἐκ "out of" and ἄγω "to bring" or "to lead" and means "to lead out." Luke and John agree (see Luke 23:32-33, and John 19:16-17, the same as Matt 27:32-33). Levitical law and Roman law were both observed when the Roman soldiers led Jesus through the Jerusalem gate to the designated place of execution, Golgotha.

Historical confirmation

The noted church historian Eusebius journeyed to Jerusalem with Queen Helena, mother of Constantine the Great (272-337 AD). The purpose of the journey was to discover, confirm, and preserve the site of the Lord's crucifixion. The local Christians of Jerusalem immediately led Eusebius and the Queen Mother to a site outside of the gates of the Old City. On this site, liturgical celebrations had been held until 66 AD.[141]

The site's landscape underwent significant changes in 135 AD when Emperor Hadrian (36-138 AD) rebuilt Jerusalem as a Roman city that he named Aelia Capitolina. Hadrian built temples to Roman deities, including Aphrodite and Jupiter. Still, the local Christians knew the exact spot that Jesus' followers centuries earlier identified as the site of Golgotha and Jesus' crucifixion.

Erich Kiehl summarizes what we know about Jerusalem's execution site. "The place of execution was near Jerusalem (John 19:20), outside the walls of the city (Heb 13:12), and close to a busy street (Mark 15:29). Matthew 26:65-66 and Mark 14:63-64 note that Jesus was condemned for blasphemy. Leviticus 24:14 and Numbers 15:35-36 stipulate that blasphemers were to be executed outside the camp."[142]

THE WALL OF JERUSALEM IN JESUS' DAY

Look at a map of the Old City of Jerusalem today, and the leading contender for the location of Golgotha has a problem. The Church of the Holy Sepulchre is inside the existing wall of the Old City. Does this disqualify it as a candidate for the authentic site of Jesus' death and subsequent burial? Not if you understand the history of the walls of Jerusalem.

Visitors to the Holy City today have to be impressed with the wall that encircles the Old City. It is, indeed, massive. The average height of this wall is almost 12 meters (40 feet); the average thickness is just over 2.5 meters (8 feet); the length of the wall is about 4,018 meters (2½ miles). Walking the Ramparts Wall is something everyone who is fit should attempt on a visit to Jerusalem.[143]

The Church of the Holy Sepulchre

The current walls were built when Jerusalem was part of the Ottoman Empire. The great Sultan Suleiman the Magnificent ordered the ruined city walls rebuilt. The work took four years, between 1537 and 1541 AD. Today the Jerusalem wall contains thirty-four watchtowers and seven main gates open for traffic, with two additional gates discovered by archaeologists. In 1981, the Old City of Jerusalem, along with its walls, was added to the UNESCO World Heritage Site list.

Walls have surrounded Jerusalem throughout its history. David prayed to God asking, "Do good to Zion in your good pleasure; build up the walls of Jerusalem" (Ps 51:18). And he begged, "Pray for the peace of Jerusalem! May they be secure who love you! Peace be within your walls and security within your towers!" (Ps 122:6–7).

Table 1 is representative of the multi-layered history of Jerusalem's walls.

Table 1: The History of Jerusalem's Walls

Dates	Identification of the Wall
c. 2000–1550 BC	The Wall of the Middle Bronze Age
?? BC–1004 BC	The Wall of the Jebusites
1004–971 BC	The Wall of David around the City of David
971–31 BC	The Wall of Solomon encompassing the Temple Mount
931–586 BC	The Wall of Hezekiah "Broad Wall" for western expansion
444–42 BC	The Wall of Nehemiah and the Returning Exiles
140 BC to 37 BC	The Wall of the Hasmonean Dynasty
37 BC–4 AD	The Wall of Herod the Great
37–70 AD	The Wall of Northern Expansion
70–299 AD	The Wall of Aelia Capitolina
299–313 AD	The Wall of third-century Jerusalem
313–637 AD	The Wall expanding Jerusalem for Christian pilgrimages
637–1517 AD	The Walls of the Muslims, Crusaders, and Mamluks
1517 AD–present	The Wall of Suleiman the Magnificent

Our primary source for information about the walls surrounding Jerusalem in Jesus' day is the historian Josephus. Here is how he described the fortifications of Jerusalem in the late Second Temple Period.

> The city of Jerusalem was fortified with three walls, on such parts as were not encompassed with unpassable valleys; for in such places it had but one wall. The city was built upon two hills, which are opposite to one another, and have a valley to divide them asunder; at which valley the corresponding rows of houses on both hills end. Of these hills, that which contains the upper city is much higher, and in length more direct. Accordingly, it was called the "Citadel," by King David . . . the other hill, which was called "Acra," and sustains the lower city . . . Now the Valley of the Cheesemongers, as it was called, and was that which we told you before distinguished the hill of the upper city from that of the lower, extended as far as Siloam; for that is the name of a fountain which hath sweet water in it, and this in great plenty also (*Wars* V.4.1).

Josephus mentions three fortified walls around Jerusalem in his day, the first century AD. A brief description of each follows.

The First Wall (ca. 130 BC)

Josephus called this wall the "old one" beginning on the north at the tower Hippicus and extending as far as the cloister of the Temple. From that same northern starting point, the wall was built westward to the Gate of the Essenes, then above the Pool of Siloam, stretching around to the eastern cloister of the Temple.

The Second Wall (ca. 50–51 BC?)

Josephus notes this wall began at the Gennath Gate of the first wall and encompassed the northern quarter of the city, reaching as far as the Antonia Fortress.

The Third Wall (41–44 AD)

The third wall was more expansive than the first two. It began at the Hippicus Tower stretching around the north quarter of the city to the monuments of Helena, then passed by the sepulchral caverns of the kings, and bent at the corner tower which is the "Monument of the Fuller," and finally joined the "old wall" at the Kidron Valley (*Wars* V.4.2).[144]

From this map, we can easily see the Church of the Holy Sepulchre and the Garden Tomb are both outside Josephus' Second Wall which crosses the Tyropoean Valley southward to the First Wall. Excavations inside the Old City have shown that the Second Wall did not enclose the Holy Sepulchre church, thus making the church an acceptable location for Golgotha and Jesus' tomb.

Map 1: The Holy City

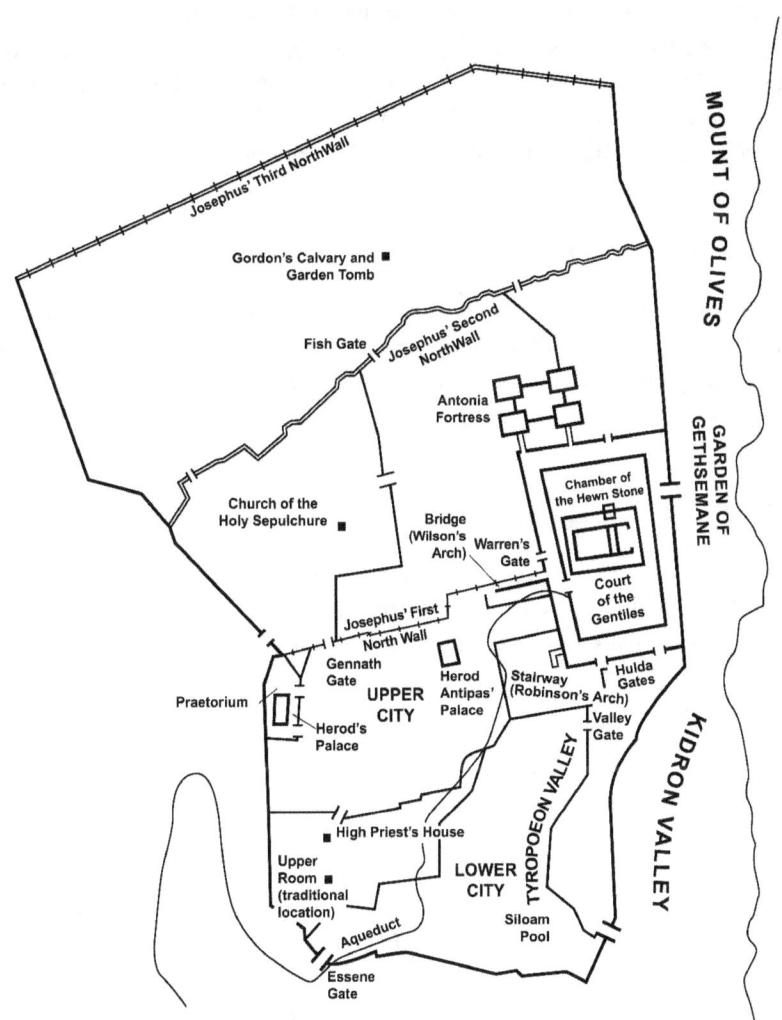

A PLACE CALLED GOLGOTHA

One would think that a location as necessary to the Passion narratives would be mentioned dozens of times in the Gospels. However, Golgotha is found in only three verses in the New Testament (Matt 27:33; Mark 15:22: and John 19:17). So why did Luke use the word "Calvary" instead of Golgotha? He didn't; he used the same word (Greek: Κρανίον; English: *Kranion*) as the other Gospel authors. The word *calvaria* is the Latin equivalent of *Kranion*, and this name for Golgotha became popular because the translators of the King James Bible chose to use *calvaria* or Calvary instead of Golgotha in Luke 23:33 (see also the NKJV and AKJV). These translators were not alone,[145] but most Bible translations today have opted for the Aramaic over the Greek meaning of "the Skull." (CEV, ESV, GNT, HCSB, JBP, TLB, NASB, NIV, NRSEV, NRES [Catholic Edition], RSV, and more).[146]

The meaning of Golgotha

From the account of John, we learn Golgotha is an Aramaic word. We know it as a Greek transliteration of the Aramaic *gulgultha'* and the Hebrew *gulgolet* coming from the root consonants *glgl* meaning "round things," such as a wheel or a human skull.

The reason behind the name

For many centuries the reason this site is called Golgotha, "the Place of the Skull" or "Skull Hill" (see MSG) has been vigorously debated. Several theories present themselves with varying degrees of plausibility.

Topography.

The first view relates to the topography of the site. Golgotha, the Place of the Skull, could refer to a geological formation resembling a skull at this execution site. The first stop on every guided tour of the Garden Tomb in Jerusalem is an overlook from where the visitor sees a rock formation that resembles the face of a skull. Garden Tomb guides admit the face of this rock outcropping could have changed over the centuries.

However, there are no references in the Bible to a skull-like rock formation, only to the fact that the site was called "the Place of the Skull." In fact, the Bible does not record that this was an elevated place or that it was called Mount Calvary, and neither do any Greek, Jewish, or Roman writers.

Cecil Frances Alexander, a nineteenth-century Anglo-Irish hymn writer, composed these words:

> There is a green hill far away,
> Without a city wall,
> Where the dear Lord was crucified,
> Who died to save us all."

Unfortunately, these wishful words may not reflect reality. The romantic notion that Jesus climbed a hill to be crucified does not appear in any of the Gospel accounts.[147] Nevertheless, the Scripture references are not irreconcilable with the suggestion that the site appeared similar to a skull. It is a rounded knoll rising from the surrounding surface.

Pilgrims in the fourth century spoke of the Calvary that existed there as a *monticulus* or small hill.[148] What remains of it today within the Church of the Holy Sepulchre stands about sixteen feet high.[149] Execution on a raised area above the surrounding roads would certainly have facilitated the Roman goal of making the punishment a public warning.

> "Calv'ry's mournful mountain climb; there, adoring at His feet,
> Mark that miracle of time, God's own sacrifice complete.
> 'It is finished!' hear him cry; learn from Jesus Christ to die."
> —James Montgomery

Nonetheless, nothing in Scripture indicates there was either a hill to climb at Golgotha or a geological formation resembling a skull at this execution site.

Boneyard

The second view holds that Golgotha, the Place of the Skull, may refer to the remains of skulls left from previous Roman executions. The site where Jesus was crucified was the customary "killing field" of the Romans. As a result, the area may have been littered with the skulls of the condemned.[150] The preeminent Christian scholar and Bible translator Jerome (347–420 AD) held this view, as did the English historian and monk, Venerable Bede (673–735 AD). "Boneyard" is the English word for a place of this type.

My favorite historic location in London is a four-minute walk south of the Old Street Underground Station. It is Bunhill Fields, directly across City Road from Wesley's Chapel. Because it was a "dissenters" cemetery, buried here are those who refused to join the Church of England. That would include such English notables as authors Daniel Defoe (*Robinson Crusoe*), John Bunyan (*The Pilgrim's Progress*), and William Blake (*Songs of Innocence* and *Songs of Experience*), plus English hymnists, Isaac Watts (*Joy To The World* and *When I Survey the Wondrous Cross*) and John Rippon (*All Hail the Power of Jesus' Name*). George Fox, founder of the Quaker movement, and Susanna Wesley, known as the "Mother of Methodism" are buried here.

The word "Bunhill" is a colloquial pronunciation of "Bone Hill." This may have been what Golgotha was like in the first century. If there was but one location outside of the city where the Roman killing fields were located, and Golgotha was that location, it is reasonable to assume there would be rotting flesh and skeletal bones scattered about the place.

Adam's skull

Another tradition claims that when David returned from the battle with Goliath, he carried the giant's bloody head to Jerusalem and buried it there, at "the place of the skull."[151] 1 Samuel 17:54 informs us, "And David took the head of the Philistine and brought it to Jerusalem, but he put his armor in his tent." From the text, we know David brought the giant's giant head to Jerusalem, but it does not tell us what he did with it. There is no indication he buried it at the place called Golgotha.

While this story has not gained much traction, there has been another Christian tradition dating from the third century AD that Golgotha was Adam's burial site. This tradition was influential in the early church. Origen (185–254 AD) speaks of it as well-known in his time (*Tractate 35 in Matthew*). So does Ambrose (340–397 AD) (*Epistle 71*), Athanasius (296–373 AD) (*Sermons de Passione Opera* ii.90), and Epiphanies of Salamis (312–403 AD) (*Panarion 46.5*).

Augustine notes, "The ancients hold that because Adam was the first man, and was buried there, it was called Calvary, because it holds the head of the human race" (*De Civitate Dei*, chapter 32). The fourth century AD Greek bishop Basil the Great remarks, "Probably Noah was not ignorant of the sepulcher of our forefather and that of the firstborn of all mortals, and in that place, Calvary, the Lord suffered, the origin of death there being destroyed" (Sermon 38 *Patrologia Graeca* 85.409).

St. John Chrysostom (349–407 AD), the Bishop of Constantinople, also wrote, "'And he came to the place of a skull.' Some say that Adam died there, and there lieth; and that Jesus in this place where death had reigned, there also set up the trophy. For he went forth bearing the cross as a trophy over the tyranny of death; and as conquerors do, so he bear upon his shoulders the symbol of victory."[152] While this is only a tradition, the tradition remains strong.

The seventeenth-century English poet and cleric John Donne wrote a hymn that demonstrates the strength of this belief in his day. The "Hymn to God my God in my Sickness" says:

> We think that Paradise and Calvarie,
> Christ's cross and Adam's tree stood in one place,
> Look Lord, and find both Adams met in me;
> As the first Adam's sweat surrounds my face,
> May the last Adam's blood my soul embrace.

Donne was expressing the widespread belief that Adam was buried at the spot where Jesus was crucified, and this was done intentionally by the Sovereign God.

The *Legend of the Rood* (*De ligno sancte crucis*) features medieval tales that are loosely based on Old Testament stories. The narrative of *The Legend of the Rood* relates how, as he was dying, Adam sent his son Seth back to Paradise to seek an elixir which would render him immortal. However, the angel guarding the gates to Paradise would not allow Seth to enter, but he did give Seth a seed from the tree where his parents picked the forbidden fruit. On his return, Seth discovered his father had died, but he put this seed under Adam's tongue and buried him at Golgotha.

As the legend goes, a tree grew from the seed but was cut down. The wood then experienced many adventures related to the motifs of many Old Testament stories. Ultimately, the wood was made into the cross (Middle English: *rood*) on which Jesus was crucified.[153]

Visitors to the Church of the Holy Sepulchre, below the site of Jesus' crucifixion, are shown a large rock streaked with red. The priest will tell you that this small cave was Adam's tomb, and the blood of Christ dripped from above onto Adam's bones so he too could be redeemed from his sins.

> "Even those scholars and critics who have been moved to depart from almost everything else within the historical context of Christ's presence on earth have found it impossible to think away the factuality of the death of Christ."
> —John McIntyre

Everyone around Jerusalem knew that Golgotha was the place you go to die. Thomas Schmidt commented:

> Crucifixion was common enough in the Roman world that major cities set aside areas for multiple and prolonged executions. Crucified bodies, some still living, others in various stages of decomposition, would there be displayed as a warning to others. In Rome, the site was called the *Campus Esquilinus*, the "place of vultures." In Jerusalem, it was given a Hebrew name

that people in Rome would not understand without a translation: *Golgotha*, "the place of a skull," or more literally, "the place of the [death's] head."[154]

So, while the Gospels tell us nothing of a hill or the outcropping of a man's face, they do tell us that the "killing field" of Jerusalem had to be outside the city wall. In the next chapter, we will examine four locations vying for the notoriety of being the place where Jesus died and the place where he was buried. Each of them meets the requirements of the Gospels, but only one of them can be the authentic location. Get ready for some scriptural sleuthing.

Chapter 6

The Location of Jesus' Crucifixion

The bottom line for any traveler to the Holy City is this: go to the Church of the Holy Sepulchre for archaeology; go to the Garden Tomb for atmosphere. Go to the Church of the Holy Sepulchre for information; go to the Garden Tomb for inspiration.

WE MUST NOW TURN our examination to the central question of Jesus' crucifixion site. Where was Golgotha where the Savior was crucified? Can the location of the most momentous event in history be identified? What do we know about those locations claiming to be the site of Jesus' crucifixion? These are important questions and beg for answers. Let's see if we can shed some light on the location of Jesus' death and resurrection.

First, we should explore the possibilities. What are the locations that claim to be the holy ground on which Jesus died and where he was subsequently buried? Some of the possibilities will surprise you, while others will not. Here are those places that lay claim to the location of Jesus' death and resurrection.

Crucifixion at Qumran

The most implausible thesis comes from Barbara Thiering. It is available to the public in her book *Jesus and the Secret of the Dead Sea Scrolls*.[155] Thiering claims to have discovered the interpretive key to the Dead Sea Scrolls and the New Testament. To understand the Gospels, Thiering says, the reader must recognize two levels of meaning. First, a symbolic surface level of miracle and mystery is designed to inspire awe and fear in the "babes in Christ." Second, a purely historical level that tells the true story of Jesus' life as a man.

Thiering believed the Dead Sea Scrolls, which include manuscripts of various Old Testament books, are the key to understanding the location of Jesus' crucifixion. The Dead Sea Scrolls contain previously unknown writings of the Essene community, many of which relate to a struggle between the "good guy" Teacher of Righteousness and his "bad guy" opponent, known as the Wicked Priest or the Man of a Lie. The twist Thiering brings to interpreting the Dead Sea Scrolls is that she believes the events recorded in the Gospels and the life of Jesus prove that Jesus is the Wicked Priest or the Man of a Lie.

She arrived at her conclusion by understanding the Gospels to be "pesher" stories that have two levels of meaning. *Pesher* is a Hebrew word meaning "interpretation." The authors of *pesharim* understand Scripture to have been written on two levels: the surface level is for ordinary readers with limited knowledge, and the concealed or deeper level is for specialists with a higher consciousness. This form of literary work became known with the discovery of the Dead Sea Scrolls.

The Caves at Qumran

On the surface, to the uninitiated reader, the Gospels simply recount stories of an itinerant teacher and miracle worker who died for his followers and then rose from the dead. Thiering claims this simplistic, surface understanding is what is understood by the Christian Church. For Jesus' inner circle and those today who have the interpretative key of the Scrolls, there is a second, coded meaning. This is accessible only to those who have the code.

Somewhere along the way, Barbara Thiering lost her way, wandering far from Christian orthodoxy. This is evident in her following beliefs:

- Jesus married Mary Magdalene for the second time on Wednesday evening before Good Friday;
- Jesus and Mary Magdalene had children;
- The Gospels do not take place in Galilee or Judea; the Gospel events all occur in the Qumran community on the Dead Sea;
- Jesus' crucifixion was real, but it took place at Qumran as well;
- Jesus did not die on the cross, but was drugged to make it appear he had died;
- When Jesus was taken down from the cross, he was placed in a cave where he was revived.
- Thiering claimed she could even identify the cave;
- Jesus' disciples were not bumbling fools as sometimes portrayed, but understood the deceptive plan and carried it out efficiently.

If some of these tenets sound familiar, it likely means you have read Dan Brown's blockbuster book and/or viewed the subsequent movie *The DaVinci Code*. Brown relied heavily on Michael Biagent's book *Holy Blood and the Holy Grail*. Biagent, in turn, relied heavily on Barbara Thiering's book *Jesus the Man*, and the theories she proposed.

Jewish scholar Géza Vermes reflected the attitude of almost all biblical scholars with his review of Thiering's book in the December 1, 1994 edition of *The New York Review of Books*. Vermes wrote:

> Professor Barbara Thiering's reinterpretation of the New Testament, in which the married, divorced, and remarried Jesus, father of four, becomes the "Wicked Priest" of the Dead Sea Scrolls, has made no impact on learned opinion. Scroll scholars and New Testament experts alike have found the basis of the new theory, Thiering's use of the so-called "pesher technique," without substance.

Harsh words, but reflective of the truth, which Thiering's theory is not. To find the truth, we must move on.

THE MOUNT OF OLIVES

The second theory for the location of Golgotha comes from Ernest L. Martin. Martin lived a fascinating life. He was a meteorologist, a minister in the Worldwide Church of God, and the author of a dozen books on biblical topics. While he is perhaps best known for his controversial works on the *Star of Bethlehem* and the *Temple in Jerusalem*, claiming to identify the location of Jerusalem's Temple, it is his book *Secrets of Golgotha* (1987) that propagates his theory that the site of Jesus' crucifixion was on the Mount of Olives.

Martin virtuously announced at the beginning of *Secrets of Golgotha* that he would use no evidence except that which comes from the Bible. While the Gospel accounts are the only Spirit-inspired primary accounts of the life and death of Jesus Christ, there is plenty of non-biblical evidence that corroborates the Gospels' accounts, and we must take that into account as well. Martin, on the other hand, appealed only to the evidence found within the pages of Scripture, but this did not serve him well.

"Outside the gate" and "Outside the camp."

Ernest Martin used mainly his interpretation of the book of Hebrews to make his case. The passage in Hebrews from which his theory on the location of Jesus' crucifixion is based is Hebrews 13:10–13:

> We have an altar from which those who serve the tent have no right to eat. For the bodies of those animals whose blood is brought into the holy places by the High Priest as a sacrifice for sin are burned outside the camp. So Jesus also suffered outside the gate in order to sanctify the people through his own blood. Therefore let us go to him outside the camp and bear the reproach he endured.

Martin maintained the two phrases "outside the gate" and "outside the camp" were not simple expressions but referred to a "specific place in the area of Jerusalem . . . to the author of the book of Hebrews, it was a specific 'gate' of Jerusalem that he emphasized. Only one area in the vicinity of Jerusalem was being referred to by the two geographical expressions mentioned above, and that was in the *eastern* region outside the city limits of Jerusalem."[156]

> "The geographical parameters mentioned in the book of Hebrews are of themselves sufficient proof to show that Golgotha was located at the southern summit of the Mount of Olives."
> —Ernest L. Martin

Claiming that most twenty-first-century people, including scholars and Christian clergy, do not understand the geographical features associated with the Temple and its ritualistic ceremonies, Martin interpreted the book of Hebrews symbolically. He embraced the idea that "the Temple at Jerusalem was patterned after the Tabernacle that Moses . . . which in turn was patterned after the geographical features of the Garden in Eden . . . The Temple and its environs were further patterned after God's heavenly palace and its celestial surroundings" (Heb 8:5; 9:23).

Appealing to the three divisions of the Temple, the Holy of Holies (the innermost portion on the west), the Holy Place (just east of the Holy of Holies), and the Court of the Gentiles (surrounding the enclosed structures), Martin believed the divisions were lined up in such a way as to point through the Eastern Gate to the Mount of Olives. In Jesus' day, the Temple area was connected to the Mount of Olives by a double-tiered arched bridge spanning the Kidron Valley.

The Mishnah indicates this bridge was constructed by the priests to facilitate the red heifer sacrifice. "They made a ramp from the Temple Mount to the Mount of Olives, being constructed of arches above arches."[157]

Focusing on the sacrifice of the red heifer and the requirement that this must occur "outside the camp" and "outside the tent," Martin saw the bridge between the Temple and the Mount of Olives as the key to understanding where the red heifer would be sacrificed.

The Jerusalem Temple

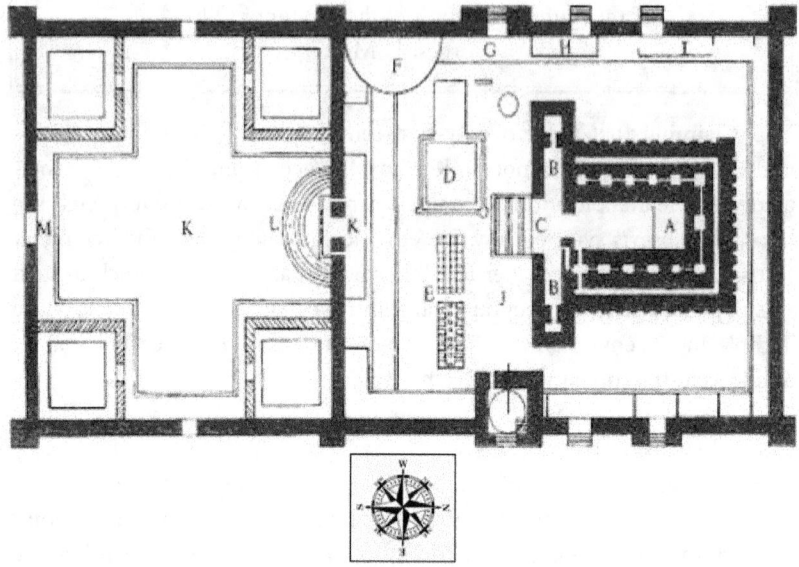

The Jerusalem Temple at the time of Jesus Christ, with the east at the bottom. (A) Holy of Holies, (B) Outer Holy Place, (C) Outer Curtain, (D) Altar of Burnt Offering, (E) Slaughter Areas, (F) Chamber of Hewn Stone (Sanhedrin Hall), (G) Counselor's Chamber, (H) House of Abtinas, (I) Chamber of Wood, (J) Court of Priests, (K) Court of Israel, (L) Steps to Nicanor Gate, (M) Credit: Eastern Gate. Diagram by Norman Tenedora.

The third altar of the Temple

Only two altars are mentioned in the Tabernacle and later in the Temple. One was in the outer court, and the other was in the Holy Place. One was without, and the other was within. They are the Altar of Burnt Offering and the Altar of Incense. The Altar of Burnt Offering (Exod 30:28) is also called the Brazen Altar (Exod 39:39), the Outer Altar, the Earthen Altar, the Great Altar, and the Table of the Lord (Mal 1:7).

The Altar of Burnt Offering was located inside the Court of the Priests, between the Chamber of Hewn Stone and the outer curtain before the Holy of Holies. This second altar was the Altar of Incense (Exod 30:1–10). It was also called the Golden Altar (Exod 39:38; Num 4:11) and the Inner Altar. It was the altar from which once a year on the Day of Atonement the High

Priest would remove hot coals in a fire pan and, along with incense, would carry them into the Holy of Holies (Lev 16:12) to make atonement for Israel.[158]

Martin believed the altar being discussed in the book of Hebrews was the third altar of the Temple. "This important Third Altar was located near the summit of the Mount of Olives where the Red Heifer was killed and burnt to ashes and where special sin offerings were burnt according to the Law of Moses (Lev 4:12)."

This outer altar, which the King James translators rendered as 'the appointed place' (Ezek 43:21), "in the words of Ezekiel, was located 'without the sanctuary,' positioned outside the sanctified area of Jerusalem. That is why it was located on the summit of the Mount of Olives," claimed Martin.[159]

> "I am now prepared with further reasons for believing that our Lord was crucified (and, necessarily, buried) to the east of the city."
> —R. F. Hutchinson

In Martin's approach, much is made about the altar being on the east. In the time of Moses, the holiest location within Israel's encampment was in front of the entrance on the east side of the sanctuary. The eastern region was also the side of the sanctuary administrated by the tribe of Judah, from which would arise both King David and the Messiah (Num 2:3).[160] Martin considered the region east of the Temple and up the slopes of the Mount of Olives to be the holiest part of the area that surrounds the Temple. He assumed there was a third altar there, a permanent altar upon which the red heifer was sacrificed.

Middoth 1:3 confirms the red heifer was taken out of the city on the east side but says nothing about there being a third altar on the Mount of Olives. Martin claimed:

> There can actually be no doubt that the "clean place" for burning the sin offerings on the Day of Atonement as well as performing the Red Heifer sacrifice was located directly east of the Temple. It was a permanent site called the Beth ha-Deshen or the House of the Ashes (Lev 4:12). It was located on a slope of a hill.[161]

Problems with the Mount of Olives site

Since Martin claimed to use only the Bible as his source, one would think the third altar would be prominently mentioned in the Old Testament. However, there is no mention of a third altar anywhere in the Bible. That is a problem for a theory based solely on the text of Scripture. So, where did Ernest Martin find the third altar in the Temple? From his interpretation of Hebrews 13:10-11. *Parah* is the Mishnah tractate that discusses the laws of the red heifer. The problem this creates for Martin's approach is that no altar is mentioned in *Parah*. In the entire tractate about the red heifer, the word "altar" (Hebrew: מִזְבֵּחַ; English: *mizbêach*) never occurs. Not once.

At one point, Martin did appear to soften his claim there was an ordinary stone altar, the third Temple altar, on the Mount of Olives. He said, "Since the ashes were not allowed to gather into a heap at the Beth ha-Deshen, the altar area was designated in such a way that it resembled more of a pit to contain the ashes rather than an altar with a ramp like we normally understand an altar to be shaped."[162] Nevertheless, the reason it resembled a pit more than an altar is that it was a pit, not an altar.

Martin also claimed that all the locals knew about this place on the mountain. However, I have an Arab friend whose family has lived on the Mount of Olives for centuries. His house is a multi-generational home, with his father living on the first level, his brother and family on the second, and his family on the fourth. The third level was empty, until the marriage of his oldest son in 2020.

From my friend's balcony facing west across the Kidron Valley toward the Temple Mount, you get the absolute best view of Jerusalem, especially at night. Nevertheless, when I asked him to show me the altar on the mountain where his family had lived for centuries, he knew nothing about it. Maybe it never existed.

The critical importance of the torn curtain

Since geographical positioning is the crux of Martin's theory, he advanced one more facet of geography he believed proved the Mount of Olives was the location of Golgotha. In *Secrets of Golgotha,* he quoted from Luke 23:47, "But the centurion having seen THE THING having occurred glorified God saying: Surely this man was righteous (Luke 23:47)." Martin emphasized the word "THING" (which he placed in all capital letters) and then explained, "It should carefully be noted that not only the centurion but also those standing beside him witnessed the effects of the earthquake."

But then Martin contradicted his emphasis on "the thing" by saying, "It must be understood that it was not simply the death of Jesus that caused the centurion to exult (because his death was quite naturally expected), but it was witnessing the tearing of the curtain at the time of his death."[163]

Martin claimed it was not the unnatural things the centurion witnessed that caused him to praise God, but a single thing, the tearing of the curtain. He asserted that since "the King James renderings are a little archaic to us moderns," he quoted Luke 23:47 in what he called a modern translation. However, he failed to identify the translation he was quoting. I searched no less than 60 translations of Luke 23:47 and did not find Martin's rendering in any of them.[164]

Martin's point was simple. Only from the eastern side of the Temple could this curtain be seen by spectators located outside the walls of Jerusalem. It would have been a physical impossibility for anyone to have seen the curtain from the south, the north, or the west. This means that anyone near the Church of the Holy Sepulchre or the Garden Tomb would only have seen the back walls of the Temple and not the tearing of the curtain.[165]

Did the centurion see the torn veil?

While this is true about the south, north, and west, it is only relevant if the centurion actually saw the veil being torn from top to bottom. Even though Ernest Martin claimed to use no evidence but the Bible in presenting his case, there is no biblical evidence that the centurion personally witnessed the tearing of the Temple curtain.

The Gospel of Matthew does not link the centurion to the tearing of the curtain at all. Matthew 27:54 says, "When the centurion and those who were with him, keeping watch over Jesus, saw the earthquake and what took place, they were filled with awe and said, 'Truly this was the Son of God!'" If any of the unnatural phenomena that occurred when Jesus died was to be singled out, Matthew says it was the earthquake, not the curtain.

Mark's reference seems to contradict what Martin earlier claimed, that it was not Jesus' death, but the tearing of the curtain that caused awe among the witnesses. "And the curtain of the temple was torn in two, from top to bottom. And when the centurion, who stood facing him, saw that in this way he breathed his last, he said, 'Truly this man was the Son of God!'" (Mark 15:38–39).

Mark says the centurion was facing Jesus, not the Temple curtain. Mark also clearly maintains that when the centurion saw Jesus take his last breath, he uttered his statement of faith regarding the deity of Jesus Christ. This had nothing whatsoever to do with the Temple veil. This is not good news for Martin's claim only to use references from Scripture for his theory.

In the third and final Gospel account of this event, Luke mentions the curtain of the Temple was torn in two, and says, "Then Jesus, calling out with a loud voice, said, 'Father, into your hands I commit my spirit!' And having said this he breathed his last. Now when the centurion saw what had taken place, he praised God, saying, 'Certainly this man was innocent!'" (Luke 23:46–47). Luke seems to parallel the account of Mark, but not Martin.

In none of the Synoptic accounts do the authors link the sole event of the torn curtain to the centurion's expression of faith. Nevertheless, Martin's theory requires the centurion to be able to see the tearing of the curtain as proof Jesus' crucifixion must have occurred on the Mount of Olives. While Ernest Martin's observations are intriguing, they are not rooted in fact, and therefore his identification of Golgotha with the Mount of Olives must be dismissed.

In our examination of the site of Jesus' crucifixion, we now come to a more plausible location, one dear to millions.

GORDON'S CALVARY

Israeli archaeologist Gabriel Barkay describes the *Sitz im Leben* into which modern archaeology took shape. At the beginning of the nineteenth century, Europeans, especially the British and Germans, fostered an interest in the Middle East. At the same time, the science of archaeology became more sophisticated. Protestants began to join Roman Catholics in their interest in exploring biblical sites.

The Archbishop of York founded the Palestine Exploration Society (PES) in 1865 to study that land from the eye of the scientist as opposed to the traveler. The society sponsored military engineers Sir Charles Wilson (Wilson's Arch) and Sir Charles Warren (Warren's Shaft) to map and record details in and around Jerusalem. It was into this climate that General Charles ("Chinese") Gordon came.[166]

In 1883, British General Gordon took a hiatus from his celebrated military career and spent January to December in the Holy Land. During that time he wrote *Reflections on Palestine* in which he argued that a skull-like outcrop and a nearby tomb discovered a few years earlier were the authentic crucifixion and burial sites of Jesus of Nazareth.[167] General Gordon was a national hero in Great Britain, the perfect embodiment of military heroics with a fervent Christian faith and Victorian Romanticism. Consequently, his argument won immediate approval, especially among Protestants in the British Isles.

General Charles Gordon

The idea that Skull Hill was Golgotha did not originate with "Chinese" Gordon. Several earlier travelers and writers proposed the same identification beginning as early as the 1840s. Among them was Claude Conder, a Palestine Exploration Society explorer and surveyor who was sent to Palestine in 1872 and recorded the idea in two of his books, *Tent Work in Palestine* (1878)[168] and *The City of Jerusalem* (1909).[169]

Additional early proponents of this site as Golgotha were English scholar and clergyman Canon Henry Baker Tristram, German archaeologist Conrad Schick, German theologian Otto Thenius, German scholar and traveler Jonas Kortens, and Protestant Bishop of Jerusalem Samuel Gobat. Many early archaeologists, geographers, and travelers were taken by the shape of Skull Hill and the nearby tomb.

> "In my opinion, the recent excavations in the neighborhood of 'Jeremiah's Grotto,' . . . all tend to confirm the view that this spot is without doubt the site of the crucifixion and of the Holy Sepulchre."
> —Edward Hull

Physical features

Just as the direction from the Temple was essential to Ernest Martin's argument that Golgotha had to be east of the Temple, so too, Charles Gordon based his argument in part on topography. He believed that, according to the Mishnah, because sacrificial animals were slaughtered in the ancient Jewish temples north of the altar, therefore Jesus must also have been crucified north of the city.

Among the contenders for the location of Golgotha, only Gordon's Calvary is north of Jerusalem and its Temple. It was outside the city wall in Jesus' day and was located well over twenty-five meters (82 feet or 55 cubits) to the north of the city.

The grounds adjacent to Gordon's Calvary, in which the Garden Tomb is located, were purchased in 1894 by The Garden Tomb Association, a Charitable Trust based in the United Kingdom. Visitors to the Garden Tomb are first taken to a platform where there is an overlook of the rocky outcropping of Gordon's Calvary.

There a friendly volunteer guide will relate the story of Jesus' crucifixion with the heart of a true believer. He will point out the general outline of a face that features two deep eye sockets. With a little imagination, they make the face look freakishly like the face of a skull.

The skull-like feature is a naturally occurring rock formation in the southern scarp of a hill called el-Edhemieh by local Arabs. This is just west of the stone quarry that has traditionally been called "Jeremiah's Grotto." On the top of the hill, there has been a Muslim cemetery for approximately two centuries. There used to be a slightly distended piece of stone sloping downward from between the two easternmost caves that gave the impression of the bridge of a skeletal nose. However, on February 20, 2015, the bridge of the skull's nose collapsed during a strong storm. Indeed, in past decades, this formation made a near-perfect skull's head, complete with eye sockets, a crushed nose, and a gaping mouth.

Some argue that "this natural formation has probably not changed significantly in the last three thousand years."[170] However, while the eye sockets were even more impressive a hundred years ago, they likely may not have been there in Jesus' day.

Gordon's Calvary 100 years ago and today

In 1610 AD, George Sandys, an Oxford-educated English traveler, made a two-year journey from Italy to Syria and Egypt. Sandys visited Jerusalem and drew pictures of some of the outstanding geographical features of the area. His drawings prominently featured the site of Jeremiah's Grotto, near the Garden Tomb.

However, they displayed no caves in the escarpment that looked like eye sockets. Possibly they were not there in the seventeenth century. Perhaps natural erosion formed the skull-like face 150 to 250 years ago, just as it is destroying it now.

> "Erosion is nothing new and the rock face [of Gordon's Calvary] likely did not have the same skull appearance 2,000 years ago."
> —Ted Bolen

Having visited this site annually for over 50 years, I have watched the face of the rock deteriorate, each year looking less and less like a skull. In the natural world, erosion is a fact of life, but rarely a friend.

The location of crucifixions

As interesting as the physical features of Gordon's Calvary are, the real question is whether or not any crucifixions were known to have been carried out in this area north of Jerusalem. We know the Romans were given to crucify their criminals in conspicuous places just outside the city wall, but still near cities and towns. Perhaps the most prominent place outside the Jerusalem wall was on the road north from the Damascus Gate over the spine of the Judean and Samaritan mountains to Nablus, Capernaum, and Damascus. It was known as the Nablus Road and still is today. The Nablus Road ran right by Gordon's Calvary. It would give the most exceptional opportunity for travelers to see the loathsomeness of crucifixion and be deterred from any criminal activity.

This leaves us with the final potential site for Jesus' crucifixion, the traditional location, the Church of the Holy Sepulchre. Eusebius said in the *Onomasticon* that Golgotha was to the north of the Mount of Sion (πρὸς τοῖ~ς βορείοις του~ Σιὼν ὄπους).[171] Jack Finegan commented, "No doubt this traditional identification of the southwestern hill with the Sion of David had something to do with the localization of the 'tomb of David' in the Church of the Last Supper."[172]

THE CHURCH OF THE HOLY SEPULCHRE

Many visitors to the Church of the Holy Sepulchre find it aesthetically distasteful. If you were looking for a quiet garden, an empty tomb, and a skull-like hill, you must go to the Garden Tomb. If you enjoy or at least do not mind, incense, icons, and priests scurrying from place to place, often being rude to visitors, you have come to the right place. The Church of the Holy Sepulchre is a shrine, with all the trappings accumulated through years of "religion."

A brief overview of the church

The modern pilgrim to Jerusalem can freely enter the church, but to see the site of Calvary, you must climb a difficult set of rock-cut stairs, ascending sixteen feet above street level. Visitors may also see the Altar of the Cross, an outcropping of rock with a fissure in it, which tradition claims was made by the great earthquake at the time of Jesus' death. Under the Altar of the Cross is a silver disk with a hole in the center which the monks and priests of the church will tell you is the exact spot where Jesus' cross was planted in Golgotha's ground.

One-hundred fifty feet to the northwest stands the ancient Rotunda and within it the traditional tomb of Jesus, hence the name—The Church of the Holy Sepulchre. This ornate enclosure is a free-standing structure within the church. While this somewhat gaudy edifice reflects the zenith of human religion, it poorly reflects the tomb of Joseph of Arimathea or the miracle of the resurrection. Only the most devout find it refreshing.

Still, they come, especially at Easter. During Holy Week celebrations, thousands upon thousands of people ascend the mountains to Jerusalem and descend on the Church of the Holy Sepulchre. The crowds in the church are jam-packed, chock-a-block as the British would say, so tightly squeezed in that you cannot move with ease. The pilgrims recite prayers, chant songs, and burn candles, as well as their eyes with the heavy scent of incense.

Eastern Orthodox tradition claims that the phenomenon of the Holy Fire happens annually on the day preceding Orthodox Pascha (Orthodox Easter). At this event it is claimed that a blue light emits within the tomb of Jesus, rising from the marble slab covering the stone bed where Jesus' body is thought to have been buried.[173] The light becomes fire and this flame is passed to thousands of candles waiting to be lit. It is a joyous celebration.

The Church of the Holy Sepulchre is known to Orthodox Christians as the Church of the Resurrection or the Church of the Anastasis (Greek: ἀνάστασις; English: *anastasis* meaning resurrection). Located within the Christian Quarter of Old Jerusalem, it is the largest and most important church in Jerusalem. According to tradition, within the church are the tenth through the fourteenth stations of the Via Dolorosa. This would include the traditional locations of Golgotha and the tomb of Jesus.[174]

Today the Holy Sepulchre church is in the hands of six Christian denominations. In 1757 AD, the Ottoman Sultan Osman III forced a compromise that came to be known as the *Status Quo* agreement. This agreement divided Jerusalem into quadrants and decreed that whoever controlled a particular site at that time would control it in perpetuity. If multiple groups laid claim to a site, all of them would have to agree to any changes, however minor.[175]

The church is the headquarters for the Greek Orthodox, the Roman Catholic (represented by the Franciscan Order), and the Armenian Apostolic Church. In the nineteenth century, these denominations were joined by the Syrian Orthodox Church of Antioch, the Copts of Egypt, and the Ethiopian Orthodox Tewahedo Church.

Unfortunately, the addition of religious groups claiming a slice of the Church of the Holy Sepulchre fostered huge resentment and anger among the groups that were the original guardians of the church. They regularly fight over turf and influence, and police are occasionally forced to intervene.

The Church of the Holy Sepulchre

In 2004, a door to the Franciscan chapel was inadvertently left open. The Greek Orthodox interpreted this as a sign of disrespect, and a fistfight broke out. No one was seriously injured, but some religious leaders were arrested.[176] On Palm Sunday in 2008, police were called to stop the fisticuffs, but they were immediately attacked by those engaged in the brawl.[177] On Sunday, November 9, 2008, another quarrel erupted between Armenian and Greek monks.[178] It appears Golgotha is still a place of brutality and bloodshed.

Before they enter, visitors to the church should look up between the two windows on the second floor. There they will see a ladder standing that has been dubbed "the immovable ladder" because almost 150 years ago a man placed the ladder on a ledge against the exterior wall of the church. Due to the imposition of the *Status Quo* and the fear of inciting violence, no one has dared touch it since.

Because of the tensions between the religious groups, almost nothing gets done quickly within the church. In 1995 the six religious traditions finally agreed on painting a section of the central dome, but only after seventeen years of debate.

As a result of the lack of trust between them, none of these religious groups controls the security of the church. In 1192, Saladin delegated the responsibility of keeping the door to the Nuseibeh family. The Joudeh al-Goudia (al-Ghodayya) family was entrusted as the keeper of the keys of the Holy Sepulchre, also by Saladin in 1187. These are noble Hashemite (Jordanian) families, descendants of the Prophet Mohammad.

When Nuseibeh arrives at the church early in the morning, he takes the key from Joudeh, climbs a small wooden ladder to unlock the top lock, then steps off the ladder to unlock the lower lock. The doors are swung open, and the church is accessible to visitors. These two Muslim families have shared this responsibility since the seventh century, protecting the holy site and keeping it open to the Christian faithful. Unlocking the church door requires strong fingers because the key is thirty centimeters (12 inches) long and weighs 250 grams or half a pound.[179]

Keys to the door of the Church of the Holy Sepulchre

The history of the church

The history of the Church of the Holy Sepulchre more-or-less parallels the history of Jerusalem; it is both diverse and violent. For the purposes of this seven-volume series on Roman crucifixion and the death of Jesus of Nazareth, history begins with the Roman Empire. No investigation goes back beyond the Roman Period. So, that's where we begin our exploration of the history of the Church of the Holy Sepulchre.

Roman Period (70–324 AD).

After the Roman General Titus Flavius reduced Jerusalem to ruins in the siege of 70 AD, the Holy City mostly remained that way until 130 AD. In that year, the Roman Emperor Hadrian began to put feet to his vision of a new Roman colony on the site called Aelia Capitolina. The name *Aelia* came from Hadrian's *nomen gentile,* Aelius. (The *nomen gentilicium,* or "Gentile name" designated a Roman citizen as a member of a *gens* or race, family, or clan. The extended Roman family all shared the same *nomen* and claimed descent from a common ancestor). *Capitolina* meant the new city was dedicated to Jupiter Capitolinus, the Roman god for whom a temple was built on the site of the former Jewish Temple. This temple remained until the fourth century. Hadrian also built a pagan temple on the destroyed site venerated by the first-century church as the site of Jesus' crucifixion.

Byzantine Period (324–638 AD).

After seeing a vision of a cross in the sky in 312 AD, Emperor Constantine the Great converted to Christianity. He signed the Edict of Milan, making the Christian religion legal, and sent his mother Queen Helena to Jerusalem to find the authentic tomb of Jesus. When three crosses were found near a tomb, leading Helena to believe she had found the location of Golgotha, Constantine ordered the Temple of Jupiter or Venus on that site be replaced by a church. The dirt and debris were removed from the cave beneath, revealing a rock-cut tomb that both Helena and Bishop Macarius of Jerusalem identified as the burial site of Jesus. In 335 AD, construction was begun on the Church of the Holy Sepulchre.[180]

First Muslim Period (638–1099 AD).

The Sasanid Empire was the last kingdom of the Persian Empire before the Islamization of Iran. In May of 614 AD, under Khosrau II, the Sasanians invaded Jerusalem capturing the "True Cross." In 630 AD, Heraclius, the emperor of the Byzantine Empire (610–641 AD), rebuilt the Church of the Holy Sepulchre after recapturing the city. When Jerusalem came under Arab rule, the early Muslim rulers protected the city's Christian sites. However, the church was severely damaged by an earthquake in 746 AD and by fire in 841, 938, and 966 AD.[181] On October 18, 1009, Fatimid caliph Al-Hakim bi-Amr Allah ordered the complete destruction of the church as part of his campaign against Christian places of worship in Palestine and Egypt.

Crusader Period (1099–1187 AD).

An agreement between the Fatimids and the Byzantines (1027–1028 AD) was made whereby the new caliph, Ali az-Zahir (Al-Hakim's son) would allow the Church of the Holy Sepulchre to be rebuilt. However, Pope Urban II called for the First Crusade in 1095. The idea of recapturing Jerusalem was the focus of the Crusade, which in 1099 became a reality. Emperor Constantine IX Monomachos spent vast sums of money to restore the church. The rebuilt church site consisted of "a court open to the sky, with five small chapels attached to it."[182] Control of Jerusalem and the Church of the Holy Sepulchre changed hands several times between the Fatimids and the Seljuk Turks until the arrival of the Crusaders.[183]

Ayyubid Period (1187–1259 AD).

The rebuilt Church of the Holy Sepulchre was taken from the Fatimids by the Crusader Knights on July 15, 1099. However, the church was lost to Saladin, along with the rest of the city, in 1187 AD. Under Saladin's leadership, the Ayyubid army defeated the Crusaders at the decisive Battle of Hattin just west of the Sea of Galilee. From that point, Saladin wrestled control of Palestine from the Crusaders, who had conquered the area eighty-eight years earlier. As a result, Jerusalem was ruled in succession by the Ayyubid dynasty (a Muslim dynasty of Kurdish origin founded by Saladin, centered in Egypt), the Bahri Mamluk dynasty (Mamluk dynasty that ruled the Egyptian Mamluk Sultanate from 1250 to 1382 AD), and the Burji Mamluk dynasty (another Mamluk dynasty that ruled Egypt from 1382 until 1517 AD).[184]

Mamluk Period (1250–516 AD).

The Muslim Caliph dismantled the walls of Jerusalem. As a result, the population of the Holy City declined rapidly. This was a period of deterioration throughout the city. The Mamluks are widely credited with a defeat over the invading Mongol forces in Syria, as well as cleansing Jerusalem and Israel of a Crusader presence. Still, Pope Nicholas IV negotiated an agreement with the Mamluk sultan to allow Latin clergy to serve in the Church of the Holy Sepulchre. With the sultan's agreement, Pope Nicholas, a Franciscan, sent a group of friars to keep the Latin liturgy going in Jerusalem. The Mamluk's control over Palestine and Jerusalem was ended by the Ottomans in 1517 AD.

Ottoman Period (1517–1917 AD)

In 1517, the same year Martin Luther tacked his 95 Theses on the church door at Wittenberg, Germany, Jerusalem fell to Suleiman the Magnificent (also spelled Suleyman). Fortunately, Jerusalem enjoyed a period of renewal and peace under Suleiman, including the construction of the present walls of the Old City. Jews, Christians, and Muslims enjoyed the freedom of religion as the city remained open to all religions. Suleiman was considered a very gracious and fair ruler.[185]

British Mandate (1917–1948 AD).

After World War I, the British were given control of Jerusalem, and worship at the Holy Sepulchre flourished. This mandate continued for some thirty-one years until Israel became a nation. The British and all other national authorities left the city, never to return. Israel had become a self-governing nation.

Divided City (1948–1967 AD).

In 1948, the State of Israel was established. Jerusalem was divided between Israel and Jordan by armistice lines. The entire Old City, including the Church of the Holy Sepulchre, was located in Jordanian East Jerusalem.

United Jerusalem (1967 AD–present).

After the "Six-Day War" in 1967, Israel claimed all of Jerusalem and reunited the city once more. While tensions still exist between Arab East Jerusalem and the Israeli government, at least most can travel somewhat freely throughout the city. The Church of the Holy Sepulchre is located near the Muristan in the Old City of Jerusalem. The Muristan is a market area situated between three churches—the Church of Holy Sepulchre to the north, the Hospitallers' Church of St. John the Baptist to the south, and the Church of the Redeemer to the northeast. The name Muristan comes from the Persian word for "hospital" because it was built over the ruins of edifices built by the Hospitallers, one of the most critical military orders of the Crusaders. In the second century AD, the Roman Forum was built in this area. Under the Roman Emperor Hadrian, the Muristan was the religious and political center of the Roman city of Aelia Capitolina. So, from antiquity, this has been a significant area of Jerusalem to many people.

Here, archaeologists have discovered the remnants of walls built by Hadrian in the second century. On one of the walls is a stone with a drawing of a merchant ship inscribed with the words DOMINE IVIMVS, "Lord, we shall go." It is believed this drawing likely dates from before the completion of Constantine's church.

Now we come to the big question about the Church of the Holy Sepulchre. Physically, is it the location of the crucifixion of Jesus? Is it geographically excluded or included? This one sizable question usually determines the answer to these questions and the legitimacy or illegitimacy of this site as the location of Jesus' crucifixion.

Is the Church of the Holy Sepulchre outside the wall of Jerusalem?

One of the reasons people have questioned the location of the Holy Sepulchre church as the site of Golgotha is because it is inside the city walls of present-day Old Jerusalem. Nonetheless, Golgotha would have to be located outside the city, following the Roman and Jewish customs of the time. Besides, the Gospels also suggest that Jesus was crucified outside of the city. John 19:17, "He went out, bearing his own cross, to the place called The Place of a Skull, which in Aramaic is called Golgotha." Matthew 27:31 and Mark 15:20 both say the same.

However, it is essential to note that the current Old City walls are not the ones from Jesus' Jerusalem. As Serr and Vieweger note below, finding the so-called Second Wall of Jerusalem, which would have been the northern wall of Jerusalem in Jesus' day, has not been easy. Several archaeological digs have been undertaken with unsatisfactory results. Josephus mentions this Second Wall (*Wars* 5.4.2), but its discovery has proven to be terribly elusive.

Renowned archaeologists Conrad Schick and Pere Louis-Hugues Vincent thought they had found the Second Wall in 1893. A wall was uncovered during the construction of the Church of the Redeemer, which is just south of the Church of the Holy Sepulchre. This appeared to answer the question and placed the church outside the city wall of Jesus' day. However, in the 1970s, German archaeologist Ute Wagner-Lux of the German Protestant Institute of Archaeology in Jerusalem excavated under the Church of the Redeemer and determined that this wall could not have been the Second Wall. "This wall was only five feet thick—far too narrow to be a city wall," as reported by Serr and Vieweger.[186]

However, from the excavations at the Church of the Redeemer, there are clues that the Church of the Holy Sepulchre is indeed located outside that elusive Second Wall. Certainly, this church has history and tradition on its side.

> "One will never be able to prove beyond doubt where
> Golgotha stood, but no candidate more credible
> than the traditional site is likely to emerge."
> —Raymond E. Brown

While careful scholars will not and cannot say with absolute certainty that the Church of the Holy Sepulchre is the site of Golgotha and the tomb of Jesus of Nazareth, the evidence strongly favors this location. The bottom line for any traveler to the Holy City is this: go to the Church of the Holy Sepulchre for archaeology; go to the Garden Tomb for atmosphere. Go to the Church of the Holy Sepulchre for information; go to the Garden Tomb for inspiration. The Garden Tomb is appreciated for feelings; the Church of the Holy Sepulchre is appreciated for facts. Most of the facts point to this church, but most of the comfort from the resurrection of Jesus comes from the Garden Tomb. When you visit the navel of the Earth, stop by both sites and get the best of both worlds.

Speaking of both worlds, there is one final consideration regarding the location of Jesus' death, burial, and resurrection. These three events occurred in the city of Jerusalem, but is there any significance to that? Does Jerusalem play a role in the centrality of the crucifixion weekend? It does, and here's why.

Jerusalem as the center of the world

Henrich Bunting was a Protestant theologian born in 1545 in Hanover, Germany in what was then the Holy Roman Empire. He attended the University of Wittenberg, graduating in 1569. Although he began pastoring in Lemgo, Germany, he was dismissed in just a few years because of his teachings. He moved to another parish in Goslar but, again, his teachings were rejected. He retired from the ministry to live the quiet life of a travel writer and geographer.

He is best known for his book, *Itinerarium Sacrae Scripturae* (*A Journey Through the Holy Scriptures*), a travel collection and commentary on the geography of the Bible. Describing the Holy Land by following the travels of Old and New Testament characters, the book provided the most complete summary of biblical geography available at the time. Published in 1571, *Itinerarium Sacrae Scripturae* was a very popular book; over sixty editions were published between 1581 and 1757.

The outstanding features of the book included many woodcut maps and three maps depicting a cloverleaf design. Each leaf represented one of the three great continents—Europe, Africa, and Asia. In the center was a circle featuring the walled city of Jerusalem with Golgotha and three crosses outside the city wall. It is this city, and the crucifixion that occurred there, that brings the world together.

An early tradition maintains the site of Jesus' crucifixion and resurrection is the center of the world. By the tenth century, Jerusalem was marked by an *omphalos*, a rounded stone representing the navel of the earth in ancient Greek mythology. For adherents of the three major religions—Judaism, Christianity, and Islam—Jerusalem is, indeed, the center of the world.

The author (left) receiving an award from the Israeli government with the tri-leaf globe showing Jerusalem as the center of the world

Bunting's tri-leaf globe showing Europe (NW), Asia NE), and Africa (S) on the author's award

The eminent Church Father Eusebius had been a follower of Apollo, Greek god of the Sun (and much more). For him, the center of the pagan world was Delphi, the seat of Apollo. In the world of the ancient Greeks and Romans, Delphi was considered the *omphalos* (or navel) of the world.

However, the Roman Emperor Constantine had been told by an Apollonian oracle that Christians were interfering with the oracle's ability to foretell the future. The emperor understood this to mean that Christianity had replaced Delphi and the adherents of Apollo. Having converted to Christianity, Constantine decided that Christianity, now the official religion of the State, should establish Jerusalem as the navel of the world.

But did Eusebius and Constantine have any grounds for establishing Jerusalem as the center of the world? Cartographer Bunting intentionally ignored the positivist rules of cartography. He knew the world did not physically look this way, but he wanted to create a map that centered on Jerusalem. No one can deny Jerusalem's physical and religious significance to the world. It is the important land bridge between the three leaves of Bunting's map. Religiously, it is most important to the three world religions—Judaism, Islam, and Christianity. But is there any evidence for Bunting's *visio mundi* ("vision of the world")? Did Eusebius know something we often forget?

> "The Sages of Israel proclaimed: The Land of Israel is the center of the world. Jerusalem is the center of the Land of Israel."
> —*Midrash Tanhuma*

The prophet Ezekiel was used by God to deliver a warning to Israel because of their habitual sin against God. In Ezekiel 38:12 the Jews are referred to as the people who live at the "center of the world." This is not a physical reference; it's a spiritual one. Jerusalem is the capital of the people of whom it was said that God "encircled him, he cared for him, he kept him as the apple of his eye" (Deut 32:10; see also Ps 17:8; Zech 2:8). In Ezekiel 5:5, the prophet quotes God as saying, "This is Jerusalem. I have set her in the center of the nations, with countries all around her." This divine declaration may be the justification for considering Jerusalem as the center of the world, the navel of the Earth.

When Constantine transferred the center of the world from Delphi to Jerusalem, he was sure to eliminate paganism by destroying Hadrian's Temple and building the Church of the Holy Sepulchre over the same site. To purge the past and discover Golgotha and Joseph's tomb, all the profane soil accumulations of two centuries were removed from the site. The underlying bedrock was used as the foundation of the Church of the Holy Sepulchre.

The site of the crucifixion of Jesus of Nazareth was huge in Constantine's thinking. Notice he did not choose the Temple Mount as the location for the new church. The Temple Mount represents Judaism and the past. Calvary represents Christianity and the future. The Temple Mount was Old Jerusalem, but Calvary was New Jerusalem and the center of the world.

Chapter 7

Did Jesus Really Die on the Cross?

"With many religious people around the world unaware of or unsympathetic toward the crucifixion of Jesus, and with many scholars within the Christian community dismissing the historicity of the Gospel narratives, is there any reason to believe that Jesus really did die on Golgotha's Cross?"

WE COME NOW TO the question of veracity. The four Gospel accounts clearly state that Jesus rose from the dead on the third day. Is it possible the evangelists were mistaken? Is it possible they had bad intel? Is it possible they outright lied to preserve the integrity of Jesus' many predictions about his resurrection? There are many questions about whether or not the Savior actually died on the cross. These questions have elicited many theories, some of them as whacky as can be. Nonetheless, these are important questions and we now examine the possible answers to them.

The facts overwhelmingly support the Gospel accounts of Jesus' death on the cross. Pilate acceded to the mob's demand to crucify Jesus and thus the Roman soldiers led him to a cross at Golgotha. He hung there. He died there. Case closed. And yet, in the face of a mountain of evidence, there are still some who deny that Jesus truly died on the cross. They have devised other theories for what happened to Jesus that day at Calvary. Some of these theories have developed into books and movies and have made their authors millions of dollars on the backs of naïve and gullible readers and movie-goers. Other theories have become the main tenets of belief in major religions. Before we examine the proof for the crucifixion of Christ Jesus, let's first think about those who deny that proof.

DENIAL OF JESUS' DEATH

No serious historian, theologian, or religious scholar doubts the existence of Jesus of Nazareth. Even atheist scholars acknowledge the reality and the effects of the Savior's life. The three great religions—Judaism, Christianity, and Islam—all teach that Jesus existed. Where these great religions part ways is with the crucifixion of Jesus and the meaning of his death. While the crucifixion and resurrection of Jesus Christ are at the heart of the Christian belief system, and while Jesus' crucifixion is acknowledged by some Jewish sources, most Muslims have been taught that Jesus was not crucified on a cross at Calvary.

If you were to ask your Muslim neighbors why they deny the crucifixion of Jesus, assuming they are somewhat conversant with the teachings of the Qur'an, they will direct you to *Surah* 4:156–59—*An-Nisa'*. The context of this *Surah* is a divine reproach on the Jews because they rejected God's prophets, spoke against Mary, and boasted of having crucified Jesus Christ. (Interestingly, none of the 'sins' of the Jews relate to Islam or the teachings of Muhammad, but two of the three relate directly to the Christian faith). Here is the passage in the Sahih International translation of the Qur'an:

> And [we cursed them] for their disbelief and their saying against Mary a great slander, And [for] their saying, "Indeed, we have killed the Messiah, Jesus, the son of Mary, the messenger of Allah." And they did not kill him, nor did they crucify him; but [another] was made to resemble him to them. And indeed, those who differ over it are in doubt about it. They have no knowledge of it except the following of assumption. And they did not kill him, for certain. Rather, Allah raised him to himself. And ever is Allah exalted in might and wise. And there is none from the people of the Scripture but that he will surely believe in Jesus before his death. And on the Day of Resurrection he will be against them a witness.

Numerous explanations of this passage have been proposed, even among Muslims. A Sunni Muslim said, "Muslims believe that Allah saved the Messiah from the ignominy of crucifixion."[187] Since Muslims see Jesus as a prophet sent from God in a long line of prophets, Muhammad being the final and culminating prophet, they have a certain respect for Jesus and see his crucifixion as a potential monstrosity. In fact, one Muslim exclaimed, "We honor [Jesus] more than you [Christians] do . . . We refuse to believe that God would permit him to suffer death on the cross."[188]

Interpretations of Surah 4:156–159

Some Muslims believe this *Surah* teaches that an angel protected Jesus from discovery while hiding in the tomb of Joseph. Others say Jesus hid in a niche in the wall of the tomb. They claim the Roman soldiers grabbed one of Jesus' disciples and he was crucified in the place of Jesus. Still, others say that Simon of Cyrene was crucified instead of Christ. Many, including the so-called *Gospel of Barnabas,* claim that God miraculously changed the appearance of the traitor Judas Iscariot to look exactly like Jesus and he was crucified in the place of Jesus.

Some say that Jesus escaped and went to India, where he died a natural death many years later. Indeed, Muslims are taught that God took Jesus away to heaven before he could be arrested, while others say it was after he had been arrested and beaten and was on the way to be nailed to the cross. Still, others believe the Savior was taken to heaven years later.

Although nuances in the Islamic interpretations of Jesus' death are many, almost all of them have one belief in common—that God somehow intervened as Jesus made his way along the Via Dolorosa or at Golgotha to change his appearance in a way to deceive the crowd and to trick the Roman killing squad into believing they were crucifying Jesus, when in fact it was another person who was executed. The bottom line belief from the Qur'an is that Jesus was never crucified as the New Testament so often declares.

Among Muslims, there is a notable exception to the belief that God switched out Jesus for someone else. That is of a South African Muslim of Indian descent named Ahmad Deedat who wrote a book with the quasi-clever title, *Crucifixion or Cruci-fiction?*[189] Sheikh Deedat broke with Islamic orthodoxy when he claimed that Jesus actually was nailed to the cross, but he did not die on the cross. Deedat declared Jesus fainted and people only wrongly assumed he was dead. Deedat subscribed to the popular, though baseless theory, that when Jesus was laid in the coolness of the tomb, he supposedly revived (see the swoon theory below).

As if this dizzying array of interpretations today wasn't enough, there are Muslims who do not believe in the crucifixion account at all. They say that the story of Jesus' death was entirely fabricated by the Gospel writers. In this, they are not much different from many liberal Christian theologians.

In Islam, a Hadith is a collection of traditional sayings of the prophet Muhammad which, with accounts of his daily practice (the *Sunna*), constitute the major source of guidance for Muslims apart from the Qur'an. Interestingly, the most reputable collections of Hadiths—Sahih al-Bukhari and Sahih Muslim—are completely silent on the question of the crucifixion. Given the divergent views held by Muslims on the forty Arabic words of *Surah* 4:157, it is incomprehensible that of all the stories preserved during the first 200 years after the life of Muhammad, none of them refers to his disciples asking him about the crucifixion of Jesus.

Problems and proponents

There are problems with all these Muslim interpretations of the crucifixion. Some of the problems are moral, e.g. God deceiving the Jews and Romans about the crucifixion. Some of the problems are factual, e.g. Jesus surviving crucifixion as well as enduring the lance driven through his side and into his heart. These problems are seen by Christians and not Muslims because of the record of the Gospels and our faith in them. Jettison the authority of those narratives and we are left with what the followers of Muhammad have—nothing in terms of salvation through God's Son, the Lamb of God, and the Savior of the world.

Those who are devotees of the Qur'an are not alone in their rejection of the crucifixion narratives. There is a *de facto* rejection of the historicity or the meaning of Jesus' crucifixion by every religion that marginalizes the death of Jesus in their faith system. This would include Hinduism, Buddhism, Taoism, Confucianism, Shintoism, Sikhism, Jainism, and all other world religions. But, unfortunately, it also includes certain strains of Christianity.

While many modern theologians and historians do not deny the existence of Jesus as a man, they often deny the efficacy of Jesus' death on the cross. Scholars and laypeople of this theological stripe are rightly called cultural Christians, they cannot rightly be called Christ-followers. The whole concept of "take up your cross and follow me" is either misunderstood or ignored. They understand well the historical Jesus, but it is not the carpenter from Nazareth but Jesus the Son of God with whom a relationship must be established if we are to be saved from the penalty of our sin.

The Bible's most popular passage still reads: "For God so loved the world, that he gave his only Son, that whoever believes in him should not perish but have eternal life. For God did not send his Son into the world to condemn the world, but in order that the world might be saved through him" (John 3:16–17).

BIBLICAL EVIDENCE FOR JESUS' DEATH

Why would Jesus leave heaven just to become a man? His life and death must have had a higher purpose than that or the incarnation makes no sense. With many religious people around the world unaware of or unsympathetic toward the crucifixion of Jesus, and with many scholars within Christian communities dismissing the historicity of the Gospel narratives, is there any reason to believe that Jesus really did die on Golgotha's Cross? What is the evidence to support this belief?

There is much, but as we have done before, we will begin with the strongest, the most accurate evidence—that of eyewitnesses or near eyewitnesses on that day at Golgotha. What is the biblical evidence for the death of Jesus on the cross?

The Bible provides so many references to Jesus' death, that we must be selective in those presented. Perhaps it is best to place the verses in categories and limit ourselves to three references per category.

Jesus predicted he would die on Calvary's Cross

While no healthy human being in the prime of life wants to die, Jesus was not afraid to die on the cross. He knew it was the eternal plan of the Godhead, and thus he often spoke of and even predicted his own death.

- Matthew 16:21, "From that time Jesus began to show his disciples that he must go to Jerusalem and suffer many things from the elders and chief priests and scribes, and be killed, and on the third day be raised."
- Luke 18:31–33, "And taking the twelve, he said to them, 'See, we are going up to Jerusalem, and everything that is written about the Son of Man by the prophets will be accomplished. For he will be delivered over to the Gentiles and will be mocked and shamefully treated and spit upon. And after flogging him, they will kill him, and on the third day he will rise.'"
- John 12:32–33, "'And I, when I am lifted up from the earth, will draw all people to myself.' He said this to show by what kind of death he was going to die."

Jesus willingly embraced the torture on Calvary's Cross

The plan for our salvation was formed in eternity past, and while humanly Jesus would have preferred another way, he knew this was God's plan, the only plan that would accomplish all of God's goals in our salvation. As a result, Jesus embraced the cross.

- Matthew 26:39, "And going a little farther he fell on his face and prayed, saying, 'My Father, if it be possible, let this cup pass from me; nevertheless, not as I will, but as you will.'"
- Matthew 26:53-54, "Do you think that I cannot appeal to my Father, and he will at once send me more than twelve legions of angels? But how then should the Scriptures be fulfilled, that it must be so?"
- John 10:17-18, "For this reason the Father loves me, because I lay down my life that I may take it up again. No one takes it from me, but I lay it down of my own accord. I have authority to lay it down, and I have authority to take it up again."

Jesus affirmed his own death on Calvary's Cross

While hanging on Calvary's Cross, Jesus himself asserted that he yielded his human spirit to God and allowed his body to die.

- Matthew 27:50, "And Jesus cried out again with a loud voice and yielded up his spirit."
- Luke 23:46, "Then Jesus, calling out with a loud voice, said, 'Father, into your hands I commit my spirit!' And having said this he breathed his last."
- John 19:30, "When Jesus had received the sour wine, he said, 'It is finished,' and he bowed his head and gave up his spirit."

Angels affirmed Jesus' death on Calvary's Cross

After the crucifixion, when the faithful women went to the tomb to anoint the body of Jesus, they were met by angels who announced that Jesus' death was now history and Jesus had already risen from the dead.

- Matthew 28:5-7, "Do not be afraid, for I know that you seek Jesus who was crucified. He is not here, for he has risen, as he said. Come, see the

place where he lay. Then go quickly and tell his disciples that he has risen from the dead."
- Mark 16:6, "And he said to them, 'Do not be alarmed. You seek Jesus of Nazareth, who was crucified. He has risen; he is not here. See the place where they laid him.'"
- Luke 24:4-6, "While they [the faithful women] were perplexed about this, behold, two men stood by them in dazzling apparel. And as they were frightened and bowed their faces to the ground, the men said to them, 'Why do you seek the living among the dead? He is not here, but has risen. Remember how he told you, while he was still in Galilee, that the Son of Man must be delivered into the hands of sinful men and be crucified and on the third day rise.'"

Eyewitnesses affirmed Jesus' death on Calvary's Cross

Those who had gathered to watch the horror of Christ's crucifixion could act as eyewitnesses in any courtroom, telling what they saw when they saw Jesus die.

- Matthew 27:54-56, "When the centurion and those who were with him, keeping watch over Jesus, saw the earthquake and what took place, they were filled with awe and said, 'Truly this was the Son of God!' There were also many women there, looking on from a distance, who had followed Jesus from Galilee, ministering to him, among whom were Mary Magdalene and Mary the mother of James and Joseph and the mother of the sons of Zebedee."
- Luke 23:48-49, "And all the crowds that had assembled for this spectacle, when they saw what had taken place [Jesus' death], returned home beating their breasts. And all his acquaintances and the women who had followed him from Galilee stood at a distance watching these things."
- John 19:32-33, "So the soldiers came and broke the legs of the first, and of the other who had been crucified with him. But when they came to Jesus and saw that he was already dead, they did not break his legs."

Matthew affirmed Jesus' death on Calvary's Cross

Each evangelist, in his own way, asserts that Jesus died on the cross.

- Matthew 27:1, "When morning came, all the chief priests and the elders of the people took counsel against Jesus to put him to death."
- Matthew 27:35-36, "And when they had crucified him, they divided his garments among them by casting lots. Then they sat down and kept watch over him there."
- Matthew 27:50, "And Jesus cried out again with a loud voice and yielded up his spirit."

Mark affirmed Jesus' death on Calvary's Cross

- Mark 9:9, "And as they were coming down the mountain, he charged them to tell no one what they had seen, until the Son of Man had risen from the dead."
- Mark 9:30-31, "They went on from there and passed through Galilee. And he did not want anyone to know, for he was teaching his disciples, saying to them, 'The Son of Man is going to be delivered into the hands of men, and they will kill him. And when he is killed, after three days he will rise.'"
- Mark 15:44-45, "Pilate was surprised to hear that he should have already died. And summoning the centurion, he asked him whether he was already dead. And when he learned from the centurion that he was dead, he granted the corpse to Joseph."

Luke affirmed Jesus' death on Calvary's Cross

- Luke 23:32-33, "Two others, who were criminals, were led away to be put to death with him. And when they came to the place that is called The Skull, there they crucified him, and the criminals, one on his right and one on his left."
- Luke 23:46, "Then Jesus, calling out with a loud voice, said, 'Father, into your hands I commit my spirit!' And having said this he breathed his last."

- Luke 23:52–53, "This man went to Pilate and asked for the body of Jesus. Then he took it down and wrapped it in a linen shroud and laid him in a tomb cut in stone, where no one had ever yet been laid."

John affirmed Jesus' death on Calvary's Cross

- John 2:22, "When therefore he was raised from the dead, his disciples remembered that he had said this, and they believed the Scripture and the word that Jesus had spoken."
- John 19:17–18, "So they took Jesus, and he went out, bearing his own cross, to the place called The Place of a Skull, which in Aramaic is called Golgotha. There they crucified him, and with him two others, one on either side, and Jesus between them."
- John 19:30, "When Jesus had received the sour wine, he said, 'It is finished,' and he bowed his head and gave up his spirit."

The Apostle Paul affirmed Jesus' death on Calvary's Cross

The Apostle Paul joins the evangelists in proclaiming that Christ died for our sins.

- Acts 13:28–29, "And though they found in him no guilt worthy of death, they asked Pilate to have him executed. And when they had carried out all that was written of him, they took him down from the tree and laid him in a tomb."
- 1 Thessalonians 4:14, "For since we believe that Jesus died and rose again, even so, through Jesus, God will bring with him those who have fallen asleep."
- 1 Thessalonians 5:9–10, "For God has not destined us for wrath, but to obtain salvation through our Lord Jesus Christ, who died for us so that whether we are awake or asleep we might live with him."

The Apostle Peter affirmed Jesus' death on Calvary's Cross

Likewise, the Apostle Peter confirms the death of the Savior on the cross.

- Acts 2:22–24, "Men of Israel, hear these words: Jesus of Nazareth, a man attested to you by God with mighty works and wonders and signs that God did through him in your midst, as you yourselves know—this Jesus, delivered up according to the definite plan and foreknowledge of God, you crucified and killed by the hands of lawless men. God raised him up."

- Acts 4:10, "Let it be known to all of you and to all the people of Israel that by the name of Jesus Christ of Nazareth, whom you crucified, whom God raised from the dead—by him this man is standing before you well."

- Acts 10:39–40, "And we are witnesses of all that he did both in the country of the Jews and in Jerusalem. They put him to death by hanging him on a tree, but God raised him on the third day and made him to appear."

The book of Acts affirmed Jesus' death on Calvary's Cross

The record of the first-century church is a record of preaching the Gospel—the death, burial, and resurrection of Jesus Christ and his power to redeem us from sin.

- Acts 17:1–3, "Now when they had passed through Amphipolis and Apollonia, they came to Thessalonica, where there was a synagogue of the Jews. And Paul went in, as was his custom, and on three Sabbath days he reasoned with them from the Scriptures, explaining and proving that it was necessary for the Christ to suffer and to rise from the dead."

- Acts 17:31, "He [Jesus] has fixed a day on which he will judge the world in righteousness by a man whom he has appointed; and of this he has given assurance to all by raising him from the dead."

- Acts 26:23, "Christ must suffer and that, by being the first to rise from the dead, he would proclaim light both to our people and to the Gentiles."

The epistle to the Romans affirmed Jesus' death on Calvary's Cross

In the most theological book of the New Testament, Paul establishes the importance of Christ's death for our eternal life.

- Romans 4:24-25, "It [righteousness] will be counted to us who believe in him who raised from the dead Jesus our Lord, who was delivered up for our trespasses and raised for our justification."
- Romans 5:6-8, "For while we were still weak, at the right time Christ died for the ungodly. For one will scarcely die for a righteous person—though perhaps for a good person one would dare even to die—but God shows his love for us in that while we were still sinners, Christ died for us."
- Romans 5:10, "For if while we were enemies we were reconciled to God by the death of his Son, much more, now that we are reconciled, shall we be saved by his life."

The letters to the Corinthians and Galatians affirmed Jesus' death on Calvary's Cross

Even in epistles to troubled churches, Paul avows the death of Jesus at Calvary.

- 1 Corinthians 15:3-5, "For I delivered to you as of first importance what I also received: that Christ died for our sins in accordance with the Scriptures, that he was buried, that he was raised on the third day in accordance with the Scriptures, and that he appeared to Cephas, then to the twelve."
- 2 Corinthians 5:14-15, "For the love of Christ controls us, because we have concluded this: that one has died for all, therefore all have died; and he died for all."
- Galatians 2:20-21, "I have been crucified with Christ. It is no longer I who live, but Christ who lives in me. And the life I now live in the flesh I live by faith in the Son of God, who loved me and gave himself for me. I do not nullify the grace of God, for if righteousness were through the law, then Christ died for no purpose."

Paul's epistles from prison affirmed Jesus' death on Calvary's Cross

While Paul languished in prison, he wrote letters of encouragement to his friends. Those letters always included the fact of Jesus' death and resurrection.

- Ephesians 1:19–20, "What is the immeasurable greatness of his power toward us who believe, according to the working of his great might that he worked in Christ when he raised him from the dead and seated him at his right hand in the heavenly places."
- Colossians 2:12, "You were also raised with him through faith in the powerful working of God, who raised him from the dead."
- 2 Timothy 2:8–9, "Remember Jesus Christ, risen from the dead, the offspring of David, as preached in my gospel, for which I am suffering, bound with chains as a criminal. But the word of God is not bound!"

The book of Hebrews affirmed Jesus' death on Calvary's Cross

Jesus' death is important to the Jews, and thus his once-for-all sacrifice that replaced the need for daily sacrifices was good news for God's chosen people.

- Hebrews 9:12, "He [Jesus] entered once for all into the holy places, not by means of the blood of goats and calves but by means of his own blood, thus securing an eternal redemption."
- Hebrews 10:28–29, "Anyone who has set aside the law of Moses dies without mercy on the evidence of two or three witnesses. How much worse punishment, do you think, will be deserved by the one who has trampled underfoot the Son of God, and has profaned the blood of the covenant by which he was sanctified, and has outraged the Spirit of grace?"
- Hebrews 13:20–21, "Now may the God of peace who brought again from the dead our Lord Jesus, the great shepherd of the sheep, by the blood of the eternal covenant, equip you with everything good that you may do his will."

Did Jesus Really Die on the Cross? 143

The epistles of Peter affirmed Jesus' death on Calvary's Cross

Peter's letters reflect his preaching, and, as the book of Acts illustrates, Peter's preaching was always about the death, burial, and resurrection of Jesus.

- 1 Peter 1:3-5, "Blessed be the God and Father of our Lord Jesus Christ! According to his great mercy, he has caused us to be born again to a living hope through the resurrection of Jesus Christ from the dead, to an inheritance that is imperishable, undefiled, and unfading, kept in heaven for you, who by God's power are being guarded through faith for a salvation ready to be revealed in the last time."

- 1 Peter 1:18-19, "Knowing that you were ransomed from the futile ways inherited from your forefathers, not with perishable things such as silver or gold, but with the precious blood of Christ, like that of a lamb without blemish or spot."

- 1 Peter 1:21, "Who through him [Jesus] are believers in God, who raised him from the dead and gave him glory, so that your faith and hope are in God."

The book of Revelation affirmed Jesus' death on Calvary's Cross

The final book of the Bible does not neglect to emphasize the importance of Christ's blood and his death for the future of humankind.

- Revelation 1:4-5, "Grace to you and peace from him who is and who was and who is to come, and from the seven spirits who are before his throne, and from Jesus Christ the faithful witness, the firstborn of the dead, and the ruler of kings on earth."

- Revelation 2:8, "The words of the first and the last, who died and came to life."

- Revelation 5:9, "And they sang a new song, saying, "Worthy are you [Jesus] to take the scroll and to open its seals, for you were slain, and by your blood you ransomed people for God from every tribe and language and people and nation."[190]

With these eighteen different categories and more than seventy-five passages in the New Testament, it is evident that the death of Jesus is important to the message of God for our time. Each of these verses affirms that Jesus actually died when he was nailed to Calvary's Cross. He was not feigning death; he was dead. It is ludicrous to say otherwise.

But these verses come directly out of God's Word. For those who accept the Bible as the written revelation of God, these passages are iron-clad proof of Jesus' death. But for those who reject the Bible as God's Word, these verses prove nothing. These non-believers require proof that is not found in the Word of God, which seems to be self-defeating. They are left with what man has to say about Jesus' death, not with Jesus' death itself.

Be that as it may, here are some pieces of evidence not found in the Bible that indicate Jesus really did die on Calvary's Cross.

EXTRA-BIBLICAL EVIDENCE FOR JESUS' DEATH

Some of the many extra-biblical texts that address the death of Jesus on the cross are mentioned below. There are others, many others, but these few should suffice to cement the fact that the crucifixion of Jesus is mentioned outside of the Bible itself.

The Talmud, Sanhedrin 43a: "On the eve of the Passover Yeshu [Jesus] was hanged [crucified].... Since nothing was brought forward in his favor he was hanged on the eve of the Passover." The Amoa "Ulla" (Ulla was a disciple of Youchanan and lived in Palestine at the end of the third century) adds: "And do you suppose that for (Yeshu of Nazareth) there was any right of appeal? He was a beguiler, and the Merciful One hath said: 'Thou shalt not spare neither shalt thou conceal him.' It is otherwise with Yeshu, for he was near to the civil authority."

Josephus, Antiquities of the Jews 18.63–64: "Pilate, upon hearing him [Jesus] accused by men of the highest standing amongst us, had condemned him to be crucified."

Justin, First Apology, 13: "Our teacher of these things is Jesus Christ, who also was born for this purpose, and was crucified under Pontius Pilate, procurator of Judæa, in the times of Tiberius Cæsar; and that we reasonably worship him, having learned that he is the Son of the true God himself."

Ignatius, Letter to the Trallians: "On the day of the Preparation, then, at the third hour, he [Jesus] received the sentence from Pilate, the Father permitting that to happen; at the sixth hour he was crucified; at the ninth hour he gave up the ghost; and before sunset he was buried."

Tertullian, Apology, XXI §2: "Yet nailed upon the cross, Christ exhibited many notable signs, by which his death was distinguished from all others. At his own free will, he with a word dismissed from him his spirit, anticipating the executioner's work."

Irenaeus, 'Against Heresies, 4.34.3: "And the points connected with the passion of the Lord, which were foretold, were realized in no other case. For neither did it happen at the death of any man among the ancients that the sun set at mid-day, nor was the veil of the Temple rent, nor did the earth quake, nor were the rocks rent, nor did the dead rise up, nor was any one of these men [of old] raised up on the third day, nor received into heaven."

Julius Africanus, Chronography 18.1: "Phlegon records that, in the time of Tiberius Cæsar, at full moon, there was a full eclipse of the sun from the sixth hour to the ninth—manifestly that one of which we speak. But what has an eclipse in common with an earthquake, the rending rocks, and the resurrection of the dead, and so great a perturbation throughout the universe?... And calculation makes out that the period of seventy weeks, as noted in Daniel, is completed at this time."

Johannes Philophonos aka. Philopon, De opificio mundi II. 21: "Phlegon also in his Olympiads makes mention of this [crucifixion] darkness, or rather of this night: for he says, that 'An eclipse of the sun in the second year of the 202nd Olympiad [summer 30 AD through summer 31 AD] turned out to be the greatest of the unknown type prior, and a night came on at the sixth hour of the day [noon]; insomuch that the stars appeared in the sky.' Now that Phlegon also makes mention of the eclipse of the sun as the event which transpired when Christ was put on the cross, and not of any other, is manifest."

Cassiodorus, Chronicon, Patrologia Latina, v. 69: "Under these co[n]s[ul]s Our Lord Jesus Christ suffered the eighth day before the Kalends of April, and an eclipse [literally: failure, desertion] of the sun occurred, such as never was before or since."

The Gospel of Peter, 5-6: "And when he [Jesus] had said it he was taken up. And in that hour the vail [sic] of the Temple of Jerusalem was rent in twain. And then they drew out the nails from the hands of the Lord, and laid him upon the earth, and the whole earth quaked, and great fear arose."

Origen, Against Celsus, 2.33: "And with regard to the eclipse in the time of Tiberius Caesar, in whose reign Jesus appears to have been crucified, and the great earthquakes which then took place."

Eusebius, Chronicle, 202 Olympiad: Speaking of the crucifixion earthquake the day Christ died, "In the fourth year, however, of Olympiad 202, an eclipse of the sun happened, greater and more excellent than any that had happened before it; at the sixth hour, day turned into dark night, so that the stars were seen in the sky, and an earthquake in Bithynia toppled many buildings of the city of Nicaea."

Eusebius, Demonstratio Evangelica, Book 8: Speaking of the darkness on the day Christ died, "And this day, he says, was known to the Lord, and was not night. It was not day, because, as has been said already, "there shall be no light"; which was fulfilled, when "from the sixth hour there was darkness over all the earth until the ninth hour." Nor was it night, because "at eventide it shall be light" was added, which also was fulfilled when the day regained its natural light after the ninth hour."

Arnobius of Sicca, Contra Gentes I. 53: "But when, freed from the body, which he [Jesus] carried about as but a very small part of himself [i.e. when he died on the cross], he allowed himself to be seen, and let it be known how great he was, all the elements of the universe bewildered by the strange events were thrown into confusion. An earthquake shook the world, the sea was heaved up from its depths, the heaven was shrouded in darkness, the sun's fiery blaze was checked, and his heat became moderate; for what else could occur when he was discovered to be God who heretofore was reckoned one of us?"

The evidence for Jesus' death on the cross is outstandingly attested both by biblical and extra-biblical accounts. To deny that Jesus actually died on the cross, one must set aside a mountain of evidence and, in its place, advance his or her own theory. This, of course, happens frequently, even with such solid proof as the death of Jesus at Calvary can produce.

INADEQUATE THEORIES ABOUT JESUS' DEATH

Over the decades, those who deny the historicity and accuracy of the Gospel narratives have developed their own theories about Jesus' death, or lack thereof, at Calvary. Some of the more popular theories are examined here. These generally are thought of in the context of the resurrection. Still, had there been no death on the cross, there could have been no resurrection. Therefore it appears there is a strong relation between these inadequate theories and Jesus' death.

The No-Death Theory

The idea that Jesus did not die on a cross permeates several of the theories we explore below. Simply stated, these theories deny the death of Jesus at the killing field of Golgotha, and in doing so, they deny the divine atonement for our sins, which leaves those who hold these theories in the unenviable position of facing God's judgment (John 3:16–17).

The Gospel of Barnabas, which appears to date to the late sixteenth or early seventeenth centuries, endorses the no-death theory. This apocryphal work claims to be written by the biblical character Barnabas. It also claims Barnabas was one of the twelve apostles. While neither of these claims is historically accurate, nevertheless, some scholars believe the Gospel of

Barnabas may contain remnants of an earlier, apocryphal work perhaps of Gnostic origin.[191]

According to this apocryphal gospel, it was not Jesus, but Judas who was crucified on the cross. The author claims when Judas led the Roman soldiers to arrest Jesus in Gethsemane, angels appeared to take Jesus up to heaven. At the same time, Judas' appearance was transformed into that of Jesus, and the Romans arrested the traitor instead of the Savior.

The Gospel of Barnabas states the transformation of Judas into Jesus' appearance not only fooled Pontius Pilate and the Romans, but the Pharisees, the High Priest Caiaphas, and even the followers of Jesus Christ, including his mother, Mary. To complete this charade, the Gospel of Barnabas alleges that after three days, Judas' body was stolen from his grave with rumors spreading that Jesus had been raised from the dead.[192]

The Docetic Theory

Docetism was an early Christian sectarian doctrine that was proclaimed a heresy by the church. Docetism comes from the word (Greek: δοκεῖ; English: *dokei*) meaning "to seem." For example, when in Athens, Paul's preaching was challenged by the Epicurean and Stoic philosophers who called him a babbler. They said, "He seems (*dokei*) to be a preacher of foreign divinities" (Acts 17:18).

Docetism taught that Jesus did not have a physical body but only that he "seemed" to have a body. Those who followed this heresy believed his body was an illusion. Consequently, the heresy taught that Jesus experienced no pain or suffering on the cross, nor was there a body to be buried or raised from the dead.

Docetism was attacked by all opponents of Gnosticism, especially by Bishop Ignatius of Antioch in the second century AD. Ignatius is mainly known for seven highly regarded letters he wrote while traveling to Rome, where he was martyred.

The Wrong Tomb Theory

Some people speculate that Mary Magdalene and the other women who went to Joseph of Arimathea's tomb early on Sunday morning simply ended up at the wrong tomb. Perhaps in the pre-dawn darkness they mistook one tomb for another. When they found a mistaken tomb and discovered it empty, they innocently but incorrectly announced that Jesus must have risen from the dead.

There are so many things wrong with this theory it's hard to know where to begin. These women had witnessed the hurried burial of Jesus less than seventy-two hours earlier. It is unlikely they would forget the location of the tomb so quickly. Maybe they became disoriented because of the pre-dawn darkness. But the Gospel account in John 20:15 indicates that there was sufficient light for Mary Magdalene to believe she saw the gardener or caretaker of Joseph's private tomb. Besides, it wasn't just the women who saw the empty tomb. Peter and John came to the same tomb when it was light enough to notice from the outside details like the grave clothes and the head cloth inside the unlit tomb.

Remember, Jesus was not buried in a typical cemetery. He was buried in a family rock-cut sepulcher. He was buried in a tomb located in a garden, not some hillside city of the dead. It would be hard to confuse the tomb of a wealthy man like Joseph of Arimathea in a well-kept garden with other dissimilar mass gravesites in unsightly places.

If the followers of Christ had presented the wrong tomb as evidence of his resurrection, many of Christ's enemies would have happily revealed their mistake. The chief priests, members of the Sanhedrin, and the High Priest Caiaphas would have been thrilled to point out the error of the Christ-followers. No, this was not the wrong tomb; it was just an empty tomb. It's not very likely that all these people were at the wrong tomb. What we have here is not the wrong tomb but the wrong theory.

The Stolen Body Theory

Some people think that three days after his crucifixion the body of Jesus did not rise from the dead but was stolen from the tomb. Some believe the Jewish authorities moved Christ's body. There doesn't seem to be any good reason for them to do so, but if the Jews did move the body and had it in their possession, why didn't they reveal it? When the disciples troubled them about preaching the resurrection, they could simply have presented Jesus' dead body and embarrassed the disciples into silence (Acts 3:14–15).

If the Jewish religious leaders knew where the body of the Lord was hidden, wouldn't it be reasonable that they would have shut down Peter's preaching by producing the body? Paul preached Christ crucified "a stumbling block to Jews and folly to Gentiles" (1 Cor 1:23; 2:2), but they couldn't object to his preaching because they did not remove the body of Jesus.

An even more absurd twist to the stolen body theory is the belief that the Romans removed Jesus' body and hid it somewhere. But what would be the reason for that? A more reasonable option for those who wish to believe that someone stole the body of Jesus would be to accuse his disciples of taking it to make the people of Jerusalem believe Jesus rose from the dead, as he had predicted. This is the most common view among those who will not permit themselves to believe the Gospel narratives. But think how unlikely even this possibility is.

These disciples had abandoned Jesus just hours earlier. The cowardice of the disciples provides a substantial argument against their suddenly becoming so daring as to face a detachment of Temple police at the tomb and steal the body. Also, these disciples had just spent nearly three years in the company of Jesus, hearing his teaching, and viewing his honesty, his compassion, and his integrity. For them to have removed the body, lied about where it was, and then continued to preach God's holy moral code and Christ's ethical teachings is highly improbable. Besides, each of these disciples except John died horrific deaths partly for their belief in the crucifixion and resurrection of Jesus Christ. If they stole Jesus' body, do you think they would have died to preserve a lie? It would be insane to die for something you knew wasn't true.

The Hallucination Theory

Another attempted explanation claims that the appearances of Jesus after the resurrection were either illusions or hallucinations. This is a stretch of the imagination. Could those who saw Jesus after his crucifixion and resurrection all have been hallucinating? Jesus presented himself to all of his disciples and friends. Paul says in 1 Corinthians 15:6 that Jesus "appeared to more than five hundred brothers at one time, most of whom are still alive."

Are we to believe that more than 500 people all hallucinated at precisely the same time? Think about how ridiculous that sounds. Frankly, I don't have enough faith to believe something that outrageous. Reason demands that we recognize there were too many witnesses for all of them to be having a hallucination.

Hallucinations are private matters; they're individual and very subjective. Christ's appearances were always public and, most often, to groups of people instead of individuals. Hallucinations usually last a few seconds or perhaps minutes; on rare occasions, they may last a few hours. But Jesus presented himself alive to witnesses for forty days after his resurrection. Hallucinations don't hang around for forty days. The hallucination theory is just too preposterous for a thinking person to believe.

The Conspiracy Theory

The conspiracy theory maintains that the disciples made the whole thing up. There was no death on the cross. There was no resurrection. It was a fanciful lie from the master deceivers who followed Jesus Christ. With the conspiracy theory, we are asked to believe that somehow these disciples, who had scattered at Jesus' crucifixion, pulled themselves together and fabricated a story that was so compelling the entire Christian faith was built upon it.

If this sounds a little unreasonable, it is. These disciples were not university professors. They were not clever lawyers. They were simple men, some of whom were fishermen.[193] What do you suppose the chances are that they could pool their intellectual resources and quickly come up with a story that would last for 2,000 years? And what a story it was—that Jesus came back to life after he had been mistreated, physically abused, and crucified. This is not to disparage these disciples. It's just recognizing that the odds of them coming up with such a story are extremely low. But there is another problem.

The disciples had spent enough time with Jesus over the last three years to know that those who wanted to think like Christ, live like Christ, and act like Christ did not go around lying about something as crucial as his resurrection. These men were not skilled deceivers. They were humble, simple, honest men who only reported what they saw with their own eyes.

Finally, what possible motive would the disciples have for deceiving us about the crucifixion and resurrection of Jesus Christ? Every lie has a motive behind it. For most people, the motive is for some selfish advantage. People want to improve their position or diminish the position of their enemies.

Lies are told for reasons. But what reason would this rag-tag group of disciples have for lying? Was it to justify Jesus' claims that he would rise from the dead on the third day? Their lies were not needed to prove that. Jesus walking around Jerusalem and Galilee is all the proof anyone would need.

If the crucifixion and resurrection were bald-faced lies, the disciples would not better their position with the Romans who wanted Jesus in their rearview mirror. If Jesus' crucifixion and resurrection were fables perpetrated on the Jewish community by the disciples, these fables would only stir up strife for embarrassing the Jewish religious leaders of Jerusalem. No, there seems to be no advantage to deceiving the Roman government, the Jewish leadership, or the residents of Jerusalem. However, there seem to be plenty of reasons for telling the truth. The deception theory has to be abandoned because it is illogical.

The Swoon Theory

The theory that has gotten the most attention over the last few decades is the swoon theory. To "swoon" means to faint, blackout, or lose consciousness. It means a person passes out or collapses and appears to be dead.

Concerning Jesus' death and resurrection, people who believe in the swoon theory claim Jesus did not die, he merely fainted from blood loss and the sheer exhaustion of his horrible crucifixion. Everyone thought he was dead—the Jewish religious leaders, the Roman soldiers, Pilate, Herod Antipas, and even his disciples—but the swooners say he was not dead. He only swooned. He fainted and was unconscious. He only appeared to be dead.

Swooners say in those hours alone in the rock tomb, where the heat of the spring sun would be shut out, in the coolness of the tomb, Jesus revived and managed from the inside to roll away the stone covering the outside of the tomb and escape. This would sound laughable if there were not many people who genuinely believed it. But this is not a very credible theory and here is why.

First, there is no way Jesus could not have survived his crucifixion. The Roman soldiers made certain of that. The spear thrust into Jesus' side eliminated any possibility that he survived and only swooned in the tomb. The Romans just would not allow Jesus to leave the cross alive. These Roman executioners were super-skilled at crucifying people. They were the best in the business. They would never have been fooled into believing that Jesus was dead if he was not.

Besides, Roman law placed the death penalty on any soldier who let a capital prisoner escape in any way, including bungling a crucifixion. The fact that the Roman soldiers did not break Jesus' legs, as they did with the two crucified on either side of him, means they were sure Jesus was dead. Besides, John, who was an eyewitness to Jesus' crucifixion, reported that he saw blood and water come from Jesus' side (John 19:33-35). This is John's eyewitness testimony. Not only does John report what he saw standing there beneath the cross, but he also certifies that what he reported is true and should be believed. John knew Jesus was dead, just like on the third day he knew Jesus had come alive again.

In your mind, come with me to the tomb. If Jesus was laid in the tomb and then in the coolness of his solitude, revived and decided to leave, he still had two enormous problems. One was the huge stone that was rolled in front of the tomb. It had to be rolled there by hand and fit over the sepulcher's opening. How would Jesus roll this stone from the inside? He couldn't just push it over because it was heavy and sat in the track in which it rolled. From inside the tomb, there was no way Jesus could get a grip on that stone to roll it away. From the tomb's interior, he could not wrap his fingers around the edges of the stone and move it. A swooning Jesus would have a real problem removing such a stone.

But there's more. Even if Jesus discovered a way to push the stone away from the opening of the tomb and made his escape possible, the Temple police just outside were there to keep Jesus securely in the tomb. How would Jesus get past them? The reasonable answer is he would not. They were there for security, to ensure that Jesus specifically did not swoon, revive, and escape. They would never be derelict in their duties.

Forensic pathologist Frederick T. Zugibe maintained, "This theory is comprised of various hypotheses all of which have been repeatedly refuted by experts in theology and science, and in some cases, the originators were frankly exposed as frauds . . . Unfortunately, like the phoenix of old, the Swoon Theory has been reduced to ashes only to reemerge over and over again."[194]

Never mind all the physical trauma Jesus had to endure before even being nailed to the cross, and put from your mind that Pilate specifically asked the centurion to confirm Jesus was dead, and forget about the fact that a spear pierced Jesus' side and out came blood and water, conspiracy theorists keep dredging up new and inventive ways to espouse the old, long-disproven swoon theory. Some of these theories had difficulty convincing even those who proposed them. The author of the apocryphal Acts of Pilate states:

> But when those men had departed to Galilee, the chief priests and the rulers of the synagogue and the elders assembled in the synagogue, and shut the gate, and raised a great lamentation, saying: "Why has this sign happened to Israel?" But Annas and Caiaphas said: "Why are you troubled? Why do you weep? Do you not know that his disciples gave much money to the guards of the tomb, and taught them to say that an angel descended from heaven and rolled away the stone from the door of the tomb." But the priests and the elders replied: "Let it be that his disciples stole his body. But how did the soul enter again into the body, so that Jesus now waits in Galilee?' (*Acts of Pilate* XIV.3).

How indeed!

While each of these theories lacks credible evidence, and some of them are well beyond ridiculous, some still seem to have legs. In the face of insurmountable evidence, there are yet some who tenaciously hold on to the swoon theory as the likely explanation for Jesus' near-death/no-death experience. Here is a brief survey of the better-known conspiracy theorists and their theories.

Did Jesus Really Die on the Cross?   153

THE SWOON THEORY IS ALIVE AND WELL

It may be surprising how many theories there are and how long some of them have been in existence. Listed are a dozen of those who have attempted to twist or flat-out deny the crucifixion as recorded by the Gospel writers. I have attempted to present them in somewhat chronological order.

Karl Friedrich Bahrdt (1741–1792)

Bahrdt was a very unorthodox German biblical scholar and theologian. He was considered an *enfant terrible* because he was one of the most immoral characters in German scholarship.[195] In his book *Ausführung de plans un Zwecks Jesu* (1784-1792), Bahrdt claimed that Jesus did not die at Golgotha but fell into a coma or deep sleep assisted by Luke the Physician, who administered drugs to Jesus to help him endure the suffering of the crucifixion. Bahrdt says the drugs wore off after his burial in the tomb of Joseph of Arimathea.[196]

The problem is, it is highly unlikely that Luke was at the crucifixion or even knew Jesus at that time. Luke was a Gentile, converted under the ministry of the Apostle Paul. The second-third century Christian Father Tertullian confirmed that Luke was never a follower of the Lord before Jesus' death. Bahrdt and his theory have both been discredited.

Karl Venturini (1768–1849)

Around 1800, Karl Venturini proposed a similar, simpler version of Barhdt's swoon theory. He suggested Jesus was a member of a 'secret society,' i.e. the Essenes, that monastic Jewish sect that forsook Jerusalem to live near the Dead Sea. They wanted Jesus to be recognized as a spiritual Messiah. However, they were caught off guard when the Romans crucified him. Venturini suggested that a group of Jesus' Essene supporters dressed in white were surprised when they heard groaning from inside the tomb. They frightened away the guards and rescued Jesus. Venturini based his theory only on the fact that Essenes always dressed in white.

The problem is, just like Bahrdt's theory, there are no facts to back it up. This theory amounts to total speculation, without theological, historical, or scientific support, and without merit.

Heinrich Paulus (1761–1851)

A rationalist theologian, Heinrich Paulus wrote multiple works from 1802 onwards proclaiming that Jesus was the victim of a temporary coma and somehow revived without any assistance in Joseph's tomb. In 1828, Paulus proposed that heavy fumes from an impending earthquake (perhaps the one related in Matt 27:5) caused respiratory problems for Jesus hanging on the cross, rendering him unconscious. Jesus was comatose but not dead. Paulus believed that Jesus then appeared to his disciples, bid them *adieu*, and disappeared into a cloud on the mountain.

The problem is, why was Jesus the only person at Calvary overcome by the fumes? That would be spectacular individualization. This theory, too, is without merit, without any scientific, historical, or theological evidence, and should be brushed aside as you would a pesky fly.

Hazrat Mirza Ghulam Ahmad (1835–1908)

In 1882 in Lahore, Pakistan, Hazrat Mirza Ghulam Ahmad founded the Ahmadiyyas, a nonorthodox branch of Islam. In his 1899 book *Jesus in India*, Ahmad claimed that Jesus survived the crucifixion and traveled to India. Ahmad said Yuz Asaf, the prophet who purportedly is Jesus, lived there and died in Mohall Khaniyar in Srinagar, not in Jerusalem. The Ahmadiyyas are committed to disproving Jesus' bodily resurrection and ascension. They also hold that the 'two angels in white' noted in John 20:12 were Essenes because Essenes dressed in white.

The problem is, Ahmad's theory runs completely counter to the four Gospels' accounts, and while stories of Jesus living in India after his crucifixion have often fluttered by as would a butterfly, there has never been any genuine, legitimate proof of his presence there. Again, eyewitnesses trump speculation.

Nikolai Aleksandrovich Notovitch (1858–after 1916)

This Crimean Jewish adventurer claimed to be a Russian aristocrat, spy, and journalist. Notovitch is best known for his 1894 book asserting that during those years of Jesus' life not recorded in the Gospels, he left Galilee for India. Before returning to Judea, he sat under the teachings of Buddhists and Hindus. Notovitch claimed to have stayed at the Hemis Monastery while in India where the chief lama told him of the existence of an unknown work called the *"Life of Saint Īssä, Best of the Sons of Men."* Īssä or Īsä is the Arabic name for Jesus in the Qur'an.

The problem is, the so-called facts of Notovitch's story don't check out. Philologist Max Müller suggested that either Notovitch was the victim of a practical joke or he fabricated the evidence. Müller wrote the head lama at the Hemis monastery to inquire about the validity of Notovitch's story. The head lama said there had been no Western visitor to the monastery in the previous fifteen years. He also said they had no documents such as the *"Life of Saint Īssä."*

Additionally, J. Archibald Douglas, Professor of English and History at the Government College in Agra, India, visited the Hemis monastery to interview the head lama, who again denied that Notovitch had ever been there and that no such documents existed. Once his story was examined by historians, Notovitch confessed to having fabricated the whole thing.

Robert Graves (1895–1985) & Joshua Podro (1894–1962)

Graves and Podro wrote a book called *The Nazarene Gospel Restored*, which is proof that scholarship is no deterrent to fantasy. Written in collaboration with the distinguished Hebrew scholar Joshua Podro, the imaginative Robert Graves drew upon Podro's knowledge of the ancient world to reveal the "true story of Jesus." In a letter to poet T. S. Eliot, Graves said he had written "a very long, very readable, very strange book." The problem is, his assessment was spot on. The book was long and exceptionally strange.

The UK-based magazine *Church Times* is known for informed and independent reporting of church and world news. However, the magazine refused to advertise *The Nazarene Gospel Restored*. Reviews of the book were extremely hostile. Twice Graves was sued for libel. Needless to say, the book had little impact on the "true" story of Jesus.

Donavan Joyce (1910–980)

Donovan Maxwell Joyce was an Australian radio producer and writer. However, he is best known as the author of the international best-selling book *The Jesus Scroll*.[197] This book was a forerunner to much of the subsequent themes found in *The Da Vinci Code* and other books of this genre. Joyce claimed that Jesus did not die on Golgotha's Cross but lived to be 80 years old [a feat in itself in the first century AD] and died at Masada during the Roman siege of the mesa [73 AD] that was occupied by Jewish zealots making their last stand against the Roman army. This would mean Jesus lived long enough to witness the destruction of Jerusalem in 70 AD. Where did Joyce get this idea? He claimed to have seen a scroll stolen from the excavations at Masada, which was signed Yeshua ben Ya'akob ben Gennesareth. In English, this would be Jesus, Son of Jacob of Gennesareth.

The problem is, when Donovan Joyce attempted to visit the archaeological dig at Masada, he was summarily prevented from doing so by the famed archaeologist Yigael Yadin, director of the dig. Thus, Joyce engaged a corrupt archaeologist named "Dr. Grosset" to help him smuggle the "Jesus Scroll" from Masada and out of Israel. Of course, no mysterious "Dr. Grosset" was ever an archaeologist at Masada, nor has any reputable archaeologist ever heard of him. Joyce proposed many spurious, controversial theories about the historicity of Jesus and received numerous death threats as a result.

Hugh Joseph Schonfield (1901–1988)

Schonfield was a British New Testament scholar specializing in the early development of the Christian religion and the church. He was a liberal Hebrew Christian who wrote over forty books, but he is best known for his 1965 blockbuster *The Passover Plot*, in which he asserted the alleged crucifixion was part of a broader, conscious attempt by Jesus to fulfill the Messianic expectations of the Old Testament prophets. Of course, *The Passover Plot* sparked worldwide controversy. The press loved it. "Enough to seriously challenge many traditional Christian beliefs, if not alter them," said the *Los Angeles Times Book Review*. *Newsweek* sensationalized the book by saying, "Like Chariots of the Gods... the plot has all the elements of an international thriller."

The problem is, Schonfield was writing more as a historical sociologist than a true biblical scholar. He based his conclusions on the social history of the time and discounted anything in the Bible that contradicted his premise. While *The Passover Plot* made quite a splash in the late 1960s, its influence waned soon afterward when the "Hollywoodesque" publicity waned.

Michael Baigent (1948–1913), Richard Leigh (1943–2007), Henry Lincoln (1930–2022)

Richard Leigh, his roommate and frequent co-author, introduced Michael Baigent to Henry Lincoln, a British television scriptwriter. The three discovered that they shared an interest in the Knights Templar, and developed the

1982 book, *The Holy Blood and the Holy Grail*. The book popularized the hypothesis that the Holy Grail was the child that Jesus and Mary Magdalene had together. This began a bloodline that later married into a Frankish royal dynasty, the Merovingians. This legend was preserved by a secret society known as the Priory of Sion. The book rapidly climbed the bestseller charts.

The problem is, almost everything in the book is historically inaccurate or unproven. Criticism came swiftly and fiercely. The book was described as "a work thoroughly debunked by scholars and critics alike."[198] A review in *The New York Times Book Review* said the book was "one of the all-time great works of pop pseudohistory."[199] The book has been described as "a work thoroughly debunked by scholars and critics alike"[200] It sounds like *The Holy Blood and the Holy Grail* doesn't have much to commend it.

Barbara Elizabeth Thiering (1930–2015)

Thiering was an Australian historian, theologian, and biblical exegete specializing in the origins of the early Christian Church. She often challenged Christian orthodoxy claiming that new findings presented better answers to the Christian's supernatural beliefs. From her study of the Dead Sea Scrolls, she argued that the miracles of the New Testament (e.g. the virgin birth, Jesus turning water into wine, the resurrection, etc.) were "deliberately constructed myths." Refer to Chapter 6 for more information about her beliefs and the rebuttals to those beliefs.

The problem is, her ideas have not received acceptance by many of her academic peers. Géza Vermes wrote, "Professor Barbara Thiering's reinterpretation of the New Testament, in which the married, divorced, and remarried Jesus, father of four, becomes the "Wicked Priest" of the Dead Sea Scrolls, has made no impact on learned opinion. Scroll scholars and New Testament experts alike have found [Thiering's theory] without substance."[201]

Former Bishop of Durham N. T. Wright wrote: "It is safe to say that no serious scholar has given this elaborate and fantastic theory any credence whatsoever ... the scholarly world has been able to take a good look at it: and the results are totally negative."[202]

Holger Kerston (1951–???)

Holger Kersten is a German writer on religion, myth, legend, and some esoteric subjects. He is best known for his books about Jesus' early years and later years in India. In 2005, Kerston led an expedition to India searching for the birthplace of Mithras, the god around whom a mystery religion was practiced in the Roman Empire from the first to the fourth century AD. In his book, *Jesus Lived in India*,[203] like others before him, Kersten followed Ahmadiyya founder Mirza Ghulam Ahmad in his sources. The book endorses Nicolas Notovich's claims about Jesus living in India during his "unknown years" (between ages 12 and 30). It also endorses Ghulam Ahmad's speculation about Jesus' years 33 to 120 in India. As evidence, Kersten cites a passage in the Bhavishya Purāna (one of Hinduism's eighteen major Purānas of Sanskrit literature) which refers to Jesus as "*Īsā*-Masih" (Jesus the Messiah). The passage describes the Hindu king Shalivahana traveling to the mountains to meet a man who calls himself *Īsā* son of a virgin. Kersten interprets this as a record of Jesus in Kashmir.

The problem is, the passage is an eighteenth-century dialogue also featuring Muhammad and not an early source as Ahmad claimed.[204] Most scholars today consider this part of the Purāna to be a nineteenth-century interpolation, not proof of Jesus being in India.[205]

Dan Brown (1964–)

Dan Brown grew up in Exeter, New Hampshire searching and confused. His father was a mathematics teacher at the prestigious Phillips Exeter Academy. Brown was raised Episcopalian, but in the eighth or ninth grade, he studied astronomy, cosmology, and the origins of the universe. "A light went off," Brown said. "The Bible doesn't make sense. Science makes much more sense to me." With this revelation, Brown gravitated away from religion.

But he drifted back later in life and came full circle. The more science he studied, the more he realized that physics becomes metaphysics and numbers become imaginary numbers. "The further you go into science, the mushier the ground gets. You start to say, 'Oh, there is an order and a spiritual aspect to science.'"[206]

In his blockbuster book *The Da Vinci Code*, Dan Brown unambiguously borrowed ideas from the aforementioned *The Holy Blood and Holy Grail*. In fact, in March 2006, Baigent and Leigh filed a lawsuit in a British court against Brown's publisher, Random House, claiming copyright infringement.

The novel promotes an alternative religious history, the main plot of which is that Jesus Christ had a child with Mary Magdalene and the Merovingian kings of France were descended from their bloodline. These ideas were borrowed from Clive Prince's *The Templar Revelation* (1997) and books by Margaret Starbird, who wrote seven books espousing the theory that Jesus was involved in a relationship with Mary Magdalene.

The problem is, not only has *The Da Vinci Code* been extensively denounced by many Christians as an attack on the Roman Catholic Church, and has been consistently criticized by others because of its historical and scientific inaccuracies. It is simply a best-selling rehash of old, discredited ideas, e.g. the marriage of Jesus and Mary Magdalene. No historical, scientific, or biblical proof has ever surfaced, or will ever surface, to support this blasphemous premise.

There are others, of course. In 2011 David Mirsch published a book entitled *The Open Tomb: Why and How Jesus Faked His Death and Resurrection*.[207] And, undoubtedly, there are more to come. But each novel attempt to deny the crucifixion, and more often the resurrection, gets mired in the same clay of conspiracy theory that those before it did. The truth is found in Jesus' own words: "Sanctify them in the truth; your word is truth" (John 17:17). No human theory can match divine revelation.

SCHOLARS VERSUS SWOONERS

The swoon hypothesis is attractive to certain people, especially those who are drawn to the sensational or who are virtually ignorant of the Gospels, but it has been criticized by many people, including medical experts, some scientists, and most biblical scholars. Here is a sampling of scholarly critiques of the swoon theory.

Medical authorities and pastor W. D. Edwards, W. J. Gabel, and F. E. Hosmer offered the following analysis concerning the New Testament Greek and the medical data in JAMA "Jesus of Nazareth underwent Jewish and Roman trials, was flogged, and was sentenced to death by crucifixion . . . The major pathophysiologic effect of crucifixion was an interference with normal respirations. Accordingly, death resulted primarily from hypovolemic shock and exhaustion asphyxia. Jesus' death was ensured by the thrust of a soldier's spear into his side. Modern medical interpretation of the historical evidence indicates that Jesus was dead when taken down from the cross."[208]

Forensic pathologist Frederick T. Zugibe, MD, Ph.D. wrote:

> In general, the Swoon Theory is completely unfounded and is refuted by the following facts: First, Jesus' physical condition was grave. The extent and severity of his injuries dictate that he would not have survived the crucifixion . . . No drugs of the time were capable of placing him into a deep sleep to feign death given his condition . . . Finally, we must ask, why would the disciples worship Jesus if he pulled a fast one? If Jesus was a quack who believed he was the Messiah . . . would they still have

relinquished all their possessions and undergone extreme hardships and dangers to preach to the world Jesus' suffering, death, and resurrection? I don't think so."[209]

Many others, including the nineteenth-century rationalist theologian David Strauss, considered it highly improbable that the faith of Jesus' followers would be strengthened by the idea that he was only capable of barely surviving a crucifixion. Strauss wrote: "It is impossible that a being who had stolen half dead out of the sepulcher, who crept about weak and ill and wanting medical treatment ... could have given the disciples the impression that he was a conqueror over death and the grave, the Prince of life: an impression that lay at the bottom of their future ministry."[210]

Christian apologist and author Josh McDowell claims that the death of Jesus in the Gospels could not have been fabricated. The reason is, as Frederick Charles Cook pointed out in his nineteenth-century work, *Jesus, a Fraud, a Lunatic or the Messiah? Resurrection: Hoax or History?* the text displays medical knowledge that was not available to the Gospel writers in the first century AD.[211]

Christian scholar and apologist William Lane Craig offered this analysis. "The extent of Jesus' tortures was such that he could never have survived the crucifixion and entombment. The suggestion that a man so critically wounded then went on to appear to the disciples on various occasions in Jerusalem and Galilee is pure fantasy."[212]

Lee Strobel adds, "He couldn't possibly have faked his death because you can't fake the inability to breathe for long. Besides, the spear thrust into his heart would have settled the issue once and for all. And the Romans weren't about to risk their own death by allowing him to walk away alive."[213]

Determining that Jesus was dead

That Jesus of Nazareth absolutely died on the cross is also confirmed by a variety of Jewish laws of the time. Several dealt with the "official" ways of determining the moment of death such that the body could be taken down from the cross. Mishnah tractate *Yevamot* 120b mentions that one of those methods of confirmation was when stray animals began to feed on the flesh of the feet and legs.

> It was taught in the Mishnah: Or even if one saw that a wild animal was eating parts of him, one may not testify that he died. Rav Yehuda said that Shmuel said: They taught this only where the animal was eating from a place on his body that does not

cause his soul to depart, i.e., does not inevitably lead to death, such as his hand or foot. But if the animal was eating from a place on his body that does cause his soul to depart, one may testify to his death.

Jesus' death was swifter than normal. He had endured such pre-cross beating at the hands of the Jews and Romans, it is amazing he was physically able even to stagger to Golgotha. His human body was half-dead before it was nailed to the cross. No wild animals would nibble at his flesh because there were plenty of humans still around watching him die.

John 19:32–34 records:

> So the soldiers came and broke the legs of the first, and of the other who had been crucified with him. But when they came to Jesus and saw that he was already dead, they did not break his legs. But one of the soldiers pierced his side with a spear, and at once there came out blood and water.

In the very next verse, John goes on to assure his readers, "He who saw it has borne witness—his testimony is true, and he knows that he is telling the truth—that you also may believe." This is the incredible power of eyewitness testimony.

DOES IT MATTER IF JESUS DIED?

Is believing that Jesus actually died at Calvary important to you? It should be. It certainly was important to the Apostle Paul. His belief that Jesus died to atone for our sin was part of the "belief package" that is the kind of saving faith God requires for our salvation. "For by grace you have been saved through faith. And this is not your own doing; it is the gift of God, not a result of works, so that no one may boast" (Eph 2:8–9). Salvation by faith is not faith in nothing; it is faith in something—specifically, the claims of the gospel, one of which is the literal death of Jesus Christ.

> "Faith is not belief without proof, but trust without reservation."
> —Elton Trueblood

The gospel's good news asserts that because of that first sin in the Garden of Eden, all who are born of Adam (and that would be every human being with Jesus as the lone exception) are born already sin-stained. We have an innate proclivity to sin. We inherit sin. We also choose to sin and because of our sin, we are condemned to death (Rom 6:23).

That's not good news at all, but the rest of the gospel is. God had a plan to redeem us from the death sentence that sin carried with it. That plan was for Jesus to die on the cross and pay the penalty for our sin. God required a perfect sacrifice and since none of us is perfect, sinless, or acceptable to God, we couldn't be that sacrifice. But Jesus was perfect, sinless, and acceptable to God and his death is the basis upon which our salvation, even our eternal future, and our hope rests.

If Jesus faked his death, there is not a thing you can trust in the Bible because the death of Jesus at Calvary is central, the main theme of the Bible.

If Jesus faked his death, he would not have been the perfect sinless substitute for us. No devious faker is sinless. Jesus, however, is God and therefore without sin.

If Jesus faked his death, we are still facing the penalty for our sin and that means our future is sealed, but not bright at all.

But, if Jesus died as he said he would, and as sixteen different books of the New Testament claim he did, the door to salvation is opened wide to us. To enter through that door all we need to do is express a genuine faith that what Jesus did at Calvary is all that God required to forgive us of our sins. Simply put by the apostle: "Believe in the Lord Jesus, and you will be saved" (Acts 16:31).

This is all true because Jesus really did die on the cross. No death, no atonement. No death, no forgiveness. No death, no heaven. No death, no hope.

"May the God of hope fill you with all joy and peace in believing, so that by the power of the Holy Spirit you may abound in hope." (Rom 15:13).

Chapter 8

The Burial of Jesus

The security of Jesus' tomb was firmly in place. They had the security of the soldiers. They had the security of the stone. And they had the security of the seal. So what kind of security did they have? Inadequate!

JESUS DIED AT GOLGOTHA. No literary or historical sleight-of-hand can alter that fact. After hanging for hours on the cross, Jesus breathed his last. He died just a short two-hour walk from where he was born. When Jesus was born, he was first taken to the Temple and in adoration Simeon held Jesus in his arms. When he was laid in the grave, in adoration Joseph held Jesus in his arms. Both were members of the Sanhedrin. They were like the believing bookends to Jesus' life on Earth.

The Roman killing squad had waited six hours for this moment. The religious leaders in Jerusalem had waited months for this. But the Holy Trinity had waited an eternity for it.

The price had been paid. The transaction was complete. However, there was still the matter of Jesus' humanity, his dead body hanging on that old rugged cross. It had to be taken down and buried quickly before sunset. It's on the burial of Jesus that this chapter is focused.

Before we examine the Jewish procedure of burying one of their own, we must settle on a more primary question. After Jesus died, was he interred?

WAS JESUS BURIED?

The Bible confirms that specific individuals were left unburied because they were obnoxious or godless during their lives. Jeremiah prophesied that the wicked people of Jerusalem would be carried into Babylonian captivity because they had turned away from God. "They shall die of deadly diseases. They shall not be lamented, nor shall they be buried" (Jer 16:4). The primary example of a person not buried but left for the dogs in the streets is Queen Jezebel. After Jezebel slaughtered the prophets of God, the message from the LORD was, "And the dogs shall eat Jezebel in the territory of Jezreel, and none shall bury her" (2 Kgs 9:10).

In the apocalyptic vision given to the Apostle John, a beast rising from the bottomless pit will kill two prophets that God will raise from the dead because they speak the truth. Revelation 11:7–9 says the beast will "kill them, and their dead bodies will lie in the street of the great city that symbolically is called Sodom and Egypt, where their Lord was crucified. For three and a half days, some from the peoples and tribes and languages and nations will gaze at their dead bodies and refuse to let them be placed in a tomb."

These examples prove that, on occasion, people were left unburied in the streets. This was the ultimate disgrace and bears on whether Jesus' body was left in the streets or buried in Joseph's tomb.

Skepticism regarding Jesus' burial

In a May 04, 2016 blog post on the Houston Baptist University site, New Testament scholar Craig Evans noted:

> The resurrection of Jesus of Nazareth . . . lies at the very heart of Christian faith and is the principal datum that accounts for the emergence of the Christian Church. Skeptics, not surprisingly, express doubt . . . In recent years a number of skeptics, including scholars who ought to know better, have charged that the story of the burial of Jesus itself is unhistorical, that Roman law did not, in fact, permit the burial of the crucified, and that the story of the burial is therefore simply part of early Christian apologetic, designed to confirm the story of the resurrection [https://hbu.edu/news-and-events/2016/05/04/craig-evans-resurrection-jesus-light-jewish-burial-practices/].

A few of these scholars have suggested that in all probability, the body of Jesus was not buried, but was left hanging on the cross or thrown into a ditch where it rotted away if it was not mauled by animals first.[214]

> "The bodies of those who are condemned to death should not be refused their relatives."
> —Ulpian, a Roman jurist

In his work simply titled *Jesus,* Charles Guignebert, late professor at the Sorbonne in Paris, claimed that Jesus' body was never buried in the private tomb of Joseph of Arimathea but was thrown into the common grave of criminals.[215] Alfred Loisy, the French Roman Catholic priest who is credited as the founder of biblical modernism in the Roman Catholic Church, also held that Jesus' body was not given a proper burial but was left lying on the ground.[216]

A more contemporary scholar, John Dominic Crossan, argues that "It was actually non-burial that made being crucified alive one of the three supreme penalties of Roman punishment."[217] Crossan goes on to guess that Jesus was buried in a shallow grave, where his body was eaten by wild dogs.[218] Of course, Crossan presents no evidence for this wildly speculative and unhistorical claim because no such evidence exists.

Crossan's views tend to run counter to reliable scholarship on many fronts. Multiple voices have been raised against his claim that Jesus' body was eaten by wild dogs. Crossan's critics have been harsh. Howard Clark Kee calls Crossan's ideas, "a triumph of circular reasoning."[219]

Why would Guignebert, Loisy, and Crossan think they knew better what happened to Jesus' body than the three eyewitnesses, Matthew and John, possibly Mark, and the non-eyewitness but careful historian, Luke? This defies both logic and common sense.

N. T. Wright says that Crossan's book, *The Historical Jesus,* "is a book to treasure for its learning, its thoroughness, its brilliant handling of multiple and complex issues, its amazing inventiveness . . . It is all the more frustrating, therefore, to have to conclude that the book is almost entirely wrong."[220] Ben Meyer says Crossan's book provides useful information, but reckons, "As historical-Jesus research, it is unsalvageable."[221] Denying that Jesus was buried after his crucifixion does not get very good reviews from reasonable scholarship.

Some theologians who deny that Jesus was buried do so partially because of a statement found in the words of Hypatius, bishop of Ephesus in 536 AD. Allegedly, in an especially weak moment, in one of the bishop's sermons, he blurted out that Jesus was "cast out naked and without a tomb." However, in a more lucid moment, he immediately corrected himself and went on to say that Joseph of Arimathea came to Golgotha to bury Jesus. Some have laid claim to the blurting but, unfortunately, not the correction.

There are many, many documented exceptions to the practice of non-burial.[222] Archaeologist Jodi Magness rightly contradicts Crossan's claim that Jesus was not buried. She also debunked his idea that Yehohanan's burial was unusual.[223] Genuine scholarship considers this issue settled.

WRITTEN RECORDS OF JESUS' BURIAL

Philo's appeal to Caesar demonstrates that Roman authorities sometimes were open to respecting Jewish burial customs. Philo says, "[The Jews] appealed to Pilate to redress the infringement of their traditions caused by the shields and not to disturb the customs which throughout all the preceding ages had been safeguarded without disturbance by kings and by emperors" (*De Legatione ad Gaium*, 38 §300).

The Jewish historian Josephus informs us that the Romans were wise enough not to forbid the peoples they conquered from continuing their religious practices. He also gives examples of how the Romans respected Jewish sensibilities.

In *Against Apion*, Josephus explained how the Romans did not demand their subjects "to transgress the laws of their countries" (2.6§73). He also recounted in *The Jewish War* that the successors to Agrippa I, as Roman procurators, kept the nation at peace, "by abstaining from all interference with the customs of the country" (*Wars* 2.11.6).

Josephus affirmed that those executed by crucifixion were, "taken down and buried before sunset." Because only the Roman authority in Samaria and Judea could execute anyone (*Wars* 2.8.1; *Ant.* 20.9.1; John 18:31), we must assume that those who did the crucifying were the Romans.

Though executed by the Romans, those crucified were nonetheless buried. If condemned by the Jewish Council, it was incumbent on the Council to arrange for the burial of the executed (Mishnah *Sanhedrin* 6.5–6). However, this was done out of concern for the purity of the land, not out of pity for the family of the crucified (Deut 21:23).

Josephus also stated those executed by crucifixion were, "buried before sunset." Here he refers to the Jewish people who did the burying. To bury the executed person "before sunset" was not a Roman concern at all (see Deut 21:22–23). This requirement was still very much in force in the days of Jesus, as seen in literature such as the Dead Sea Scrolls (e.g., 11Q19 64:7–13).

What this Jewish historian recorded for the Romans is entirely consistent with what the Jewish historians of the Gospels recorded for the Church. The Romans crucified Jesus and two other men, but it was up to the Jews to bury them. To argue that just because the Romans executed a malefactor he would not be buried, flies in the face of the evidence that the Roman authority in Jewish Palestine, during peacetime, did accommodate Jewish customs and sensitivities.

The burial of crucified individuals is further supported by the 1968 discovery of the ossuary at Giv'at ha-Mivtar, a suburban neighborhood of Jerusalem. It contained evidence of the burial of a man named Yehohanan who had been crucified. The remains of an iron spike 11.5 centimeters (4.52 inches) in length were found that still pierced Yehohanan's right heel bone.

The Gospel record

The claim must be rejected that removing Jesus' body from the cross and burying it would contradict Roman lack of respect for Jewish sympathies. This position contradicts eyewitness accounts that are recorded in all four Gospels. The Gospels are the best historical accounts of Jesus' death, burial, and resurrection available to us. They provide the only eyewitness accounts of Jesus' disposition and burial by Joseph of Arimathea.

The Gospel of Matthew records the burial of Jesus with these words:

> When it was evening, there came a rich man from Arimathea, named Joseph, who also was a disciple of Jesus. He went to Pilate and asked for the body of Jesus. Then Pilate ordered it to be given to him. And Joseph took the body and wrapped it in a clean linen shroud and laid it in his own new tomb, which he had cut in the rock (Matt 27:57–60).

Mark adds a few more details. "And Joseph bought a linen shroud, and taking him down, wrapped him in the linen shroud and laid him in a tomb that had been cut out of the rock. And he rolled a stone against the entrance of the tomb" (Mark 15:46).

Luke does as well: "Then he took it down and wrapped it in a linen shroud and laid him in a tomb cut in stone, where no one had ever yet been laid" (Luke 23:53).

Furthermore, John adds his own details. "Now in the place where he was crucified there was a garden, and in the garden a new tomb in which no one had yet been laid. So because of the Jewish day of Preparation, since the tomb was close at hand, they laid Jesus there" (John 19:41–42).

Every source we have indicates that, during peacetime at least, the practice in Israel, especially in the vicinity of Jerusalem, was to allow the Jews to bury their dead before nightfall. The Roman authorities permitted the families of the crucified to remove the body from the cross and give it a proper burial.

During times of war, however, this was another matter. When Titus besieged Jerusalem from 69 to 70 AD, thousands of Jews were crucified, and very few of them were permitted a burial. The dead or dying bodies hung helplessly from Roman crosses (*Wars* 5.6.5; 5.11.1).

While the four Gospels present differing details about Jesus' burial, they are united in their confidence that Jesus of Nazareth was, in fact, buried after his body was removed from the cross. Still, these biblical declarations continue to be challenged by modern liberal theologians.

The testimony of the Apostle Paul

To say Jesus was never buried not only conflicts with the Gospel records but also with what was written in the first century by the Apostle Paul. About 55–56 AD, Paul wrote to the believers at Corinth. He declared, "For I delivered to you as of first importance what I also received: that Christ died for our sins in accordance with the Scriptures, that he was buried, that he was raised on the third day in accordance with the Scriptures" (1 Cor 15:3–4).

This ancient tradition confirmed the Gospel narratives and was written long before any supposed legendary elements could be added to the facts. While Paul wrote this letter in the middle of the first century AD, there is evidence that suggests the formula of 1 Corinthians 15:3–4 dates back even further. When Paul said to the Corinthians, "For I delivered to you ... what I also received" and then spoke of Christ's death, burial, and resurrection, he was indicating what he received came from God (2 Cor 12:1–4; Gal 1:11–12). But the apostle was also aware that others had believed the same message before him. Paul names some of those who embraced Jesus' crucifixion, burial, and resurrection before he ever came on the scene. These included: Cephas (Simon Peter), the Twelve Disciples, 500 believers in Jerusalem, James, and all the apostles of that day (I Cor 15:5–7).

The knowledge of Jesus' burial was both established and recorded early in the first century AD, but how early? According to Paul elsewhere, as early as six years after Jesus' death. In Galatians 1:18, Paul mentions that he went to visit Peter and James in Jerusalem three years after his conversion—Peter and James being two witnesses of the resurrected Jesus (see 1 Cor 15:5–7). Since Paul's conversion was presumably in 36 AD, his visit with Peter and

James would have been in 39 AD. It is here that Paul most likely received the formula regarding Jesus' death, burial, and resurrection.

Jesus' death, burial, and resurrection are central to the Christian faith, as is demonstrated by the great creeds of Christendom. The Apostle's Creed states: "[Jesus] suffered under Pontius Pilate, was crucified, died, and was buried; he descended to the dead. On the third day, he rose again." The Nicene Creed also says, "He [Jesus] suffered, was crucified, was buried, rose again on the third day."

To deny that Jesus was buried suffers from more than a lack of faith; it suffers from a lack of facts as well.

WHY WAS JESUS' BURIAL UNUSUAL?

A tiny amount of detective work will answer the question of why Jesus' burial was unlike any other. For those crucified as criminals, being buried in a sepulcher, especially one owned by a wealthy member of the Jewish Sanhedrin, is an unlikelihood "to infinity and beyond." Even though Pontius Pilate found no guilt in Jesus, he permitted the criminal proceedings to go forward to their natural end—death on the cross. This was not only unjust, but it was also unusual. Criminals were typically thrown into a common grave where their bodies would rot or be eaten by scavengers. How unlikely is it that Jesus was spared that fate? Had it not been essential in the eternal plan of God for our salvation, Jesus' burial would not have taken place.

Remember the context in which Jesus was sent to Golgotha. He was tried and convicted of blasphemy by the Jewish Council. Then he was sent to Pilate to pronounce the death sentence. Here are the pertinent facts.

- Jesus was condemned to be crucified as a criminal (Matt 27:20–22).
- Jesus was treated as a criminal who had to bear his cross to the killing field of Golgotha (John 19:16–18).
- Jesus was treated as a criminal and was crucified between two other criminals (Mark 15:27).

The Roman authorities crucified the Lord Jesus at the bidding of a lawless mob. Speaking to the residents of Jerusalem, the Apostle Peter declared, "[Jesus] you crucified and killed by the hands of lawless men" (Acts 2:23). The best a crucified criminal could hope for was a quick death. The worst was a slow, painful death that lingered for days. The Latin poet Horace tells us it was the Roman custom to leave a body until it was "feeding crows on the cross" (*Epistle* 1.16.46–48).

Because Jesus of Nazareth was creating so much turmoil for the Jews, and consequently for the Roman government, why would the governor be inclined to allow Joseph of Arimathea to receive the body and give it a proper burial? There are several reasons.

Roman Law, as recorded in the ancient *Digest* of Justinian, verified that the bodies of executed persons at the time were required to be given to anyone who requested them for burial. *Digesta* 24.48 contains valuable and relevant material that helps us understand the nuances of Jewish law and burial customs.[224]

Secondly, Joseph was a respected member of the Jewish community. As a member of the Sanhedrin, he was from the highest class of Jews. Josephus carried some weight in Jerusalem, and giving Jesus' dead body to him would be another effort by Pilate to keep the Jews peaceful.

However, there is more going on here. While the arrest, trial, conviction, and execution of Jesus appear to take the disciples by surprise, they should not. Jesus warned his disciples of his death, burial, and resurrection frequently and for a long time (Matt 16:21; 17:22–23; 20:17–19; Mark 8:31–32; 9:30–31; 10:32–34; Luke 9:21–22; 18:31–33). In Christian theology, Jesus' crucifixion and resurrection are inseparably linked. They are co-equally important and complement each other in the eternal plan of God.

Nevertheless, these two gigantic theological events are linked by what is very common among humans—burial. Jesus' burial is the connection that binds together the two most significant events in Christendom—Jesus' crucifixion and resurrection. Each time Jesus predicted his death, he also predicted his rising from the dead. You cannot have a resurrection without some sort of burial. Thus, whether it was stated or not, in the final paragraph his burial was implied in each of the Synoptic passages. It was part of God's eternal plan for this Passover weekend, and nothing would change that.

Was releasing Jesus' body for burial, especially to a non-family member, unusual in the Roman Empire? It was. Was there a chance it would not happen? There was not.

THE DISPOSITION OF JESUS' BODY

The act of removing Jesus' dead body from the Roman cross is referred to as the "Deposition." John records the account with these words.

> After these things Joseph of Arimathea, who was a disciple of Jesus, but secretly for fear of the Jews, asked Pilate that he might take away the body of Jesus, and Pilate gave him permission. So he came and took away his body. Nicodemus also, who earlier

had come to Jesus by night, came bringing a mixture of myrrh and aloes, about seventy-five pounds in weight. So they took the body of Jesus and bound it in linen cloths with the spices, as is the burial custom of the Jews (John 19:38-40).

Nicodemus figures prominently in medieval depictions of the Deposition in which Joseph of Arimathea and he are shown removing the dead Christ from the cross, often with the assistance of a ladder. There was very little time to prepare Jesus' body for burial before sundown. Joseph and Nicodemus had to work rapidly.

Metal Cross with a Ladder

But why these two men? Where are the rest of Jesus' men—his disciples? Moreover, where are his family members—his brothers and sisters? Removing a dead body after a Roman crucifixion and burying it was not a suitable task for two elderly men and a handful of faithful women. Both Joseph and Nicodemus were members of the Sanhedrin, so they would have known each other. Nevertheless, neither of them likely knew the other had become a follower of the Messiah. Imagine Joseph's surprise when Nicodemus showed up at Golgotha to help him remove Jesus' body and carry it to Joseph's tomb.[225]

> "Not only the rich, but even those moderately well-to-do, had tombs of their own, which probably were acquired and prepared long before they were needed, and treated and inherited as private and personal property."
> —Alfred Edersheim

It was not uncommon for wealthy Jews to employ servants who were not Jews so they could perform tasks on the Sabbath without breaking the Sabbath prohibitions. Probably these men first lifted the *patibulum* off of the *stipes crucis* and laid Jesus on the ground, still attached to the crossbeam. Together they pulled the Roman spikes from his hands. The Master's muscles already have become rigid from the trauma of crucifixion. *Rigor mortis* usually does not set in until the fourth hour postmortem. This is when chemical changes cause a stiffening of the muscles. Likely it had not been four hours since Jesus' death, so there was still some flexibility to his body as they removed it from the cross.

A Typical First-century Tomb

There may have been no such thing as a "typical" sepulcher in the first century. Most tombs in Jesus' day had two chambers hollowed out of solid rock. The first chamber was kind of a vestibule or foyer and the entranceway into the tomb itself. The second chamber was where the bodies would be laid to rest.

Some tombs of this era were cut into a square or near-square with long, narrow niches (*kokhim* in Hebrew) cut into the rock walls.[226] These niches were slightly larger than a man's body. Into these niches, the enshrouded body would be slid until all its flesh had decomposed, usually a year later. The bones would then be taken from the niche and placed in a bone box called an ossuary. *Sanhedrin* 47b says, "Once the flesh of the deceased had decomposed, they would gather his bones and bury them in their proper place in his ancestral burial plot."

The second primary type of tomb had no niches. Instead, an arched recess called an *arcosolium* was carved into the wall. The word *arcosolium* comes from two Latin words, *arcus* meaning "arch," and *solium* meaning "throne." It was a place to honor a loved one as if he were a king, or she a queen. Examples of *arcosolia* may be seen in the catacombs of Rome.

But what about the tomb of Joseph of Arimathea? In which type of sepulcher was Jesus' body placed? We cannot say for certain. The interior of the Garden Tomb in Jerusalem gives the appearance of an *arcosolium* and perhaps the tomb in the Church of the Holy Sepulchre as well.

In 2016, a Greek restoration team undertook a reinforcing project of the Edicule at the Church of the Holy Sepulchre. The four-million-dollar project took nearly a year to complete. On October 26, 2016, the marble slab over what has traditionally been believed to be the burial site of Jesus was removed. Archaeologist and Franciscan priest Father Eugenio Alliata was there, among the few to look into the grave.

From his observations, Father Alliata explained, "We are not certain about the kind of [funeral chamber] that is in question here. Today, we can exclude the possibility of a *kokhim* tomb—literally 'oven,' in Hebrew—that is to say, a cavity dug into the rock the size of a body." From his limited observations, then, Father Alliata suggested that this was an *arcosolium* tomb, a "type of shelf tomb on which the body was placed."

While the archaeologist and priest was confident the supposed tomb of Jesus was not of the *kokhim* type, he also took note that the grotto appeared to be "too narrow" to be a tomb with an *arcosolium*. Father Alliata concluded that this tomb was not "strictly one type or another."[227] Thus, while it is currently believed that Joseph's family tomb was of the *arcosolium* type, we cannot be dogmatic about it.

Corroborating evidence for the Gospels' descriptions of the tomb in which Jesus was buried is impressive. "More than sixty examples of similar tombs used at the time Jesus lived, with large rolling stone boulders that seal the entrance, just as described in the Gospels, have been found in and around Jerusalem."[228]

WAS JESUS EMBALMED?

The science or art of embalming has been practiced for thousands of years. Its beginnings are usually associated with the ancient Egyptians. Because of their arid climate, preserving a body using the correct embalming techniques was entirely possible. The ancient Egyptians perfected the art of embalming. So skilled were they that people mummified four thousand years ago still have skin, hair, and recognizable features such as scars and tattoos (see Gen 50:1–3).

In 2019, Egyptian archaeologists discovered thirty ancient wooden coffins in Luxor, Egypt with more to follow. "It is the first large human coffin cache ever discovered since the end of the nineteenth century," according to Egyptian Antiquities Minister Khaled El-Enany.[229] The 3,000-year-old coffins were exceptionally well-preserved and brilliantly colored. The bodies inside were yet another example of the science and art of embalming in ancient Egypt. It seems as if almost monthly we receive news of another discovery of an Egyptian field of tombs.

- The 4,400-year-old tomb of royal priest Wahtye in Saqqara, was unearthed in 2018.
- Hundreds of mummified animals and statues were discovered in 2019 in Saqqara.
- Fifty-two burial shafts in Saqqara with more than fifty wooden coffins inside, dating back 3,000 years, were uncovered in 2020.
- The funerary temple of Queen Nearit, the wife of King Teti, the first pharaoh of the Sixth Dynasty of Egypt, was unearthed in Saqqara in 2020.
- Five tombs at Saqqara, more than 4,000 years old, were discovered in 2021. The burial chambers are in a good state of preservation with hieroglyphics, carved walls, and relics all being discovered.
- In 2023 Egyptian archaeologists uncovered several 4,300-year-old tombs in Saqqara, which is nineteen miles south of Cairo. The tombs date back to the Fifth and Sixth dynasties of the Old Kingdom (2686–2181 B.C.)
- You can update information about more recent discoveries at Home—Biblical Archaeology Society

The Egyptians, however, were not alone in embalming their dead. The prehistoric Paraca Indians of Peru embalmed their dead as well. Japanese and Peruvian archaeologists have discovered a 3,000-year-old tomb in northern Peru that is thought to have been a tribute to a priest. On the Canary Islands, although not universally across the islands, Guanches aborigines employed embalming methods eerily similar to the Egyptians. Many Guanches' mummies have been found in an extreme state of desiccation, each weighing not more than 3 kg (7 lb). Two almost inaccessible caves in a vertical rock by the shore 5 km (3 mi) from Santa Cruz on Tenerife are said still to contain remains.

The ancient Babylonians, Sumerians, and Greeks practiced only the most superficial kind of embalming. Instead, they anointed the body with unguents, perfumes, and spices. Most important for the subject of this book, with the notable exception of Joseph, great-grandson of Abraham, the Jewish people did not normally embalm their dead.

God's promise to the disobedient Adam was, "By the sweat of your face you shall eat bread, till you return to the ground, for out of it you were taken; for you are dust, and to dust you shall return" (Gen 3:19; see also Eccl 12:7). Judaism has always been a "dust to dust" religion, not one that embalms or preserves the body of the dead.

JEWISH BURIAL CUSTOM

The Apostle John records that Joseph and Nicodemus followed the traditional Jewish burial custom of burying the body of Jesus (John 19:38–40). The stench of decaying flesh can be overwhelming. For family or friends visiting the tomb of the deceased, the Jews perfumed or spiced the body of the deceased to neutralize the odor. This was the practice of the first-century Jews with their dead.

Jewish burial law has not changed in 3,500 years. There were only two elements to Jewish burial customs. Those were the linen cloths in which the body would be wrapped and the spices that were inserted between the folds of the cloth. The Jews buried their dead before sundown on the same day that death occurred. Thus, there would be no coffin, no vault, no service of remembrance—just cloth and spice, accompanied by the reverberation of weeping and wailing.

The linen cloth

Some scholars understand the cloth in which Jesus' body was wrapped to be strips of cloth, something akin to bandages. Others see it as a single, long piece of cloth. Usually, one's understanding is influenced by the Shroud of Turin. Kenneth E. Stevenson and Gary R. Habermas observe, "It is quite difficult to determine from the Gospels the precise method used to wrap Jesus' body in the cloth since the four evangelists use several different Greek verbs to describe the process."[230]

Matthew 27:59, Mark 15:46, and Luke 23:53 all say Jesus' body was wrapped in a linen sheet or shroud (Greek: σινδόνι; English: *sindoni*). Each of the Synoptic Gospels uses the word *sindoni* to describe the cloths. Each also uses the word "wrapped" (Greek: ἐνετύλιξεν; English: *enetylixen*) to describe how the linen was applied to the body of Jesus.

While the Synoptics say Joseph and Nicodemus "wrapped" the body of Jesus in a *sindōn*, John says they "bound" (Greek: ἔδησαν; English: *ed ēsan*) Jesus' body in linen cloths (Greek: ὀθονίοις; English: *othoniois*). In John 19:40, he uses both a different noun and a different verb to describe the preparation of Jesus' body for burial. While these words are similar, they are not identical and do not connote the same method of preparing the body.[231]

One possible solution to this difference between the Synoptics and John is offered by Stevenson and Habermas.

> It is likely that *othonia* refers to all the grave clothes associated with Jesus' burial—the large *sindon* (the shroud), as well as the smaller strips of linen that bound the jaw, the hands, and the feet. This interpretation of *othonia* is supported by Luke's use of the word. He says (23:53) Jesus was wrapped in a *sindon*, but later (24:12) Peter saw the *othonia* lying in the tomb after Jesus' resurrection. Luke, then, uses *othonia* as a plural term for all the grave clothes, including the *sindon*.[232]

On Sunday morning, Peter and John entered the empty tomb. Both Luke and John describe the grave clothes left behind. Luke says Peter saw the *othonia*, the broad, generic term for all the grave clothes, which would include the *sindōn*, and the smaller pieces used to bind the head, hands, and feet.

However, John was there too, and he says they saw "the linen cloths (*othonia*) lying there, and the face cloth (Greek: σουδάριον; English: *soudarion*), which had been on Jesus' head, not lying with the linen cloths but folded up in a place by itself." (John 20:6–7). The *othonia* was lying on the ground, but the *soudarion* was folded (Greek: ἐντετυλιγμένον; English: *entetyligmenon*) and lying in a place by itself, apart from the *othonia*.

The Mishnah gives these guidelines for preparing the dead. "One may perform all the needs of the dead: One may anoint him with oil and wash him, provided that no limb of his is moved . . . One may tie up the jaw, not in order that it should close but that it should not further [open]." (*Shabbath* 23.5).

Binding the chin of a corpse to keep it closed was commanded in The *Code of Jewish Law*.[233] John's mention that the linen facecloth was twisted and lying separately appears to corroborate that both Joseph of Arimathea and Nicodemus had strictly followed Jewish burial customs in their hurried preparation of Jesus' body.

The spices

The linen cloth constituted the first component of Jewish burial customs. The spices were the second. Concerning the spices brought to the tomb of Jesus, two questions come to the fore. First, what did Nicodemus bring? And second, if the men had already "spiced" the body of Jesus, why did the women seek to "spice" it again on Sunday morning? These are two very appropriate questions.

John 19:39 informs us, "Nicodemus also, who earlier had come to Jesus by night, came bringing a mixture of myrrh and aloes, about seventy-five pounds in weight." What appears to be an excessive amount of spices is thoroughly explored in Book 2 of this series, Watching Jesus Die.

First, a brief word about myrrh and aloes. Myrrh (Hebrew: מֹר; English: *môr*; Greek: σμύρνα; English: *smýrna*) is a natural gum or resin that is extracted from various small, thorny trees. It is not native to Israel but is found nearby. The extraction process necessitates wounding the tree so that it "bleeds" out the gum. Myrrh gum is waxy and coagulates very quickly, becoming hard and glossy with a yellowish color that may be either clear or opaque. As it ages, it darkens.

Aloe comes from a genus of plants with over 500 species. The best known of these species is *aloe vera* or "true aloe." Aloe is native to tropical and southern Africa, Madagascar, the Arabian Peninsula, and Jordan, along with some of the islands of the Indian Ocean.[234] While aloe species are frequently cultivated as ornamental plants both in gardens and in pots, it is mainly used as alternative medicine.

Joseph and Nicodemus in preparing Jesus' body for burial used aloe as a preservative.[235] The properties that made it useful for first aid also made it useful as a burial aid. What the Gospel writers say about the use of myrrh and aloe squares with what we know about its usage during the Roman era.

> "Dead bodies and graves are noisome and offensive;
> hence sin is compared to a body of death and an open sepulchre;
> but Christ's sacrifice, being to God as a sweet-smelling savour,
> hath taken away our pollution."
> —Matthew Henry

The fourth-century AD theologian Gregory of Nazianzus, when speaking of his brother Caesarius, said, "He lies dead, friendless, desolate, miserable, favored with a little myrrh."[236] The Orthodox Church calls Gregory of Nazianzus (330–389 AD) "The Theologian," which is a high honor indeed since they accorded this title to only one other, St John the Apostle. His authority and accuracy are rarely questioned.

The women and their spices

Because of the hastening Sabbath, Joseph, Nicodemus, and those who assisted them were in a real hurry to do as much of the Jewish burial ritual as they could. Nevertheless, it appears that the approach of the Sabbath caused them to curtail some of the usual Jewish rituals (Luke 23:54–56). Since the Gospels do not record the washing of Jesus' body, it could be inferred that the washing was not accomplished.

Since the women observed Joseph and Nicodemus emerge from the tomb and learned the burial ritual was not complete, they planned to return on Sunday morning as soon as it was light. They would join the men and add their spices as Jesus was placed in Joseph's tomb.

SECURITY AT THE TOMB

Everybody is concerned about security these days—security for our homes, at the office, the bank, and the ever-increasing number of online financial accounts people have today. A McAfee study indicated hacking costs consumers and companies as much as $575 billion each year. Believe it or not, security was a big issue in the first century as well, especially at the tomb of Jesus of Nazareth.

Keeping Jesus on the cross was no problem: he wanted to be there. Keeping him in the tomb was another matter: he wanted out. Caiaphas and his crew did not have the problem with cybersecurity we have today, but they clearly had a security problem.

The Jewish leaders knew they needed to secure the tomb of Joseph of Arimathea because it had been a wild weekend so far, and they wanted no more difficulty, such as would be caused by someone stealing Jesus' body from the grave. That is why they went back to Pilate to request Roman security at Jesus' gravesite. Matthew records the story.

> The next day, that is, after the day of Preparation, the chief priests and the Pharisees gathered before Pilate and said, "Sir, we remember how that impostor said, while he was still alive, 'After three days I will rise.' Therefore order the tomb to be made secure until the third day, lest his disciples go and steal him away and tell the people, 'He has risen from the dead,' and the

last fraud will be worse than the first." Pilate said to them, "You have a guard of soldiers. Go, make it as secure as you can." So they went and made the tomb secure by sealing the stone and setting a guard (Matt 27:62–66).

Of Pilate's retort, Matthew Henry, the seventeenth-century English nonconformist minister, wrote, "Methinks that word, 'Make it as sure as you can,' looks like a banter, either [1] Of their fears; "Be sure to set a strong guard upon the dead man;" or rather, [2] of their hopes; "Do your worst, try your wit and strength to the utmost; but if he be of God, he will rise, in spite of you and all your guards."[237]

Pilate was at the point in his ongoing dispute with the Jewish leaders where he could lampoon them. In essence, his response to their demand was, "Do the best you can. We'll see if you can secure the tomb."

Pilate's response was classic. As he attempted to push the blame for Jesus' crucifixion back on these Jews, now he tried to push the responsibility to guard his dead body back on them.

What did Pilate mean by his classic response? Father Pierre Benoit defines the options. "The Greek text reads, 'You have a guard,' and this may be understood in two ways. Either it means, 'Here is one, I give you one,' in which case it is composed of Roman soldiers. Or 'You have a Jewish guard, the Temple soldiers, use them,' in which case it is the Jews who provide the guard and seal the tomb."[238]

The apocryphal Gospel of Peter confuses the issue when it says, "Pilate gave over to them Petronius the centurion with soldiers to safeguard the sepulcher. And with these the elders and scribes came to the burial place" (Gos of Pet 31). According to this work, both a centurion with a contingent of Roman soldiers and a similar contingent of Jewish elders and scribes made up the guard at Jesus' tomb.

However, I am inclined to think that Pilate had "had it up to here" with these fastidious and pesky religious leaders. They had goaded him into releasing an innocent man to be crucified. They had used the "no friend of Caesar" ploy as a knife in his back. For Pilate, this would have been the equivalent of the "nuclear option." Now they want Roman soldiers to do the work the Temple police should be doing. It appears they have finally pushed the Roman prefect a bit too far. He refused.

Sabine Baring-Gould comments:

> The watch set by the priests was the same Temple guard who was employed in the taking of Christ in Gethsemane. This guard was allowed to the Jews to protect the Temple from profanation, but they might not employ it outside the Temple precincts,

without permission from the Roman governor; this is why the priests approach Pilate with their request, and why he answers, "You have a watch." He gave them the requisite permission.[239]

When Pilate sarcastically said, "You have a guard," he was speaking about the Temple guard, those charged with keeping order in the Temple precincts and keeping out those who were not allowed in. These were trained militia at the disposal of the High Priest and chief priests. They were not a volunteer army but rather a trained auxiliary fighting force selected by the clan.

When King David was organizing Israel, he placed individual members of particular clans to be musicians, others became officers in his military, and some were designated as gatekeepers, in essence, the Temple police force (1 Chr 24-26). These were the authorities that arrested Jesus in Gethsemane and shoved him along the way to the house of Annas. Pilate's position was clear: the Jewish religious leaders could use their own Temple police to guard the tomb. "You already have a guard of your own. You'll get none from me!"

The security of the soldiers

The verses in Matthew 27:62-66 are a goldmine of information. First, they tell us when the Jewish religious leaders went to Pilate with their request—"the next day," that is, "after the day of Preparation." Matthew was talking about Saturday morning. However, this was the weekly Sabbath. Should not they be at home with their families? Even more, it was the Passover Sabbath—the most solemn day of the year. How threatened must they feel that they leave their homes, meet together to decide upon a plan, and go to Pilate with their frightened request?

Second, we also learn from these verses that the religious leaders were aware of Jesus' teaching. "Sir, we remember how that impostor said . . ." This must have become public knowledge because every time Jesus spoke of going to Jerusalem, it was a private conversation with his disciples (Matt 16:21; 17:22-23; 20:17-19; Mark 8:31-32; 9:30-31; 10:32-34; Luke 9:21-22; 18:31-33). Still, somehow, the religious leaders knew what Jesus said.

Third, as noted, the religious leaders demanded the Roman governor provide a Roman guard at the tomb until the third day passed. "Therefore order the tomb to be made secure until the third day." "Order" (Greek: κέλευσον English: *keleuson*) is a rather strong demand from these religious leaders. They are ordering the Roman government to do something they do not want to do themselves. Maybe these leaders are still basking in the enabling glow of their "You are no friend of Caesar" accusation.

> "It is striking that now the watch kept on the Temple should be weakened, in order that part of it might be sent as a guard to him Who rests in the grave."
> —Sabine Baring-Gould

Fourth, the Jewish leaders clearly understood the concept of the third day, asking the Roman guard to be placed at the tomb so it would "be made secure until the third day." It has taken them one whole day of the three to get their wits about them enough to know the tomb needed to be guarded. Furthermore, they think they already know who would cause them trouble at the gravesite—"lest his disciples go and steal him away and tell the people." Their concern was that a stolen body would enable the disciples to disseminate a "gospel lie"—that he has risen from the dead, as he said he would.

Finally, the Jews believed Jesus was an imposter, and the missing body from the grave would make "the last fraud will be worse than the first." Jesus claiming to be the Messiah, the Savior of the world, and the Son of God was bad enough. If the disciples stole his body from Joseph's tomb, his pretended resurrection would be worse than that of his pretended messiahship.

The security of the stone

Both Matthew 27:66 and Mark 15:46 mention that Joseph, with the help of others, rolled a stone over the face of his tomb with Jesus' body inside. Neither Luke nor John mentions the stone in their crucifixion chapters, but they do refer to it in their resurrection chapters (Luke 24:1–3; John 20:1).

Thus, all four Gospels note that to keep Jesus in the tomb and his disciples out, a vast stone was placed at the entranceway. The stone was not placed there by the Jewish police force. It was rolled in place by Joseph of Arimathea and those friends and servants with him.

It was the Jewish burial custom to place "a great stone," (Hebrew: גלל; English: *galal*) to close the entrance to a tomb. In *Sanhedrin* 47b, which discusses the laws regarding burial and the retrieval of bones from a grave, Rabbi Ashi asks, "When do the mourning rites commence? From the closing of the grave with the gravestone?"

First-century sepulcher stones often rolled slightly downhill in a trough or channel cut from the rock parallel to the tomb itself. When the giant circular stone was pushed back from the doorway, they would place a smaller stone, called *Dopheq*, as a wedge to keep the larger stone in place. When they left the tomb, they would remove the wedge, and gravity would return the rolling stone to its place.[240]

The security of the seal

In addition to the soldiers and the stone, the third type of security used to make certain Jesus' body was not stolen was a seal around the stone. Before we examine the kind of seal the Temple police would have used, it will be beneficial to think about what a seal meant. What was the purpose of a seal in the Old and New Testament days?

Ancient Hebrew Seal.

Briefly, a seal was used for the following reasons.

#1. A seal indicated a completed transaction.

A seal was never applied until the work was done. The Prophet Jeremiah bought a piece of property from his cousin in Anathoth. Jeremiah 32:9-11 describes the legal procedure used. "[Then I] weighed out the money to him, seventeen shekels of silver. I signed the deed, sealed it, got witnesses, and weighed the money on scales. Then I took the sealed deed of purchase, containing the terms and conditions and the open copy." The final step in the legal purchase of a piece of property was the seal applied to the deed indicating a completed transaction.

#2. A seal certified authenticity.

When the property deed purchased by Jeremiah was sealed and handed to the purchaser, that seal bore witness to the fact that Jeremiah now owned the property in Anathoth. The same is true today. When I purchased my house more than 25 years ago, the deed was stamped with "The Great Seal of the State of Nebraska." My name was on the deed, but it was certified as authenticated by the state with its official seal.

#3. A seal guarantees security.

When the Temple police sealed the stone that had been rolled in front of the entrance to Joseph's tomb, they could come back on the third day, and if the seal was unbroken, it meant the tomb was secure. Every package we receive today is sealed with tape or by another process. When the package arrives, if the seal is broken it is an indication that the package is not secure, and perhaps it was tampered with.

That's the purpose of the seal around the stone of Joseph's tomb. The Jewish religious leaders and Temple police came to Joseph's tomb, placed a cord of clay or wax around the stone, and put the High Priest's imprint on it to make the seal official. No one dared break the High Priest's seal.

> "If a door had to be sealed, it was first fastened with some ligament, over which was placed some well-compacted clay [or wax], and then impressed with the seal, so that any violation of it would be discovered at once."
> —John McClintock

The priests affixed wax to the *galal* that closed the opening into the grave, drew a string through it, and sealed the stone just as people did for centuries. Darius (Dan 6:17) sealed the stone door that closed the lions' den; and we learn from history that, in like manner, Alexander the Great sealed the grave of Cyrus.[241]

The security at Joseph's tomb designed to make sure no one entered the tomb until the third day was as impressive as it could be. The Temple soldiers were there to make sure none of Jesus' disciples tampered with the tomb. None did. The stone was there to keep people from entering the tomb. None did. And the seal of wax or clay with the impression of the High Priest was the ultimate precaution to keep Jesus in the tomb. Did anyone enter? None did.

Nevertheless, Mark records this on the third day:

> When the Sabbath was past, Mary Magdalene, Mary the mother of James, and Salome bought spices so that they might go and anoint him. And very early on the first day of the week, when the sun had risen, they went to the tomb. And they were saying to one another, "Who will roll away the stone for us from the entrance of the tomb?" And looking up, they saw that the stone had been rolled back—it was very large (Mark 16:1–4).

The security of Jesus' tomb was firmly in place. They had the security of the soldiers. The security of the stone. And the security of the seal. So what kind of security did they have?

Inadequate!

Upon seeing the tomb was empty, and speaking with an angel who was sitting on the rolling stone, the women hurried off to tell Peter, John, and the others. What happened to the Temple police? Matthew 28:4 says "the guards trembled and became like dead men." You can be sure when the trembling stopped, they ran directly to the High Priest's palace to report the bad news to Caiaphas. Jesus had left the building.

The burial of Jesus of Nazareth was both complete and incomplete. It was complete in that his body was placed in a rock-cut tomb and closed off with a stone. It was incomplete in that Joseph and Nicodemus were unable to finish preparing his body thoroughly because of the time crunch of the approaching Sabbath. And, of course, it was incomplete because burying Jesus was not enough to keep him in the grave, and for that, we should all be grateful.

> Death cannot keep his Prey,
> Jesus, my Savior;
> He tore the bars away,
> Jesus, my Lord!—Robert Lowry

Chapter 9

The Location of Jesus' Tomb

Go to the Church of the Holy Sepulchre for information; go to the Garden Tomb for inspiration. Go to the Church of the Holy Sepulchre for facts; go to the Garden Tomb for feeling. Go to the Church of the Holy Sepulchre for the evidence; go to the Garden Tomb for the experience.

ONE OF THE MOST controversial issues related to Jesus' crucifixion is the location of his tomb. Where was the most famous person in history buried after the most famous crucifixion in history? With so much speculation surrounding the authentic tomb of Jesus, are there any ways we can identify its location for certain? This chapter begins with a few essentials for Jesus' tomb and then explores the locations that claim to be the actual tomb of Jesus of Nazareth.

TOMB ESSENTIALS

There are some things that the historical record requires of any location claiming to be Jesus' tomb. Everything else must be judged by our most reliable historical record, the Gospel narratives. If these five tomb essentials are not met, the contender for Jesus' tomb, regardless of its veneration, history, or speculation, cannot be the tomb of Joseph of Arimathea in which Jesus of Nazareth was buried.

Essential #1: The tomb must be near Jerusalem

The Gospels' references are numerous indicating Jesus' death and burial are associated with the Holy City. Any tomb not somewhere in the vicinity of Jerusalem is automatically disqualified. Some of those biblical references are presented here.

- At his transfiguration, Moses and Elijah spoke of Jesus' death, which would occur in Jerusalem (Luke 9:31).
- As Passion Week approached, Jesus "set his face to go to Jerusalem" (Luke 9:51, 53; 13:22).
- Jesus declared that "it cannot be that a prophet should perish away from Jerusalem" (Luke 13:33).
- Jesus revealed to his disciples he must go to Jerusalem and be crucified, buried, and raised from the dead (Matt 16:21; 20:17–18; Mark 10:32–33; Luke 18:31–33).
- Jesus triumphantly entered Jerusalem at the beginning of Passion Week (Matt 21:1, 10; Mark 11:1, 11; Luke 19:28; John 12:12
- Herod Antipas was in Jerusalem when Pilate sent Jesus to him for trial (Luke 23:7).
- On the Via Dolorosa, as Jesus carried his cross to Golgotha, he addressed some women in the crowd as "Daughters of Jerusalem" (Luke 23:28–31).
- After betraying Jesus, Judas hanged himself in what became known as Akeldama, the "Field of Blood," which everyone in Jerusalem knew (Acts 1:19).
- On the road to Emmaus, Cleopas questioned whether Jesus was a stranger in Jerusalem because he was unaware of the day's events (Luke 24:13, 18).
- Cleopas and his friend returned to Jerusalem after meeting Jesus (Luke 24:33).

The historical accounts of the Gospels require that Jesus be crucified and buried near the Holy City of Jerusalem.

Essential #2: *The tomb must be outside the city walls*

In almost every society of antiquity, burials took place outside the city, beyond the city walls. The City of the Dead, the Necropolis of Cairo, is a series of vast cemeteries and graves on the edges of historic Cairo, Egypt. They are located outside the old city walls, north and south of the Cairo Citadel. The *Kerameikos* of ancient Athens is another city of the dead, as is the Mayan cemetery at Campeche, Mexico.

In ancient Rome, the *Campus Martius*, although an essential part of Rome, was beyond the *pomerium* or city limits during the Republic and part of the Empire. It was the place for those buried at public expense. Private burial spots were along the roads leading into Rome, especially the Via Appia.

In Jewish thought, because God dwells with his people inside the camp, all practices that would defile his holiness were to be conducted outside the camp or city (Num 15:35–36).

Executions were always conducted outside the city. This is why Stephen was stoned outside of Jerusalem (Acts 7:58), as well as Ananias and Sapphira (Acts 5:5–6, 10).

The Gospels suggest Jesus was crucified outside of the city as well. John 19:17 notes, "He went out, bearing his own cross, to the place called The Place of a Skull, which in Aramaic is called Golgotha." Matthew 27:31 and Mark 15:20 both say the same. If Golgotha was outside the walls of Jerusalem, so was the tomb in which Jesus was buried.

Essential #3: *The tomb must be in a garden near Golgotha*

John 19:41–42 declares, "Now in the place where he was crucified there was a garden, and in the garden a new tomb in which no one had yet been laid. So, because of the Jewish day of Preparation, since the tomb was close at hand, they laid Jesus there." This represents the best clue given in Scripture to pin down the location of the Joseph of Arimathea's tomb. John is not saying crucifixions took place in a garden, but that not far from where they took place, there was a garden (Greek: κῆπος; English: *kēpos*). This same word was used to identify the place called Gethsemane (John 18:1, 26).

Judah's King Amon was buried in a tomb in a garden (2 Kgs 21:26). A garden implies greenery. It implies peace. It implies quiet. From the chaos of Calvary, Jesus' body was taken to the tranquility of a garden. As a wealthy man, Joseph of Arimathea could afford a choice spot for his family tomb, a spot in a garden, just as the Gospels describe.

Essential #4: The tomb must be a rock-cut tomb

Matthew 27:59–60 says, "And Joseph took the body and wrapped it in a clean linen shroud and laid it in his own new tomb, which he had cut in the rock." Mark 15:46 indicates the same. Tombs cut out of solid rock were not uncommon in the Middle East. There was plenty of rock from which to cut them.

Sometimes caves were used or even enlarged to accommodate family tombs (Gen 25:8–9; see 23:7–9; 49:29–30; 2 Chr 16:13–14). Read the Prophet Isaiah's divine oracle against Jerusalem (Isa 22:16). Within a chamber cut into a rock, there was a significant difference in temperature from the hot sun outside. A tomb provided a "cool spot" for family visiting deceased relatives buried in a rock-cut tomb. The coolness of the tomb also helped keep the body from decaying as rapidly.

Essential #5: The tomb must be a new tomb

Luke 23:52–53 notes, "This man went to Pilate and asked for the body of Jesus. Then he took it down and wrapped it in a linen shroud and laid him in a tomb cut in stone, where no one had ever yet been laid." Matthew 27:60 also confirms Jesus was buried in a new tomb.

The fact that Joseph's tomb was "a new tomb" and one "where no one had ever yet been laid" likely means two things. First, it was a family tomb because the description of who would be placed in the tomb was not solely about Joseph. And second, the tomb was not yet complete when Jesus was laid in it. Other burial sites were still being cut into the rock. From the primary choices for this tomb, in either case, one or more arcosolium was complete, but it appears more were yet to be carved out of the rock.

Jesus' life was wrapped in virtue. It was bookended in purity. Think about it. His life began in a virgin womb and ended in a virgin tomb.

LESSER CONTENDERS

All this being said, there are five main contenders for the location of the tomb owned by Joseph of Arimathea. Three of these are lesser contenders and can be dismissed quickly.

The Roza Bal Shrine, India

The Roza Bal (aka Rouza Bal or Rozabal) is a shrine located in Srinagar, India. Srinagar lies in the Kashmir Valley on a tributary of the Indus River. Locals believe two Muslim holy men are buried there. The shrine is housed in a small unlikely-looking building. It was relatively unknown until Mirza Ghulam Ahmad espoused the theory that Jesus was buried there. Ahmad claimed both to be the promised Mahdi (Guided One) and the Messiah expected by Muslims to appear in the end times to give Islam a final triumph.

Nothing historical, biblical, or consequential can be said of the genuineness of this location as the tomb of Jesus of Nazareth. Therefore, it can be rejected with no consequence.

> "For everything genuine in God's world there
> will be a counterfeit in man's world."
> —Woodrow Michael Kroll

The tomb of Jesus in Shingo, Japan

Shingō is a small village in northern Japan, with a population of about 2,500. The village would pass without notice were it not purported to be the location of the tomb of Jesus (*Kirisuto no haka*), as well as where Jesus' last descendants reportedly still live. The family of Sajiro Sawaguchi claims that Jesus did not die on the cross at Golgotha as both the Gospels and history claim. Instead, Jesus' Japanese brother, Isukiri, took his place on the cross while Jesus fled across Siberia to northern Japan. Once he arrived in Japan, the legend goes, he changed his name to Torai Tora Daitenku and became a rice farmer. He married a twenty-one-year-old Japanese girl named Miyuko and raised three daughters in Shingō.

As farfetched as the claims about Jesus and Mary Magdalene are in *The Da Vinci Code*, they are tame compared to this one. Think of how unlikely it is that Jesus had a brother named Isukiri. or that he crossed Siberia on his way to Japan, just to become a simple rice farmer. Jesus as the husband of Miyuko and father of three daughters is not only not historically sustainable, but the idea is fairytale-like and fictitious. This site, too, must be dismissed out of hand as the location of Jesus' tomb.

The Talpiot Tomb, Jerusalem, Israel

Coming closer to Jerusalem, as the result of a construction project, the Talpiot tomb was unearthed on March 28, 1980. The Israel Antiquities Authority (IAA) promptly recorded the tomb as IAA-80, and its ten ossuaries were cataloged with the numbers 500–509. The tomb is carved from solid limestone bedrock. Inside the tomb were located six *kokhim* and two *arcosolia*. Also found were ten ossuaries, of which 6 were inscribed. The 6 inscriptions bear the names of 7 individuals, using 8 names:

- Jesus ("Jesus, son of Joseph")
- Joseph
- Mary (there are two)
- Judah
- Yose (or Joses to a Greek speaker)
- Matthew

These are important names in the Gospel story. The question is, do they refer to the figures in the Gospel narrative? To that question, there is yet no definitive answer.

While biblical and archaeological scholarship is divided on whether or not this is Jesus' tomb, with the vast majority of scholars rejecting it, the discovery does shed light on popular New Testament names of the first century. Each of the names represented on the ossuaries was a common name in the late Second Temple Period. They could refer to anyone at that time.

While the Talpiot tomb is interesting and meets some of the requirements to be the tomb of Jesus, it does not meet all of them. If either Gordon's Calvary adjacent to the Garden Tomb or the Church of the Holy Sepulchre is the location of Jesus' crucifixion, then the tomb at Talpiot cannot be the site of Jesus' burial. While it is in the vicinity of Jerusalem, it is not close enough to either location to be the nearby tomb of Joseph of Arimathea. Reference John 19:41–42 again. "Now in the place where he was crucified there was a garden, and in the garden a new tomb in which no one had yet been laid." At 2.6 miles from the Church of the Holy Sepulchre or 3.6 miles from the Garden Tomb, the Talpiot tomb appears not to be Jesus' tomb.

> "If Jesus already had a family tomb in Talpiot, there would be no need to bury him in a temporary tomb, despite the onset of the Sabbath. It's little more than a half-hour's walk from Golgotha to Talpiot."
> —Hershel Shanks

That leaves our investigation with the two top contenders for the location of Jesus' burial—The Garden Tomb and the Church of the Holy Sepulchre.

THE GARDEN TOMB

All four Gospels help to identify the location and appearance of the tomb in which Jesus was buried. As noted above, the tomb was near Golgotha, a new tomb cut out of sheer rock, and located in a garden. In Jesus' day, a garden did not mean a place where you grow carrots, lettuce, okra, and squash. It usually indicated a working vineyard, orchard, or olive grove.

A description of the Garden Tomb

In 1874, a brief report on the tomb was prepared by the German architect and archaeologist Conrad Schick. This was the earliest detailed investigation of the tomb itself. In the late twentieth century, Gabriel Barkay, professor of Biblical Archaeology at the Hebrew University of Jerusalem, made the fullest archaeological study of the area to date.

When you enter the Garden Tomb, you immediately find yourself in the first of two separate chambers. This is the vestibule or "weeping chamber" of the tomb with a bench against the back wall. This chamber is roughly rectangular, approximately 10 feet long, almost 7 feet wide, and about 6 feet high.

To the right (south) of the entry chamber was the burial chamber. Today most of the wall separating these two chambers is missing. Now an iron gate separates the two chambers. The inner chamber is nearly 8 feet long by 11 feet wide, with a 7-foot ceiling.

Along each wall of the inner room, except for the entry wall, are burial places carved out of the rock. They resemble sarcophagi in that they are carved as a box, but with the front wall missing. The trough-shaped burial spot opposite the inner chamber entranceway entrance is only 4 ¾ feet long, whereas the other two are 7 ½ feet long each.[242]

Perhaps more interesting are the distinct Christian symbols painted on the east and south inner chamber walls. They are crosses painted in dark red. Above the horizontal crossbar of the Greek crosses are the letters IS and CS in Greek. These letters are *iota sigma* and *chi sigma*. Iota is the initial letter of the Greek word for Jesus (Ἰησοῦς) and *sigma* is the last Greek letter in Jesus' name. The *chi* stands for the Greek Christos (Χριστός), and the *sigma* is the last letter of Christos. Beneath the horizontal crossbar of the crosses are the letters A and Ω. *Alpha* and *Omega*, the first and last letters of the Greek alphabet, were used to designate the Alpha and Omega of Revelation 21:6.

The history of the Garden Tomb

The Garden Tomb was first discovered in 1867 by a Greek peasant. He was attempting to cultivate the land at the site and to make the land fertile he needed to cut a cistern into the rock. While doing so, he accidentally came upon a cave. Soon after its discovery, a Jerusalem correspondent for several European academic societies named Conrad Schick visited the cave. According to Schick's 1874 account, the cave was half-filled with dirt and human bones. After Schick's initial visit, the owner cleared the cave to use it.

Perhaps the key figure in the history of the Garden Tomb, and the adjacent hill thought to be Golgotha, is General Charles "Chinese" Gordon. General Gordon, who had served with distinction in the Crimean War and later successfully suppressed the Taiping Rebellion in China, arrived in Jerusalem in 1883. He was in Palestine less than a year when, in January 1884, he was dispatched to Khartoum, where he was killed in battle.

Horatio Spafford was a prominent nineteenth-century American lawyer and devout Christian. Spafford is best known for writing the words to the hymn, *It is Well With My Soul*, following a family tragedy in which his four daughters died aboard the S.S. *Ville du Havre* on a transatlantic voyage. After four of his daughters perished, Spafford, his wife, Anna, eleven other adults, and three children settled in Jerusalem and established the American Colony on Nablus Road, just north of the Old City of Jerusalem.

The colony engaged in philanthropic work among the people of Jerusalem regardless of their religious preferences, gaining the trust of the local Muslim, Jewish, and Christian communities.[243] The American Colony remains at the same location today as an exquisite boutique hotel.

General Charles Gordon was also a Christian and when he arrived in Jerusalem he stayed with the Spaffords at the American Colony. Just a thousand meters (1,093 yards) south on Nablus Road was a hill with a rock escarpment. Because of its physical characteristics, it caught Gordon's eye and he immediately identified it as Golgotha. The Garden Tomb was cut into the vertical escarpment on the western slope of that hill, just 250 meters (820 feet) north of Damascus Gate.

It would be incorrect to say that General Gordon "discovered" Gordon's Calvary and the Garden Tomb. It appears that honor goes to Otto Thenius, a German scholar, who suggested this site was Golgotha in 1842. In 1894, the area of the cave and the surrounding garden were purchased by the British Garden Tomb Association for £2,000 sterling ($2,545.80 today). This association still owns, operates, and maintains the site. The lovely garden has well-maintained paths and benches for visitors to sit and meditate.

EVIDENCE FOR THE AUTHENTICITY OF THE GARDEN TOMB

With this background, what evidence can be presented in favor of the authenticity of the Garden Tomb as the genuine tomb of Jesus? It is to this our attention is now turned.

Evidence #1. Location, location, location

There is no question about the location of Jerusalem's wall and the Garden Tomb. It is outside the walls of Jerusalem. Sultan Suleiman I of the Ottoman Empire built the existing wall between 1537 and 1541 AD. This wall does not provide evidence that the Garden Tomb is outside the wall of Jerusalem for it was not built until 1500 years after Christ's death. It has no bearing on the location of the tomb.

What does bear on the location of the tomb is the first wall of Jerusalem. This was the wall around Jerusalem in the days of Jesus. Originally built by King Hezekiah of Judah in the late eighth century BC, it was rebuilt by the Hasmoneans in the second century BC. Until the first century BC, the northern limit of Jerusalem's residential district was the east-west line of this first wall. The location of the Garden Tomb is beyond this wall, making it a candidate for the burial location of Jesus.

Josephus refers to three fortified walls around Jerusalem in his day, the first century AD. A brief description of each follows.

Josephus calls the first wall (ca. 130 BC) the "old one" and indicates it began on the north of the tower Hippicus and extended to the Temple, as well as westward to the Gate of the Essenes. The first wall stretched to the Temple on the east, passing above the Pool of Siloam. The second wall (ca 50–51 BC) began at the Gennath Gate of the first wall and ended at the Antonia Fortress, encircling the northern quarter of the city. The third wall (41–44 AD) began at the Hippicus Tower, stretching around the northern sector of the city, before bending south to join the "old wall" at the Kidron Valley (*Wars* 5.4.2).[244]

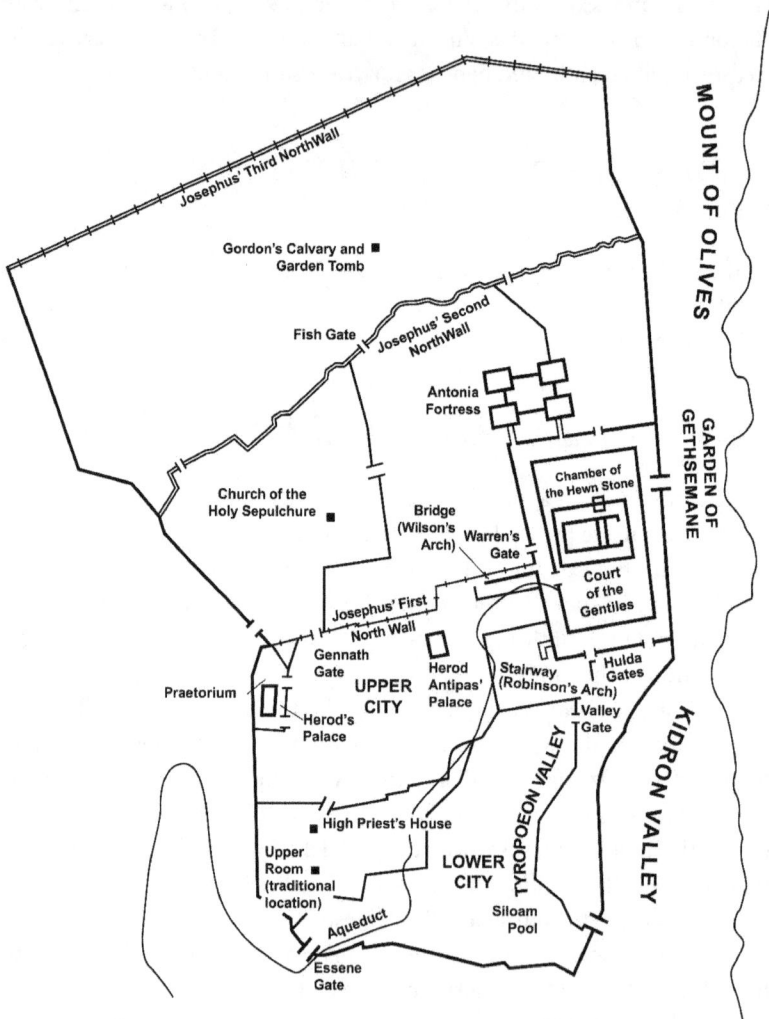

Map 1 *Jerusalem's Three Walls*

The question that has divided many scholars is not whether the Garden Tomb is outside the first and second walls, but whether the Church of the Holy Sepulchre is.

Evidence #2. The date of the Garden Tomb

Over the years, various shifts in the dating and interpretation of the tomb have come with the light of new archaeological evidence. This has been true with the dating of the Garden Tomb. In my lifetime, the prevailing opinion has shifted from the Byzantine era, which followed the collapse of the Roman Empire, to the seventh or eighth century BC, with a brief stop in the first century AD along the way.

As a member of the nineteenth-century Corps of Royal Engineers, Claude Reignier Conder surveyed Palestine between 1872 and 1873. Conder was an early proponent of the authenticity of the Garden Tomb area. Among the twenty-seven or so publications of his survey work, his best known is *Tentwork in Palestine*, first published in 1879. In it, he wrote:

> We have yet another indication—namely, that Calvary should be near the cemetery in which was the tomb of Joseph of Arimathea, in the garden beyond the city. Now the great cemetery of Jewish times lies north of Jerusalem, on either side of the main north road; here we have the sepulchre of Simon the Just, preserved by Jewish tradition; here is the magnificent monument of Helena, Queen of Adiabene, fitted with a rolling-stone, such as closed the mouth of the Holy Sepulchre. The first of these tombs dates from three centuries before Christ; the second was cut in the first century of his era. Thus the northern cemetery was probably that which was in use in his time.[245]

Conder argued that the Church of the Holy Sepulchre cannot have been the tomb of Jesus of Nazareth because it features *kokh* tombs. Originally used by the Jews, with this type of tomb, the whole body was slid head or feet first into a niche in the wall of the burial chamber. Conder pointed out that a *kokh* tomb would afford no place for two angels to sit, "one at the head and one at the feet" (John 20:12). He remarked, "It must have been one of the later kinds of tombs, in which the body lay in a rock sarcophagus under a rock arch parallel with the side of the chamber. This is the kind of tomb which throughout Palestine we find closed by a rolling-stone; it is the kind in use in the late Jewish times, and the kind, moreover, which is found north of Jerusalem."[246]

Conder concluded:

> These considerations would lead us to fix Calvary, the place of execution, north of Jerusalem, near the main road to Shechem, and near the northern cemetery. Now, close to this road, on the

east, is a rounded knoll, with a precipice on the south side, containing a cave known to Christians as Jeremiah's Grotto.[247]

He is describing the area of the Garden Tomb, which he dates to the "late Jewish times," i.e., the first century AD.

Several older archaeologists who examined the Garden Tomb believed it to be a Jewish tomb of the Herodian Period, the first century BC to the first century AD. These included Dame Kathleen Kenyon, Sir Charles Marston, Sir Flinders Petrie, and others (see the London *Daily Telegraph Magazine* of March 27, 1970). They pointed out that the type of chiseling on the face of the cliff both outside and inside the tomb resembles that found in the "Sanhedrin Tombs." These are tombs in the Kidron and Hinnom valleys, the so-called "Tomb of the Kings," and the "family tomb of Herod," all of which are Jewish tombs dating to the Herodian Period.

Evidence #3. The schema of the burial chamber

If you look closely at the inner chamber of the Garden Tomb, there is a visible location for a body. Its area gives the impression that the south end was extended from the original space allocated. It has been suggested that this represents a hurried elongation of the burial site.

The essential arrangement of the two chambers in the Garden Tomb may provide a clue to its date. This tomb consists of two adjoining rooms, one beside the other. The entrance from the outside to this two-chamber burial cave is through the northern weeping chamber. To the right of the first room is the second, where the bodies of the deceased would have been placed. This is not the typical configuration of a two-chamber burial tomb. Ordinarily, the inner chamber would be cut further into the rock, behind the weeping chamber. This would provide added safety against grave robbers.

Typical of a Second Temple Period burial cave are burial niches (*kokhim*) cut vertically into the cave wall. First-century burial caves typically featured *arcosolia*, arches hewn into the wall of the cave forming a shelf for stone coffins and ossuaries. The Garden Tomb has none of the features typical of a Second Temple burial cave.

Also, Second Temple tombs give evidence of a so-called "comb chisel." The comb chisel had a toothed edge that left small parallel lines, called combing, on the rock surfaces. The Garden Tomb displays no sign of comb chiseling. This makes a Second Temple Period dating for the tomb unlikely.

The Interior of the Garden Tomb

A burial cave with this plan was found very near the Garden Tomb. It is on the premises of the Convent of the White Sisters on Nablus Road. The tomb features right-angled cornices where the walls join the ceiling and raised burial benches similar to other Iron Age tombs. Burial caves from the First Temple Period with this same plan have been discovered in places other than Jerusalem.[248]

As more discoveries are made, the evidence mounts that the schematic plan of the Garden Tomb appears to be more in line with the seventh or eighth century BC than it is with the first century AD. To date, no Second Temple-era tombs have been found anywhere in the vicinity of the Garden Tomb.[249]

Evidence #4. The great cistern

Near the Garden Tomb is an underground cistern, a reservoir for storing rainwater. Cisterns were quite common in the ancient Near East. There are two of them beneath the grounds of the Garden Tomb. The smaller one lies beneath the rock floor very close to the tomb, left of the entrance. In 1921 this was filled in because it was no longer needed.

198 *The Trials, Crucifixion, and Burial of Jesus of Nazareth*

The Great Cistern

The larger one, which is further back but still not far from the tomb, measures 10.16 meters (33'4") wide, 17.27 meters (56'8")' long, and 10.97 meters (36') tall.

I am quite familiar with cisterns. I grew up on a farm and helped my father build a cistern for our house. I thought it was huge; it held 11,221 gallons of water. However, the great cistern under the Garden Tomb grounds holds 200,000 gallons (some say 250,000 gallons). That is almost eighteen times larger than our tiny cistern on the farm. This is one of the largest cisterns in Israel and the third largest in Jerusalem.

Evidence #5. The winepress

As you enter the Garden Tomb compound, directly ahead of you and slightly below ground level is a nicely restored winepress. It is lined with stone and shaped somewhat like a giant keyhole or a baby grand piano. This press was excavated in 1924, and it, too, is one of the largest in Israel. It's believed to be of pre-Christian origin and often is pointed out as evidence that a rich man owned the garden and there was an extensive vineyard at this location.

The Garden Tomb winepress

While archaeologists have uncovered numerous winepresses around Israel, most of them, like those at Mt. Gerizim, Apollonia (Arsuf), and Hippos (Sussita) are Byzantine presses. There are some Roman presses at Shiloh (Early Roman), Achziv (Late Roman), Usha (Roman), and Manot (Roman), all of which show both the essentials of a press and the variety of shapes depicting those essentials.

Typically, winepresses were a complex consisting of the treading floor, a channel that lets the grape juice flow through a filter down to the collecting pool. There were also steps to access the juice, jars to transport it, and a storage area to keep it. The Garden Tomb winepress shows only the collection area; the rest presumably is under the ground of the tomb area.

Evidence #6. The great stone

"And Joseph took the body and wrapped it in a clean linen shroud and laid it in his own new tomb, which he had cut in the rock. And he rolled a great stone to the entrance of the tomb and went away" (Matt 27:59–60; see Mark 16:3–4; Luke 24:2–3). All three Synoptic Gospels mention a great stone was rolled in front of the door to the tomb, closing Jesus in. All three comment that when the women arrived at the tomb early Sunday morning the stone was already rolled back from the door. Matthew 28:2 notes, "There was a great earthquake, for an angel of the Lord descended from heaven and came and rolled back the stone and sat on it."

Although this was the second earthquake within forty-eight hours (it could have been an aftershock), Matthew is careful to tell us that it was an angel who rolled back the great stone, not Jesus, not his disciples, not even the earthquake, and certainly not the faithful women.

Rolling stone at "Herod's Family Tomb"   *Example of a rolling stone sepulcher*

That the stone was super large is borne out by the words used to describe it. It was a "great stone" (Greek: μέγαν λίθον; English: *megan líthon*—Matt 27:60) and "it was very large" (Greek: σφόδρα μέγας; English: *sphódra mégas*—Mark 16:4). We use the word in much the same way today. Many people shop at a mega mart. To make their voices larger so they can be heard, cheerleaders use a megaphone. We speak of megabytes, megahertz, mega-hits, mega millions and so much more. Everybody understands the meaning of the word.

As is evident from Table 1, the word *megas* has multiple applications and is used to describe many types of people and things. Nevertheless, its meaning is always "superior" or "more than usual." Concerning other people or things, whatever is described as *mégas* is much larger, greater, or superior.

Table 1: *The Use of the Greek mégas in the New Testament*

Scripture	Usage
Matt 5:35	"Jerusalem, the city of the *megalou* king."
Matt 8:24, 26	"There arose a *megas* storm … there was a *megalē* calm."
Matt 22:38	"This is the *megalē* and first commandment."
Mark 4:37, 39, 41	"A *megalē* windstorm arose … and there was a *megalē* calm."
Mark 5:11–13	"A *megalē* herd of swine ran down the steep bank into the sea."
Mark 14:15	"He will show you a *mega* upper room."
Luke 1:32	"He will be *megas* and will be called the Son of the Most High."
Luke 22:12	"He will show you a *mega* upper room."
John 11:43	"He cried out with a *megalē* voice, 'Lazarus, come out.'"
Acts 8:1	"There arose a *megas* persecution against the church in Jerusalem."
Acts 10:11; 11:5	"A *megalēn* sheet descending, let down by its four corners."
1 Cor 16:9	"A *megalē* door for effective work has opened to me."
Titus 2:13	"The appearing … of our *megalou* God and Savior Jesus Christ."
Heb 4:14; 10:21	"We have a *megan* high priest … Jesus, the Son of God"
Heb 13:20	"Our Lord Jesus, the *megan* shepherd of the sheep."
Revelation	The book of Revelation uses *megas* more than eighty times.

The word *megas* is frequently used in the Gospel narratives of Jesus' crucifixion.

- Jesus cried out with a loud (*megalē*) voice, saying, "*Eli, Eli, lema sabachthani*" (Matt 27:46; Mark 15:34)
- "Jesus cried out again with a loud (*megalē*) voice and yielded up his spirit" (Matt 27:50).
- "And Jesus uttered a loud (*megalēn*) cry and breathed his last" (Mark 15:37).
- "Then Jesus, calling out with a loud (*megalē*) voice, said, 'Father, into your hands I commit my spirit!'" (Luke 23:46).
- "And behold, there was a great (*megas*) earthquake, for an angel of the Lord descended from heaven and came and rolled back the stone and sat on it." (Matt 28:2).

- "So they departed quickly from the tomb with fear and great (*megalēs*) joy, and ran to tell his disciples" (Matt 28:8; see also Luke 2:10 and Acts 15:3).

Without argument, the stone rolled in front of Joseph's tomb was *megas*. It was larger than customary stones of the time.

Evidence #7 The stone channel

Every person who has ever visited the Garden Tomb has taken notice of a stone channel running parallel to the face of the tomb. You had to step over it to enter the small doorway to the tomb.

This channel runs the full length, 8.5 meters (27 feet 7 inches), of the tomb's face. It measures 15 inches wide and has often been thought of as a track, which would have enabled the rolling stone to hug the face of the tomb. This explanation is plausible and the great stone of Abu Badd fits this track perfectly (see below).

The earliest photographs of the Garden Tomb show a stop-stone in the correct position to hold the *mégas* stone directly in front of the door of the tomb. So the pitch of the channel itself is no detriment to the authenticity of the Garden Tomb.

Evidence #8. Traditional execution site

Death by stoning was not accomplished just by people throwing rocks at you. Stoning was achieved by throwing the person from a high building or a cliff. If the guilty person survived the fall, the executioners would then drop a huge rock onto his chest from the building or cliff. If the person still survived, as unlikely as that would be, the guilty person would be pelted with rocks by his accusers until death was certain.

Significant support for the authenticity of the Garden Tomb comes from the claim that this site has long been known as an execution site. When in 1874–1875, the British surveyor Major Claude Conder was examining the site, he was told of a Jewish tradition that the site is where for centuries the Jews stoned those who broke their law.[250] Another of those Jewish traditions is that it was here the prophet Jeremiah died.

However, several ancient authors, including Jerome, Epiphanius, Tertullian, Elmacin, and Abulpharagius, were quoted by later historians as indicating that Jeremiah was stoned by his countrymen in the Egyptian city of Tahpanhes. If this established tradition is correct, and I suspect it is, Jeremiah could not have been stoned at the Garden Tomb.

There is also an old tradition that this place was the site of the martyrdom of Stephen, the deacon of the Jerusalem church mentioned in Acts 7:54–60.[251] This tradition is more likely to be correct than the one about Jeremiah. The Crusaders originally called the main northern gate of Jerusalem "St. Stephen's Gate" (Latin: *Porta Sancti Stephani*). This was because of the proximity of the site to the location of Stephen's stoning. Acts 7:58 says, "They cast him out of the city and stoned him."

A Christian pilgrim named Luciana, writing in 415 AD, also notes that the northern gate of Jerusalem was called the "Gate of St. Stephen." From the end of the Crusader Period, after the disappearance of the Byzantine Church, the name "Saint Stephen's Gate" shifted to a still accessible gate, just north of the Eastern Gate. Today this gate is also referred to as the "Lions Gate."[252]

Just a few hundred feet to the north and adjacent to the Garden Tomb, a part of the same rock escarpment, is the Church of Saint-Étienne (St. Stephen's Church). It was built in 460 AD by Empress Eudocia, the highly cultured wife of the Eastern Roman Emperor Theodosius II.[253] The discovery of this fifth-century St. Stephen's Church in 1882 provided further evidence in support of the early tradition placing Stephen's execution near here.

When excavations were done in the late nineteenth century, the area around the ruins of Saint-Étienne revealed numerous Christian burial vaults and in-ground gravesites. Two tombstones were found in one of the underground burial vaults so close to the Garden Tomb that it almost touches it.

One displayed the inscription: "To Nonnus Onesimus deacon (or "Nonnus and Onesimus Deacons"–the inscription was somewhat marred) of the church of the [witness] of the resurrection." This strongly suggests that Jesus' resurrection was nearby, else why would you build the church there?

The second inscription is even more direct. It reads "buried near his Lord." This may be one of the most persuasive arguments for the authenticity of the Garden Tomb as the tomb of Jesus.

PROBLEMS WITH THE EVIDENCE FOR THE GARDEN TOMB

While the Garden Tomb has much to commend it, much of the same evidence for the Garden Tomb is also evidence against it. We must probe some of the problems associated with identifying the Garden Tomb as Jesus' tomb.

In March 1986, *Biblical Archaeology Review* published what was then a controversial article by Gabriel Barkay, a Hungarian-born Israeli archaeologist who has taught at various universities in Israel. In 1974-1975, Amos Kloner, the District Archaeologist of Jerusalem, and Barkay conducted an archaeological investigation of two large complexes of burial chambers in the courtyard of the Monastery of St. Étienne, just north of and adjacent to the Garden Tomb. Their excavations shed much light on the Garden Tomb because of its proximity.

The date of the Garden Tomb

Because the Garden Tomb is at the same location as these burial chambers, Barkay wrote, "I have concluded that the cave of the Garden Tomb was originally hewn in the Iron Age II, sometime in the eighth or seventh century BC. It was reused for burial purposes in the Byzantine Period (fifth to seventh centuries AD), so it could not have been the tomb of Jesus."[254]

Professor Barkay advanced three fundamental propositions to support his stark conclusion:

1. The Garden Tomb could not have been a "new tomb" (Matt 27:60; Luke 23:53) in Jesus' day if it was originally an Iron Age II triple-bench sepulcher;

2. Four to six hundred years after Jesus' death, the tomb's benches were carved into fixed sarcophagi for the burial of Byzantine Christians. This would never have occurred if the site were venerated as the tomb of Jesus; and

3. The features in the garden outside the Garden Tomb, which have been misinterpreted, do not lend themselves to corroborating the site as the first-century tomb of a rich man like Joseph of Arimathea.

While these reflect Barkay's determination that the Garden Tomb could not have been a Second Temple tomb, other considerations about the date of the tomb should be noted.

#1. There is no long history of identifying the site as Jesus' tomb. While the earliest recorded tradition about the Holy Sepulchre being the place of Jesus' burial is only three centuries after the crucifixion, there is no such history for the Garden Tomb. The identification of the Garden Tomb as the tomb of Jesus did not become a consideration until the nineteenth century. Thus, its identification is relatively new, with no tradition behind it.

#2. The Garden Tomb is in the middle of tombs dated to the Iron Age. North of the Damascus Gate, there are numerous burial caves, most of which were excavated when archaeology was in its infancy—about 100 years ago. The Garden Tomb is situated between the St. Étienne tombs to the north and two Iron Age tombs to the south.[255] The link between the St. Etienne tombs and the other Iron Age tombs suggests both a geographical and chronological relationship.

#3. There appears to be a link between the Garden Tomb and the St. Etienne tombs. Amos Kloner and Gabriel Barkay's 1974–1975 archaeological survey of the burial chambers in the courtyard of the Monastery of St. Étienne led them to date the St. Etienne tombs to the Iron Age B Period (1000–539 BC). The Garden Tomb appears to be part of the same cemetery as the St. Étienne tomb complexes and is hewn out of the very same cliff. This would appear to date the Garden Tomb to the Iron Age Period as well.

#4. Not a single Second Temple tomb has been found in the area of the Garden Tomb. Jesus of Nazareth lived in the late Second Temple Period. The Second Temple was destroyed by the Romans in 70 AD when General Titus sacked the city. It appears that by this time, the people of Jerusalem relocated their cemeteries further north. The southernmost burial cave of the Second Temple Period is the so-called "Tombs of the Kings," about 600 meters (1,970 feet) north of the Garden Tomb. Since a large number of tombs from the Second Temple Period have been discovered in other areas of Jerusalem, if the Garden Tomb was from Jesus' era, it would be entirely out of place.

The schema of the burial chamber

It has been suggested the apparent elongation of the burial site within the Garden Tomb was to accommodate the height of Jesus. One person even wrote, "[Jesus] must have been taller than Joseph of Arimathea who had the tomb constructed for himself and was presumably 5' 8" tall. The cutting of the stone was hastily completed to accomplish the task of burial before the Sabbath hours, Friday at sunset" (https://arkdiscovery.com/aoc-1.htm).

Unfortunately, as evidence for the Garden Tomb, these calculations of Joseph and Jesus' height are unsupported in any biblical, literary, historical, or archaeological records. They are the speculations of an adventurer and amateur archaeologist, not a biblical scholar or professional archaeologist. Even the Garden Tomb Association would not endorse these conjectures.[256]

This anomaly in the length of the burial location cannot, therefore, reasonably contribute to the evidence for the Garden Tomb as the location of Jesus' burial. There was barely enough time to get Jesus' body to the tomb and leave before sundown, let alone enough time to chisel away at lengthening the rock-cut tomb.

The winepress

Identifying the "winepress" of the Garden Tomb as part of a vineyard has a linguistic problem. John 19:41 says, "Now in the place where he was crucified there was a garden, and in the garden a new tomb in which no one had yet been laid."

The word for "garden" (Greek: κῆπος; English: *kēpos*) is used only five times in the New Testament: once in the parable of the mustard seed (Luke 13:19); twice about the Garden of Gethsemane (John 18:1, 26); and twice referring to the garden where Joseph's tomb was located (John 19:41). Also, when Mary Magdalene first saw the risen Christ, she mistook him for the gardener (John 20:15), which comes from the same root word, *kēpos*. However, the word *kēpos* bears no relationship to a vineyard. It relates to an orchard or garden of trees, like olive trees.

A word for "vineyard" (Greek: ἀμπελώνα; English: *ampelōna*) does exist. Jesus used it frequently in his parables, such as the parable of the laborers in the vineyard (Matt 20:1–8), the parable of the two sons (Matt 21:28), and the parable of the wicked tenants (Matt 21:33–41; Mark 12:1–9; Luke 20:9–16). Had John wanted to identify a winepress in the garden of Joseph's tomb he more likely would have used the word for "vineyard" (*ampelōn*), not the word for "garden" (*kēpos*). The fact that no winepress or vineyard is mentioned concerning the burial of Jesus moots any evidence the winepress might provide for authenticating the Garden Tomb.

Additionally, the term John 20:15 uses for the caretaker of this garden is "gardener" (Greek: κηπουρός; English: *kēpouros*). When Jesus was obviously talking about a vineyard; he used the word vinedresser (Greek: γεωργός; English: *geōrgos*) ("husbandman" in KJV). There just does not seem to be sufficient linguistic evidence to support the Garden Tomb area as having a vineyard in Jesus' day.

The great stone

The stone rolled in front of Joseph's tomb was larger than normal. However, there is no *mégas* stone at the Garden Tomb today. It has been missing for hundreds of years. In the last few years, there has been some buzz about the stone being found in Jordan. The Abu Badd stone is a large stone used as a fortified door for a sixteenth-century Byzantine monastery in the old village of Faisaliyah, Jordan. Some believe this stone is the one rolled in front of Jesus's tomb in Jerusalem. They point to these considerations:

- The stone is the perfect thickness for the 15-inch-channel in front of the Garden Tomb;
- The diameter of the stone is large enough (9 feet, 8 Inches) to cover both the doorway and the "spirit" window of the Garden Tomb, essentially covering much of the tomb face;
- The stone is carved from the same color, same texture, and same kind of rock as the Garden Tomb;
- The chisel marks on the stone are like those found on the face of the Garden Tomb.

The Abu Badd Stone

This sounds like positive evidence in favor of the Garden Tomb. However, presently there is no way to prove beyond doubt that this stone was the rolling stone that sealed the Garden Tomb. The arguments for its genuineness are reasonable but circumstantial. Many questions have yet to be answered, like why was the stone removed from Joseph's garden, and why would it be taken down into the Jordan Valley, across the river, and up to the mountains of Moab. Surely if someone wanted to preserve this stone, they could have done so in the area of Jerusalem where its transport would have been much easier.

Some who believe this to be the rolling stone of Joseph's tomb suggest a theological reason for removing it to Mount Nebo. They assert that the top of Mount Nebo is where Moses lifted up the serpent in the wilderness, which relates to Jesus' words, "as Moses lifted up the serpent in the wilderness, so must the Son of Man be lifted up" (John 3:14).

There are at least two problems with a theological identification of Mount Nebo and the Garden Tomb. First, this connection may be appropriate for Golgotha, but not for the tomb. Jesus was "lifted up" at Golgotha, but Joseph, "laid it [Jesus' body] in his own new tomb" (Matt 27:59–60). At the crucifixion site, the Savior was "lifted up," and at the tomb, he was "laid" down. The comparison is therefore flawed.

It is also important to remember Moses did not lift the serpent on Mount Nebo but in the wilderness. Numbers 21 indicates the Israelites were at Mount Hor more than 200 kilometers (125 miles) south of Mount Nebo when Moses raised the bronze serpent into the air.

Another consideration concerning the rolling stone is its shape. Each of the Synoptics (Matt 27:60; 28:2; Mark 15:46; 16:3–4; Luke 24:2) reference the stone as being "rolled" (Greek: προσκυλίσας; English: *proskylisas*) to and from the door to Joseph's tomb.

Such rolling stones for tomb entrances are known from other Jewish tombs of the time of Jesus. Examples would be the so-called Herod's Family Tomb near the King David Hotel; the so-called "Tomb of the Kings" across from St. George's Cathedral; the Nicophoria tomb, east of Herod's family tomb; the church at Bethphage on the Mount of Olives approaching Bethany; the Hinnom Valley tomb; the Kidron Valley tomb; and the tomb on the road from Mount Carmel to Megiddo near the Jezreel Valley. Except for the last, each of these tombs featured rolling stones and is near Jerusalem.[257]

In an article in *Biblical Archaeology Review,* Israeli archaeologist Amos Kloner suggested that Jesus' tomb was not sealed with a disk-like "rolling stone" of the type generally imagined. Kloner claims that "98 percent of the Jewish tombs from this period ... were closed with square blocking stones."[258] He asserted that the Synoptic accounts of Jesus' burial and resurrection are likely referring to a square stone about a meter wide.

Kloner concluded, "Matthew, Mark, and Luke all describe the stone being 'rolled' (in John it is 'taken away'), and thus it is only natural to assume that the stone was round. But we must remember that 'rolled' is a translation of the Greek word *kulio*, which can also mean 'dislodge,' 'move back' or simply 'move.'"[259]

However, Kloner's interpretation of *kulio* to mean "dislodge" is misleading. While "dislodge" is a possible translation of the Greek, it is not the preferred translation or even the usual translation. The word *kulio* [which is part of the word προσκυλίσας above] comes from the root word (Greek: κῦμα; English: *kŷma*) meaning "to bend" or "curve" like a wave of the sea. "And behold, there arose a great storm on the sea, so that the boat was being swamped by the waves (Greek: κυμάτων; English: *kymatōn*) but he was asleep" (Matt 8:24). This certainly implies roundness. Another word of the same derivation (Greek: κύκλῳ; English: *kýkloi*) in the dative case means a "ring" or "cycle." Therefore, I believe assuming this stone was not a block but was indeed a "rolling stone" is the more accurate assumption.

The stone channel

While the stone-cut channel running parallel to the face of the Garden Tomb gives the appearance of a track for a rolling stone, some archaeologists and historians have offered other considerations that would give us pause before accepting this as a rolling-stone track.

For one, if the Garden Tomb channel were the track for a *mégas* stone disk, you would expect the low point of the channel, that is, the resting point of the stone in the channel, to be directly in front of the cave opening. However, the channel continuously slopes westerly downward to the end.

In his oft-quoted article in *Biblical Archaeology Review*, Gabriel Barkay maintained that the groove outside the tomb has a diagonal edge. This means the inside face of the channel's outer edge was not cut straight up and down like the façade of the tomb, but was cut at a 45-degree angle leaning away from the tomb's face. As a result, the channel is a full 37 centimeters wide (15 inches) at the bottom, but 50 centimeters wide (19 inches) at the top.

This configuration reduces the contact with the rolling stone and thus reduces the stability of the great stone in the track. It also diminishes the possibility that this is a channel for the rolling stone.

The other rolling-stone tombs, such as the Tomb of the Kings and the tomb at Midras in the Shephelah (*Shfēlah*), place the stone between a higher wall and the façade of the tomb. This wall, often a meter or more high, is built straight up parallel to the façade of the tomb. In reality, because the outside support for the rolling stone is a wall itself with the stone rolling between two walls—the façade of the tomb and the outer support wall, Barkay claims, "There is no archaeological precedent for a low-cut track for a stone-disk door, particularly a track with a slanted outer edge as we see at the Garden Tomb."[260]

If a higher wall would give more stability to the stone, and this smaller outside edge of the track would be insufficient to hold such a *mégas* stone, what was the purpose of the track? Again, Barkay contends it was not for drainage (there is no outlet for water), nor was it the channel of a rolling stone. He says it was used as a trough for watering animals. Barkay suggests Crusader workmen cut it as a water trough for an eleventh-century donkey stable, which was built directly in front of the Garden Tomb.

Since a watering trough would not need a higher outside wall, and since the outside edge of this channel was well below the opening of the door (so water would not flow through the open door and into the tomb cave), Barkay is convinced that during Crusader times the cave was probably used as a storage room for fodder.

If this were the case, do the dimensions and configuration of the trough fit the needs of a watering trough? In fact, they do. The trough was raised above the bedrock floor in front of the tomb so the donkeys could comfortably drink from the water.

The channel's outer edge being tapered at a 45-degree angle away from the cave's façade would provide a more comfortable angle for the head and throat of the donkeys as they drank from the trough. It is entirely possible, however, that the current channel of the eleventh century was cut down from its original wall to be repurposed as a watering trough. In Jesus' day, the trough wall may have been much higher.

However, if this was a Crusader-era watering trough for animals, is there any evidence of a stable at the site? There is an arched feature on the face of the cave that is six meters (19 feet 7 inches) wide and some 5.5 meters (19 feet) high. It appears to be the beginning of a vaulted roof that extended outward from the tomb façade and covered the bedrock floor in front of the tomb.

One of the pieces of evidence for the Garden Tomb is the long-held tradition that this was the normal, established site for Roman crucifixions and Jewish stonings. If this is where Stephen was stoned and was the recognized place of execution, this would also be the place where Jesus was crucified. Nevertheless, how likely is it that the Jews stoned their offenders in the same place the Romans crucified theirs? Quite unlikely, I'd say.

Given the general revulsion of the Jews toward crucifixion and their equal distaste for the Romans, it does not seem reasonable that Jews would be pushing other Jews off the cliffs where the Romans were crucifying people below.

Wheaton College Professor of New Testament Emeritus, the late John McRay, said the two tomb inscriptions were used improperly as supporting evidence for this as the site of Jesus' tomb. On its own, the 1889 inscription simply marked the site of "Deacon Nonnus Onesimus of the Holy Resurrection of Christ and of This Monastery."[261] Late professor at the École *Biblique* Jerome Murphy-O'Connor examined this inscription and its confusing application as proof of the authenticity of the Garden Tomb site.

A full accounting of why this inscription cannot be used to authenticate the Garden Tomb is found in his *BAR* article of 1986.[262]

Thus, while there is evidence for the Garden Tomb being the authentic location of Jesus' crucifixion and resurrection, that evidence is inconclusive. Some of what has been presented as evidence in the past has since been disqualified. That means we must consider the alternative site that has claimed authenticity.

Whether or not the Garden Tomb is the actual tomb of Joseph of Arimathea, thousands of pilgrims each year come here to remember, reflect, and reverence this possible site of Jesus' crucifixion. That in itself, for them, makes this place holy ground.

THE CHURCH OF THE HOLY SEPULCHRE

For many Christians, the most venerated site in Jerusalem is the Church of the Holy Sepluchre. Just as a visit to the Garden Tomb is essential, so too is this site, the preferred location for Roman Catholics and Eastern Orthodox pilgrims to Jerusalem. Our investigation now must turn to the Church of the Holy Sepulchre as the possible location of Jesus' tomb.[263]

Before we launch into that investigation, however, we must deal with the elephant in the room. If the Church of the Holy Sepulchre has been venerated as the location of Jesus' tomb since the third century AD, why did so many people latch onto the Garden Tomb as the location of Jesus' tomb in the nineteenth century? Asked differently, why do some pilgrims to Jerusalem avoid the Church of the Holy Sepulchre? The reason is that visitors to the church today are in for a shock. At first sight, the church may be a disappointment. Frankly, for many, it is aesthetically repulsive. If you enjoy incense, icons, and the scurrying of priests from place to place, you will be pleased with the Church of the Holy Sepulchre. If you are looking for a quiet garden, an empty tomb, and a skull-like location, you must look elsewhere.

The Church of the Holy Sepulchre is noisy, busy, and the scene of recurrent fights between priests of the Latin (Roman Catholic), Greek Orthodox, Armenian Orthodox, Syriac Orthodox, Ethiopian Orthodox, and Egyptian Copts. All of them have laid claim to their corner of the church. Six denominations, six church traditions–you can imagine the chaos. There is an understanding among the religious communities called the Status Quo. It is designed to maintain order within the church. The Status Quo began with a decree (known as a *firman*) from Ottoman Sultan Osman III in 1757 AD. This decree preserved the division of ownership and responsibilities of various Christian holy places, including the Church of the Holy Sepulchre.

For those who belong to a brand of Christianity that is not given to ritual, formalism, and hierarchy, the Church of the Holy Sepulchre is often not on their list of places to visit in Jerusalem. While I fully understand their feelings, this is a mistake. This church may be the authentic location of Jesus' crucifixion and resurrection. However, unless you are a devout Catholic or Orthodox Christian, you are likely going to come away from your visit with an empty feeling. The place is so unlike what your spirit longs for.

> "There is very little as entertaining as watching monks hitching up their cassocks and laying into each other."
> —R. Cohen

This church is the poster child for divisions within the Christian faith. It is a territorial battlefield. Nevertheless, somehow, it comes out as the winner in the contest for the authentic sites of Jesus' Passover Weekend.

The location of the tomb vis-à-vis Golgotha

As you enter the church, immediately ahead of you is the Stone of Anointing (also known as the Stone of Unction). Tradition says this is where Jesus' body was prepared for burial by Joseph of Arimathea. This tradition, however, does not go back to the first century but comes from 1288 AD, and Italian Dominican friar, travel writer, and Christian apologist named Riccoldo da Monte di Croce. The present stone is of Italian pink marble and was added in the 1810 reconstruction of the church, and therefore cannot be original.[264]

To the left is the rotunda, located under the dome on the far west side of the church. In the center of the rotunda is a box-like structure that is a small chapel called the Edicule or *Aedicula* in Latin. In ancient Roman religion, an *aedicule* was a small shrine with altars. The word *aedicula* is the diminutive of the Latin *aedes*, meaning a temple building. The Edicule in this church encloses the Holy Sepulchre, believed to be the burial place of Jesus. There are approximately 23 meters (75 feet) between the Rock of Golgotha and the tomb of Jesus.

The Edicule consists of two rooms. As you enter, the first room is called the Chapel of the Angel. Here is a stone that tradition claims to be a fragment of the large stone that sealed the tomb (Matt 28:2).

The second chamber, deeper into the Edicule, is the assumed location of the tomb of Jesus. You cannot see the tomb because, in the fourteenth century, a marble slab was placed over the tomb to prevent damage from pilgrims eager to take home a piece of the authentic tomb of the Savior.²⁶⁵

The Stone of Anointing, Church of the Holy Sepulchre

Restoration of the Edicule

Visitors to the Church of the Holy Sepulchre before 2016 remember the ghastly-looking supports and iron beams on the outside of the Edicule. They were paced there to keep it from crumbling to the ground. Finally, the Israel Antiquities Authority declared the structure unsafe because it was ready to collapse. Something had to be done.

From May 2016 to March 2017, the Edicule underwent restoration and repairs. It was a $3 million project, much of which was funded by the World Monuments Fund.²⁶⁶ The delicate restoration was carried out by a team of about fifty experts from the National Technical University of Athens, which had previously worked on the Acropolis in Athens and the Hagia Sophia in Istanbul. These Greek experts worked mainly at night, so visiting pilgrims could have access to the church during the hours when it was open.

Unsightly supports that held up the Edicule for decades

Perhaps the most exciting moment was one night in October when the marble slab covering the rock-cut tomb was raised. It was the first time in more than two centuries anyone had seen beneath that slab of marble. The workers, archaeologists, and priest watchdogs were afforded the first opportunity to examine the original rock shelf on which Jesus's body is thought to have rested.

Using radar, laser scanners, and drones, the Greek team was able to stabilize the shrine with titanium bolts and mortar. They also cleared away thick layers of candle soot and pigeon droppings.

Is the tomb of Jesus located within the church?

After Constantine the Great converted to Christianity and signed the Edict of Milan which legalized the Christian religion, he sent his mother, Queen Helena, to Jerusalem to look for Jesus' tomb. With the help of Eusebius, Bishop of Caesarea, and Macarius, Bishop of Jerusalem, legend has it that Helena and the work team she took with her discovered three crosses at the site now occupied by the Church of the Holy Sepulchre. This led the queen to believe she had found Golgotha, the place where Jesus died.

Inside the Edicule

As a result, in 326 AD, Constantine ordered the Temple of Jupiter/Venus that Hadrian had built on that site to be removed. A colossal church was built in its place. Work began immediately. The soil and debris were removed from the cave, revealing a rock-cut tomb that Helena and Macarius identified as the burial site of Jesus.[267]

The Church of the Holy Sepulchre was built as separate buildings over the two holy sites: the great Basilica (the *Martyrium* which was visited by Egeria in the 380s AD), the Triportico (an enclosed colonnaded atrium with the traditional site of Golgotha in one corner), and across a courtyard the *Anastasis* (a rotunda housing the tomb).[268] Archaeologist Dan Bahat points out that "the *Triportico* and *Rotunda* roughly overlapped with the Temple building itself."[269] The new church was consecrated on September 13, 335 AD.

Since the presumed site of Golgotha and the tomb of Jesus are nearby, both are now housed under the roof of the Church of the Holy Sepulchre. If there is proof for the authenticity of one, it is reasonable to assume there is proof for the authenticity of the other.

Archaeologist John Wilkinson comments:

> The Garden Tomb and Gordon's Calvary have been shown to people as the place of Jesus' death and burial for more than a century, but the location where the Church of the Holy Sepulchre stands has been shown to people since before AD 135 and has been regarded as the place of Jesus' burial since its recovery by Emperor Constantine in about AD 325.[270]

This means there is a long tradition in favor of the Church of the Holy Sepulchre which does not exist for the Garden Tomb.

EVIDENCE FOR THE AUTHENTICITY OF THE CHURCH OF THE HOLY SEPULCHRE

So, what is the evidence for the authenticity of the tomb in the Church of the Holy Sepulchre? Presented are the following arguments.

Evidence #1. The presence of a quarry

The Muristan (from the Persian word meaning "hospital") is a complex of shops, churches, and other buildings within the Christian Quarter of the Old City of Jerusalem. Adjacent to the Church of the Holy Sepulchre, it was the location of the first hospital of the Knights Hospitaller. The bedrock under the Muristan, the Church of the Holy Sepulchre, and the Lutheran Church of the Redeemer exhibited traces of a quarry that had been used until the first century BC. This is precisely what British archaeologist Dame Kathleen Kenyon discovered in the 1970s.

Present-day archaeologists have confirmed that the 198.12 x 144.78 meters (650 x 475 feet) area known as Golgotha was a quarry for building materials.[271] When the quarrying ended, the next higher (later) stratum of soil washed into the area, making it suitable as gardens or fields in the first century AD.

The fact that a first-century BC quarry was found at this location supports the argument that it was outside the city wall in Jesus' time. This also means the Second Wall was somewhere east of today's Church of the Redeemer, making it east of the Church of the Holy Sepulchre as well.

John 19:41 tells us, "Now in the place where he was crucified there was a garden, and in the garden a new tomb." The stratum above the quarry that shows traces of fields or gardens can be dated to the first century AD. This is possible positive evidence for the Church of the Holy Sepulchre's authenticity.

Around my rural and rustic hometown of Ashland, Nebraska there are many former quarries, the most famous being the Quarry Oaks Golf Course. If there were ever two words that do not belong together, they are "quarry" and "golf." Nevertheless, after the quarrying finished, dirt was brought in to landscape the area and created the premier golf course in Nebraska, named by Golf Digest as one of "America's 100 Greatest Golf Courses." Clearly, former quarries can become something much more useful.

> "The Church of the Holy Sepulchre is 1700 years of religion wrapped around a rock."
> —Max Lucado

When you visit the Holy Sepulchre church, to get to the height of Golgotha, you must ascend eighteen stone steps that are on your right. It's believed by many that this was a raised hill in the ancient quarry. This identification comes from three similar verses: "There were also women looking on from a distance" (Mark 15:40); "The women who had followed him from Galilee stood at a distance watching these things," (Luke 23:49); and Matthew 27:55, "There were also many women there, looking on from a distance."

It is assumed that, if the women could see Jesus dying on the cross from a distance, he must have been at a higher elevation. However, this is not necessarily so. The women could just as easily have been at a higher elevation, enabling them to see the cross. Alternatively, being a filled-in quarry, the area may have been quite level allowing the women to see from a distance.

Remember, nowhere in Scripture does it say that Golgotha was a hill or in an elevated location. Many adopted this view because of Cecil F. Alexander's old hymn: "There is a green hill far away, outside a city wall," but a nineteenth-century hymn is not positive evidence for a fourth-century church.

Evidence #2. Hadrian's Temple foundation

Born January 24, 76 AD near Naples, in 117 AD Publius Aelius Hadrianus became Caesar Traianus Hadrianus Augustus, or just Hadrian. In 135 AD, Emperor Hadrian conquered Jerusalem, razed much of it, and constructed in its place a Roman city, which he renamed Aelia Capitolina. *Aelia* came from Hadrian's *nomen gentile*,[272] while *Capitolina* meant the new city was dedicated to the chief Roman deity Jupiter, whose monument Jupiter Capitolinus was located on Capitoline Hill. Aelia Capitolina was built according to the plan of a typical Roman town. Hadrian also renamed the *Iudaea Province* as *Syria Palaestina* so he could eliminate the name Judea.[273]

While Hadrian viewed the Bar Kokhba Revolt as a failure for his PanHellenic ideal, there was an even more troubling threat to unifying the disparate peoples of the Roman Empire. This was the new start-up religion of the Christians. They saw Jesus Christ as the unifier of peoples where, in his church, "There is neither Jew nor Greek, there is neither slave nor free, there is no male and female, for you are all one in Christ Jesus" (Gal 3:28).

To thwart the rapid growth of this new religion, Hadrian was determined to squelch the message and squash any reminder of it. The veneration of the location thought to be where Jesus was crucified and where he rose from the dead, became a prime target for Hadrian's campaign of eradication. He removed anything "Christian" from these locations and attempted to wipe them from memory. When he razed this district, the area of Golgotha and the tomb were simply filled with dirt and debris. Terraces were built for the construction of Hadrian's Forum.

On top of this reconstructed site, Hadrian built a temple to Venus (also variously held to be to Jupiter, Juno, or Minerva) to prevent Christians from worshiping there (Eusebius, *Life of Constantine* 3.26). Archaeologists have uncovered remains from this temple. John Wilkinson describes the situation. "Eighty or ninety years after this official Roman temple was built practically no Christians were left who had known it [Golgotha and the tomb] as it was before. Two centuries later, or to be exact, in AD 325, no living eye had seen what was beneath the temple."[274] It seemed the site where first-century Christians imagined the place of Jesus' death and burial would presumably be gone forever by the second century AD.

Coins were found in the debris of the beaten-earth floor that came after the quarry was abandoned. They have been dated to the First Jewish Rebellion against Rome (66–70 AD). This would confirm both traces of Hadrian's rebuilding of Jerusalem as Aelia Capitolina and his suppression of the Second Jewish Revolt. It would also lend credence to the claim that within the Church of the Holy Sepulchre is a tomb from the time of Jesus of Nazareth.

Evidence #3. Beneath the Lutheran Church of the Redeemer

In an article entitled, "Site-Seeing: Archaeological Remains in Holy Sepulchre's Shadow," Boston University's Professor of Religion Jonathan Klawans implores his readers not to miss taking in the Lutheran Church of the Redeemer on their visits to Jerusalem. This is the church adjacent to the Church of the Holy Sepulchre with the tall bell tower. Climb the 177 steps, and from there, you get the best photos of Jerusalem from deep within the Old City itself.

The Redeemer Church is strategically located. On the north side runs the traditional route of the Via Dolorosa. To the west is Muristan Street, the thoroughfare to the Muristan, a kind of gathering place. To the south, Muristan Street connects to David Street, which runs west past Herod's Jerusalem palace and out the Jaffa Gate. Between the Muristan and the Church of the Redeemer is the Holy Sepulchre church itself.

Today this is a busy, thriving area with shops, restaurants, residences, and more, but not so in the first century AD. This was just outside the city. It was a part of the former rock quarry, now a garden. The only hustle and bustle here was on the day of Jesus' crucifixion.

These two churches are inexorably connected, not by time, but by location. They both sit over the site formerly occupied by Hadrian's forum and temple. When Jerusalem expanded in the seventh century BC, this area was inhabited for the first time. Excavations beneath the floor of the Lutheran Church revealed the area was covered with a beaten-earth floor in which seventh-century BC pottery, tested by Carbon-14, was found.

Today's Church of the Redeemer was built on the site of an old Crusader church. That earlier church was known as Santa Maria Latina. While some ruins are to be seen in the yard north of the church, the most interesting ruins lie beneath the church. Before the church was constructed, excavations were undertaken underneath it.[275] You may access these ruins by descending a staircase near the entrance to the bell tower. Here you will find remnants of walls built by Hadrian (117–38 AD), as well as later periods.[276]

That archaeological evidence of Hadrian's Temple wall was found beneath the Lutheran Church of the Redeemer is significant because of its proximity to the Church of the Holy Sepulchre. They are both located in the area filled with dirt and debris by Hadrian to erase any memory of Jesus and his tomb.

Evidence #4. Beneath the Alexander Nevsky Church

Alexander Yaroulavitz was a thirteenth-century Russian warrior-prince who expelled Swedish and German invaders from Russia in 1242 AD at the "Battle of the Ice." The name "Nevsky" comes from a river called Narva, where the Swedish army was defeated. The prince became a Russian saint under the name Alexander Nevsky.

There are cathedrals named after Alexander Nevsky all over the world. I have visited these cathedrals in Tallinn (Estonia), Sophia (Bulgaria), and Paris (France).[277] The entrance to the Alexander Nevsky Church in Jerusalem is about 70 meters (230 feet) from the entrance to the Church of the Holy Sepulchre. It is just across the street from the Lutheran Church of the Redeemer. As such, it is located in the same area as the original quarry of Jerusalem and the forum and temple built by Emperor Hadrian.

Excavations of the Alexander Nevsky Church were led by the Archimandrite Antonin Kapoustin, Chief of the Russian Ecclesiastical Mission in Jerusalem. Since the church is Russian Orthodox, as you would expect, there is an iconostasis replete with icons and crosses. Behind the iconostasis, there are stairs with a huge cross standing inside the arcade to mark the place where Jesus used to go in and out of the city in his day.

Remnants of a Hadrianic triple arch that opened onto the forum of *Aelia Capitolina* and part of the retaining wall of the Temple precinct are visible above ground in the basement of the Alexander Nevsky Church (*'Alexandrovsky Hospice'*) of the Russian Mission in Exile.

As you enter the excavated area in the basement of the church, you descend a set of stairs to an archway. The stonework on the left-hand column is part of an entrance to the main forum built by Emperor Hadrian in the second century. This arch is the remains of a large arch, one of four Hadrian built in Jerusalem. Another more famous would be the *Ecce Homo* Arch at the beginning of the traditional Via Dolorosa.

Passing through the underground arch of the Alexander Nevsky Church and to the left is a reconstruction of the broad stairway that led to the original Church of the Holy Sepulchre (which was much larger than the present basilica). New Testament scholar Jerome Murphy-O'Connor noted that this corresponds precisely to the eastern end of Constantine's fourth-century Holy Sepulchre church, as it is depicted in the sixth-century Madaba Map.

Straight ahead, under a glass covering, is the gate threshold once thought to have been where Jesus left the city on the way to Golgotha. Today archaeologists think the gate probably dates to the second century AD. Next to the threshold is a large piece of the rock of Calvary, purchased by the Russians when the church was built. Above it stands a crucifix.

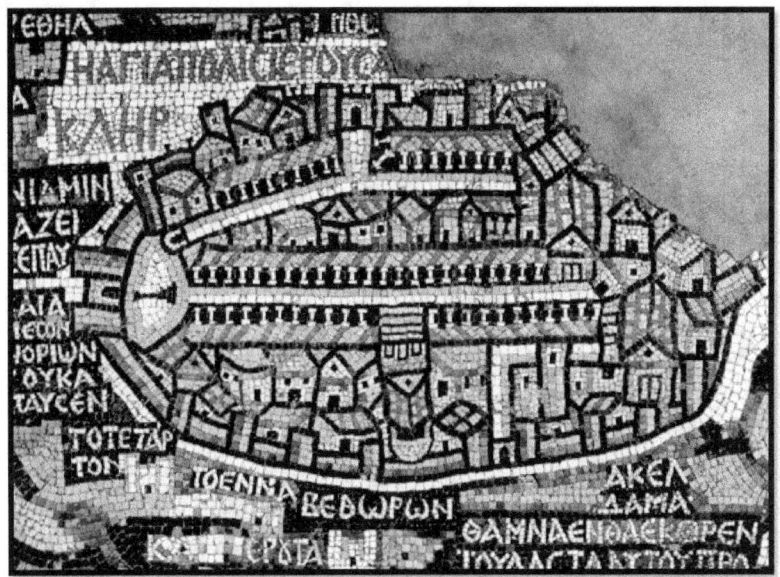

The Madaba Map

Those who believe the Church of the Holy Sepulchre is the authentic location of Golgotha and the tomb of Joseph of Arimathea find beneath the Alexander Nevsky Church evidence to support their belief.

Evidence #5. The Indiana Jones of the fourth century AD

Tradition is just that—tradition. Sometimes it is based on fact; sometimes it is not. But whatever the root of the tradition, the fact that a tradition lasts for centuries has to be taken into account.

Tradition claims that in the days of Constantine the Great, the cross on which Jesus died was "rediscovered" in Jerusalem by Constantine's mother, Queen Helena. Whether this occurred or not is not the point here. Because of this alleged discovery, Helena was named a saint by the Roman Catholic and Eastern churches. In recent decades, she has been hailed as the first biblical archaeologist. Perhaps she is better called the female Indiana Jones.[278]

It appears that Helena converted to Christianity after 312 AD when her son began to protect and favor the Christian Church. Eusebius reports that Constantine was instrumental in Helena's conversion and is responsible for leading her to become a devoted servant of God (Eusebius, *Life of Constantine* 3.47). Sometime after she became a Christian, Helena transformed part of the *Palatium Sessorianum,* her palace in Rome, into a church called the *Basilica Heleniana,* now known as *Santa Croce in Gerusalemme.*[279]

Emperor Constantine the Great

After Constantine defeated Maxentius at the Milvian Bridge, Helena came to live in Rome as a member of her son's court.[280] Helena's prominence at the imperial court is confirmed by the title *Nobilissma Femina* ("The Noble Lady"). Roman coins from that era bear witness to this.

Helena is best known for her journey to Palestine in 326–27 AD. Helena's adventures are lavishly expressed by the Church Father Eusebius in his *Life of Constantine* (3.41–47). Eusebius describes her religious enthusiasm and ascribes the construction of the Constantinian churches in Bethlehem and on the Mount of Olives to her. However, most importantly, he connects her with the construction of the Church of Holy Sepulchre in Jerusalem.

In his definitive work on Helena, Jan Willem Drijvers claims her greatest fame was acquired by an act for which she was credited but probably did not accomplish, *i.e.*, the discovery of the "True Cross."[281] The origin of the legend that Helena found the "True Cross" arose in Jerusalem during the second half of the fourth century. Three different versions of the legend exist and are known as the Helena legend, the Protonike legend, and the Judas Kyriakos legend.[282]

Drijvers, from the Department of History and Classics at the University of Groningen in the Netherlands, maintains that Helena's presence in Jerusalem, and Eusebius' detailed account of her visit, ultimately led to connecting Helena with the discovery of the cross.

Remains of the cross were reportedly already venerated in the Church of the Holy Sepulchre near the end of the 340s AD. This is verified in the sermons of Cyril (*Catecheses* 4.10, 10.19, 13.4 *PG* 33, 467ff, 685–87, 777). The Roman Emperor Julian believed the discovery of the relic to be authentic, but he rebuked Christians for worshipping the cross (*Contra Galileos* 194c).

Does Helena's visit to Jerusalem and her alleged discovery of the "True Cross" prove the Church of the Holy Sepulchre is the authentic location of Golgotha and Joseph of Arimathea's tomb? No, they do not. Nevertheless, the staying power of the legend and the many historical references to Helen's pilgrimage to Jerusalem connecting her to the site of the tomb, lend secondary credence to the church.

Evidence #6. The confirmation by Eusebius

Perhaps the most prolific literary source confirming much of the story of the discovery of the Church of the Holy Sepulchre built by Constantine comes from Eusebius. "Eusebius seems to have been present at its discovery when a boy; he speaks as an eye-witness."[283] Consider the following corroborations from Eusebius' *Church History*.

- *That the Holy Sepulchre had been covered with debris and idols.* "For it had been in time past the endeavor of impious men (or rather let me say of the whole race of evil spirits through their means), to consign to the darkness of oblivion that divine monument of immortality to which the radiant angel had descended from heaven, and rolled away the stone for those who still had stony hearts, and who supposed that the living One still lay among the dead" (book 3, chapter 26).

- *How Constantine commanded the debris from the idol temple and the soil itself, to be removed at a considerable distance from the sacred area.*

"Nor did the emperor's zeal stop here, but he gave further orders that the materials of what was thus destroyed, both stone and timber, should be removed and thrown as far from the spot as possible; and this command also was speedily executed. The emperor, however, was not satisfied with having proceeded thus far: once more, fired with holy ardor, he directed that the ground itself should be dug up to a considerable depth, and the soil which had been polluted by the foul impurities of demon worship transported to a far distant place" (book 3, chapter 27).

- *The discovery of the tomb of Jesus.* "But as soon as the original surface of the ground, beneath the covering of earth, appeared, immediately, and contrary to all expectation, the venerable and hollowed monument of our Saviour's resurrection was discovered. Then indeed did this most holy cave present a faithful similitude of his return to life, in that, after lying buried in darkness, it again emerged to light, and afforded to all who came to witness the sight, a clear and visible proof of the wonders of which that spot had once been the scene, a testimony to the resurrection of the Saviour clearer than any voice could give" (book 3, chapter 28).

> "On the seventh day God rested in the darkness of the tomb;
> Having finished on the sixth day all his work of joy and doom."
> —N. T. Wright

- *Constantine commented about the preservation of the holy sites.* "Such is our Saviour's grace, that no power of language seems adequate to describe the wondrous circumstance to which I am about to refer. For, that the monument of his most holy Passion, so long ago buried beneath the ground, should have remained unknown for so long a series of years until its reappearance to his servants now set free through the removal of him who was the common enemy of all, is a fact which truly surpasses all admiration" (book 3, chapter 30).

- *Constantine commissioned an unsurpassed church to be built on the site.* "It will be well, therefore, for your sagacity to make such arrangements and provision of all things needful for the work, that not only the church itself as a whole may surpass all others whatsoever in beauty, but that the details of the building may be of such a kind that the fairest structures in any city of the empire may be excelled by this. That whatever quantity or sort of materials we shall esteem from your letter to be needful may be procured from every quarter, as required... for it is fitting that the most marvelous place in the world should be worthily decorated" (book 3, chapter 31).

- *Constantine built a "New Jerusalem" from the site of Golgotha.* "This was the emperor's letter, and his directions were at once carried into effect. Accordingly, on the very spot which witnessed the Saviour's sufferings, a new Jerusalem was constructed... It was opposite this city that the emperor now began to rear a monument to the Saviour's victory over death, with rich and lavish magnificence" book 3. chapter 33).

- *The splendor of Constantine's church.* "This temple, then, the emperor erected as a conspicuous monument of the Saviour's resurrection and embellished it throughout on an imperial scale of magnificence. He further enriched it with numberless offerings of inexpressible beauty and various materials—gold, silver, and precious stones, the skillful and elaborate arrangement of which, in regard to their magnitude, number, and variety, we have not leisure at present to describe particularly" (book 3. chapter 40).

- *Helena's piety toward God.* "While, however, her character derived luster from such deeds as I have described, she was far from neglecting personal piety toward God. She might be seen continually frequenting his church, while at the same time she adorned the houses of prayer with splendid offerings, not overlooking the churches of the smallest cities. In short, this admirable woman was to be seen, in simple and modest attire, mingling with the crowd of worshipers, and testifying her devotion to God by a uniform course of pious conduct" (book 3. chapter 45).

Eusebius of Caesarea was a first-rate historian of Christianity. He was also an exegete, Bible scholar, and Christian polemicist. He is regarded as the most extremely learned Christian of his time.[284] Eusebius came to see himself as a spiritual advisor to Constantine. This relationship led to the famous posthumous biography, Eusebius's *Life of Constantine.*

However, did Eusebius' close friendship and evident admiration for Constantine blind his eyes when it came to writing about Helena and her escapades in Jerusalem? Certainly his panegyric eulogy of Constantine I paints the emperor in the most favorable light. But does that nullify the facts? It does not. The truth is Helena did make a journey to Palestine and did determine the location she believed was the site of Golgotha and the tomb. That location is where the Church of the Holy Sepulchre stands.

Eusebius, the historian, attests to that regardless of his personal feelings for the emperor.

Evidence #7. Additional literary corroboration

While Eusebius was the most famous and most prolific historian describing the Church of the Holy Sepulchre in antiquity, he was not alone. Others describe the church or the discovery of the "True Cross" as well. Among them are these.

Egeria—fourth century. About half a century after Helena made her famous trip to Palestine, another female pilgrim headed for the Holy Land. Egeria may have hailed from Galicia in Spain or the southern region of France. She visited most of the known sites of interest to fourth-century AD Christian pilgrims. What we know of her travel itinerary comes from those pieces of her travelogue that have survived, as well as the accounts of other travelers such as the Pilgrim of Bordeaux and some later writers who quote Egeria's words.

Egeria described her travels in one of two letters she addressed to her *sorores*, which is Latin for "sisters." Some believe her references to *sorores* indicate Egeria belonged to a religious society and may have been a nun. Egeria does demonstrate a high level of understanding of the details of the Christian liturgy.

Having arrived in Jerusalem just before Easter, Egeria gave a day-by-day description of the Holy Week festivities at the Church of the Holy Sepulchre. Significantly, Egeria—like our other early sources—never mentions Helena in connection with the church.

Egeria's most significant contribution to our understanding comes from her descriptions of church services she attended in the Church of the Holy Sepulchre, conversing with monks, and her observations of the "Jerusalem liturgy," which greatly influenced the expression of the Christian liturgy today (*Travels of Egeria* 37.1–7).

Unfortunately, the text of Egeria's travels was lost for almost 700 years. In 1884, the Italian scholar Gian Francesco Garmurrini discovered the *Codex Aretinus* in the monastic library of Santa Maria in Arezzo, Italy. Known today as *Itinerarium Egeriae* or *The Travels of Egeria*,[285] only about a third of her text remains, which means we lack some fundamental information about Egeria herself. What we do have is a remarkably detailed account of her three-year stay in Jerusalem and her trips to Egypt, Syria, Turkey, and beyond.

Abbot Daniel—twelfth century.

The travels of a Russian abbot named Daniel are usually dated to 1125 AD during the reign of Baldwin II. Abbot Daniel describes the ruins of the place where Helena found the Holy Cross. "It was a very large church with a wooden roof; now, however, there is nothing but a small chapel. Towards the east is the large doorway to which Mary the Egyptian came, desiring to enter the church . . . She passed out of this door on the way to the desert of Jordan. Near this door is the place where St. Helena recognized the True Cross."

Daniel then describes the Holy Sepulchre. He tells us that at the beginning of the twelfth century, the Church of the Holy Sepulchre was protected by a wall enclosing it. This wall was encased with marble.

> The Holy Sepulchre . . . the Emperor [Constantine I] caused to be decorated with the greatest care, and with magnificent columns. Outside was a vast court, open to the sky, paved with polished stone, and with long porticoes on three of its sides. Towards the east, opposite the tomb, was joined a basilica, an admirable work of immense proportions.[286]

The abbot expressed that in the interior of the chapel, on the northern side, there was a bench upon which Jesus' body was laid. This bench was cut into the rock of the cave and covered with marble slabs. The stone that was rolled away was three feet in front of the entrance to the sepulchral chamber. Abbot Daniel then describes the "holy rock." "Approached by a little door through which a man can scarcely get by going on bended knees. The sacred rock was visible through a covering of marble slabs by three small round openings on one side."[287]

Daniel's description of the church is significant because he saw the church before the Crusaders renovated it into its present form. He mentioned, "The Navel of the Earth" in a small oratory just outside the wall of the eastern apse, as well as "Golgotha" or "Calvary" in a small building outside the church.[288] He also alluded to the "place of the descent from the cross" and the locations of "the parting of the vestments," "the crowning with thorns," "the mocking," "the striking of Jesus," and "the prison," all under a single roof not far to the north of Golgotha.

Finally, the abbot described the site where Saint Helena discovered the Holy Cross called "the Invention of the Cross," located east of the place of the crucifixion. At the time of Abbot Daniel's visit, there was only a small church at the location of the crucifixion and resurrection.

Later, Sæwulf, probably the first English pilgrim to Jerusalem following its conquest in the First Crusade, recorded a huge church built in honor of St. Helena. This large church was utterly destroyed but it is likely this large church mentioned both by Daniel and Sæwulf was the Basilica of Constantine itself. The small church must then have been the Chapel of St. Helena.

Sæwulf—Twelfth century.

During the First Crusade, Christian knights from Europe captured Jerusalem after a seven-week siege. When the Holy City fell to the Christian forces, traveling to Jerusalem for European Christians became feasible. Sæwulf was an English pilgrim who is known mostly from the *Relatio* or written account he left of his pilgrimage to Jerusalem in 1102 AD. This was just a few years after the Crusaders recaptured the city in 1099 AD.

In the *Relatio*, Sæwulf describes how he sailed from the Apulia region of southeastern Italy and eventually docked at Jaffa where he began a tour of Palestine. Sæwulf's description of the Lord's Sepulchre, "surrounded by a very strong wall and roof, lest the rain should fall upon it," squares with Abbot Daniels' description of the same. The Chapel of the Holy Sepulchre is and always must have been a small building.

Evidence #8. Optically Stimulated Luminescence

An exciting scientific discovery came as a result of refurbishing the Edicule in 2016–2017. It relates to the mortar found between the limestone surface of the tomb and the marble slab that covered it. Experiments conducted on the mortar indicate it dates to 345 AD.

Antonia Moropoulou, the chief scientific supervisor for the Edicule restoration project, tested the mortar with a technique called Optically Stimulated Luminescence (OSL). OSL is a method for measuring ionizing radiation. It's used in the luminescence dating of ancient materials. The difference between radiocarbon dating and OSL is that the former is used to date organic materials, while the latter dates minerals.[289]

The energy within mineral grains like quartz builds up when they are not exposed to sunlight. Through the OSL technique, scientists can measure this energy to determine how long it has been since the mineral was visible to light. In turn, this enables dating the burial associated with the mortar.

Moropoulou and his team discovered that the quartz mineral in the mortar from this tomb dates back to the fourth century AD. That strengthens the case for the authenticity of the Church of the Holy Sepulchre as the site of Jesus' burial.

It also provides the first piece of non-literary, non-traditional evidence related to dating the church Constantine built to venerate the presumed tomb of Jesus.

Evidence #9. *The Holy Sepulchre ring*

During 1974 excavations south of the Temple Mount in Jerusalem, directed by Professor Benjamin Mazar of the Hebrew University, a gold ring was discovered in a Byzantine house near the Triple Gate. It was the mid-1970s, and at the time, there was a great deal of skepticism by scholars at the suggestion the ring depicted the Holy Sepulchre or the tomb of Jesus.

Positively dating the ring is fraught with difficulty. Rings are often best-dated by their style. Unfortunately, the style of this ring does not pinpoint any date within multiple centuries. It likely dates anywhere from the twelfth century to the sixteenth century AD, when rings of this type—featuring the Holy Sepulchre as rebuilt in the Crusader Period—were being sold in Jerusalem as souvenirs and carried back to Europe.

There are, however, rings similar to this one found in several other collections. In the Benaki Museum in Athens, for example, a very similar ring is displayed. Another is a sixth- seventh-century gold ring found near Milan, now in the British Museum. It presents itself in the same manner as the Holy Sepulchre ring.

The band encircling the finger is made of ornamented wire. The head or bezel (the part that protrudes upward from the band) is in the form of a square structure with a pyramidal roof. The walls of the building are pierced with rounded arches. The sides of the roof are decorated with pellets arranged in triangles.[290] Many of the Monza ampullae and the Bobbia ampullae come from Jerusalem and date from the Byzantine Period.[291] They, too, depict the Anastasis—the domed structure—over Jesus' tomb in a way similar to the Holy Sepulchre ring.[292]

Yaakov Meshorer was, at the time, the Chief Curator for Archaeology at the Israel Museum in Jerusalem. After studying the ring, he gave this assessment:

> It is my impression that the ring is Christian because of the design of the vaults: The shaft with two branches resembles a stylized lily with a long central petal reaching the top of the vault ... The lily was a well-known Christian symbol during the Crusader Period. We should, therefore, look for an important building from the Christian world to identify the structure.[293]

Ring featuring the Holy Sepulchre

We do not have to look far. There is a remarkable similarity between the building on the ring and the Crusader Holy Sepulchre. The Crusader Holy Sepulchre is depicted on marble screens, which were part of the Crusader lintels on the facade of the Holy Sepulchre church before it was damaged in a fire. These screens are now housed in the Rockefeller Museum in Jerusalem.

PROBLEMS WITH THE EVIDENCE FOR THE CHURCH OF THE HOLY SEPULCHRE

As with the Garden Tomb, the Church of the Holy Sepulchre enjoys a fair amount of evidence for its authenticity but has some difficulties with that evidence. While there are others, two major problems exist in identifying this church as the site of Jesus' crucifixion and resurrection. Let's probe these two difficulties.

The Kokhim-type tombs.

A huge problem for the Church of the Holy Sepulchre housing the tomb of Jesus is the tombs at this site are *kokhim*-type tombs. This is where the body was slid into a niche about 2 feet wide, 3 feet high, and 6–7 feet deep and cut into the rock wall. In essence, the body was placed in a tube-like chamber holed out of the rock.

Burial kokhim in the Church of the Holy Sepluchre

How is it when Mary Magdalene looked into the tomb "she saw two angels in white, sitting where the body of Jesus had lain, one at the head and one at the feet" (John 20:12)? *Kokhim* would not permit an angel to sit in such a cramped niche in the wall.

The location of the church

And then there is the problem of the location of the Church of the Holy Sepulchre. Certainly, it has been established that the church was outside the wall of Jerusalem in Jesus' day. However, there may be a problem with the direction of the church outside the wall.

From the tenth century BC through the first century AD, which corresponds to the archaeological Iron Age through the Herodian Period, no tombs were constructed west of the inhabited areas of Jerusalem. The only exceptions were tombs located over one thousand meters (3,280.83 feet) west of the city walls. West of the wall was simply avoided as a burial area, and the reason seems to be geographic meteorology.

Jerusalem sits high on the ridge of mountains that runs north to south down the spine of Israel. If you walked down the mountainside from Jerusalem west toward Ashdod on the Mediterranean Sea, you would walk approximately 68 kilometers (42 miles). Except on those occasions when a haboob or sirocco blows from the deserts toward the west, Jerusalem enjoys breezes coming right off the Mediterranean. More than 350 days a year, the wind is from the west, from the sea.

Because of these prevailing winds from the west, the Jews did not bury their dead on the west side of Jerusalem. They had tombs and cemeteries to the east, north, and south of the city, but archaeological research has shown that the west of the city was off-limits for the dead.

A map in the *New Encyclopedia of Archaeological Excavations in the Holy Land* indicates the locations of Jerusalem's *necropoli* (burial grounds). It shows hundreds of tombs on the Mount of Olives, east of Jerusalem, and large cemeteries on the north and south, but none on the west within a kilometer of ancient Jerusalem's western wall.[294]

If tombs were located to the west of Jerusalem, that presented two problems for the Jews. First, the stench of decomposing corpses would sweep over the city pushed along by the sea breezes from the west. Second, Jews believed ritual impurity from the "city of the dead" could cause the inhabitants of Jerusalem, or any Jewish town, to become "defiled" or unclean. The first is a practical reason for not permitting a cemetery or burial ground to be on the western side of the city. The second is a religious reason.

The Mishnah says:

> One must distance animal carcasses, graves, and a tannery [*ha-burseki*], a place where hides are processed, fifty cubits [75 feet] from the city. One may establish a tannery only on the east side of the city because winds usually blow from the west and the foul smells would therefore be blown away from the residential area. Rabbi Akiva says: One may establish a tannery on any side of a city except for the west, as the winds blowing from that direction will bring the odors into the city, and one must distance it fifty cubits from the city (*Bava Batra* 24a).

The stench of a dead carcass, including a dead human, produces an unbearable smell. Anyone who has passed "roadkill" day after day before it was removed by the highway department knows how true this is. It was merely a matter of practicality not to put a cemetery on the western side of the city.

The lack of ritual purity

But more to the point was the religious reason why cemeteries were not placed west of the city. The Jews were super careful about being defiled by death. "There were certain men who were unclean through touching a dead body so that they could not keep the Passover on that day" (see Num

9:6–10). Ritual impurity removed a Jew from the reasonable requirements of Jewish life, as well as the usual social interaction of that life.

This presents a problem for the Church of the Holy Sepulchre's location as it was west of the Temple area. It presents a problem for the Temple as well. University of Haifa archaeologist Rami Arav and researcher John Rousseau have noted that Pharisaic tradition would not have allowed a cemetery or killing ground anywhere west of the expanded Temple Mount because the wind from the Mediterranean would pass over the cemetery before it would reach the Temple Mount, defiling everyone who breathed it in.[295]

Arav and Rousseau argue that "tombs found in this area [west of the city] are either older than the first century C.E. or are located more than a distance of 2,000 cubits (3,000 feet) from the Temple Mount."[296] They concluded that since "burial customs in the first half of the first century C.E. preclude burials and their attendant impurities west (windward) of the Temple, then the crucifixion and burial of Jesus could not have taken place at the site of the Church of the Holy Sepulchre, which is almost exactly due west of the Holy of Holies."[297]

What we know for sure.

With so much speculation and tradition surrounding the Church of the Holy Sepulchre, what is it that we know for certain?

- Until the first century BC, there was a functioning quarry at the location of the present Church of the Holy Sepulchre.
- In the early Roman Period, however, this quarry was covered with soil, and the area was cultivated. This corresponds with what John 19:41 says: "Now in the place where he was crucified there was a garden, and in the garden a new tomb in which no one had yet been laid."
- About 135 AD, according to the historian Eusebius, Emperor Hadrian built a temple to Venus over the presumed site of Golgotha and the tomb to prevent Christians from worshiping there (Eusebius, *Life of Constantine* 3.26).
- Archaeologists have uncovered remains of Hadrian's Temple which stood on the presumed site of Golgotha throughout the second and early third centuries.
- In the fourth century AD, both archaeological and historical sources corroborate that Emperor Constantine ordered this pagan temple destroyed and a church built on the site. The Church of the Holy

Sepulchre still stands in the Christian Quarter of the walled Old City of Jerusalem at that location.

- When layer after layer was excavated, Eusebius wrote, "The testimony of the Savior's resurrection [that is, Jesus' empty tomb], was against all expectation revealed, and "the cave, the holy of holies, took on the appearance of a representation of the Savior's return to life" (Eusebius, *Life of Constantine* 3.27–28).

- In multiple sources from the early to mid-fourth century AD, such as the pilgrim Egeria and Abbot Daniel, it is recorded that in the church there were relics, including the "True Cross." However, none of these earliest sources, including Eusebius, associates Helena with the actual construction of the Holy Sepulchre church. Constantine, in letters describing the construction of the church, does not. The Bordeaux pilgrim visited Jerusalem in 333 AD. He describes the building of the Holy Sepulchre but does not mention Helena or the discovery of the cross.

- Gregory of Nyssa (died c. 385), St. Jerome (c. 340–420), John Chrysostom (c. 347–407), and the female pilgrim Egeria (380s) all mention the relics of the cross in the Holy Sepulchre—but none credits Helena with their discovery.

- Even Bishop Cyril of Jerusalem—who later commissioned his nephew to write the *Church History* that included the legend of Helena's discovery of the cross—does not mention Helena in his earliest writings about the cross. Around the year 350 AD, Cyril—whose seat was the Holy Sepulchre—mentions in his *Catecheses* the presence of the *lignum crucis* (wood of the cross) but nothing about Helena discovering it.

- A year later, Cyril wrote that the cross was found in the days of Constantine the Great, but again says nothing about Helena (Cyril, *Letter to Constantius*).

- Eusebius also quotes a letter Constantine wrote to Bishop Macarius of Jerusalem, in which he told the bishop that his excavations on the site of the church had uncovered "the token of that holiest passion," which had long been hidden under the ground and which had now been found (Eusebius, *Life of Constantine* 3.30). The "holiest passion" is Jesus' death by crucifixion, and the "token" of that passion, must be a reference to the cross, but no reference to Helena's discovery of it.

- The fact remains that we have no reliable historical evidence linking Helena to the discovery of the cross. She did not live long enough to hear the stories that would make her famous. Within a year or two after her journey to the East, and several decades before her name came to be associated with the cross, Helena died, in the presence of her son Constantine.[298]

A splintered fragment of the cross Helena was alleged to have discovered eventually made its way to Rome. You can see it today in the *Santa Croce di Gerusalemme* (Holy Cross of Jerusalem) church. By the late fourth century, pieces of the "True Cross" had made their way to many places distant from Jerusalem. Today, churches, basilicas, monasteries, and private collectors the world over claim to have a piece of the authentic cross of Jesus. According to Bishop Cyril of Jerusalem, "The whole world had been filled with pieces of the wood of the cross."

CONCLUSIONS

So, where does that leave us in determining the location of Calvary? Perhaps with more questions than answers. The truth is, there is no "smoking gun" that forces you to say, "This is definitely the site." The Church of the Holy Sepulchre has more archaeological evidence in its favor than the Garden Tomb. It also has literary evidence that goes back to the fourth century; the Garden Tomb has no such literary evidence. And then there's the historical evidence. The Garden Tomb has been celebrated as the potential site of the crucifixion, burial, and resurrection of Jesus for more than 130 years, while the Church of the Holy Sepulchre has been celebrated for more than 1,700 years. The Church of the Holy Sepulchre has more hard evidence for authenticity than the Garden Tomb. It also has more years of tradition behind it.

> "We may not be absolutely certain that the site of the Holy Sepulchre church is the site of Jesus' burial, but we certainly have no other site that can lay a claim nearly as weighty, and we really have no reason to reject the authenticity of the site."
> —Dan Bahat

Nevertheless, the Garden Tomb remains a viable option, especially for Protestants who are repulsed by the cacophony of smells, sounds, sites, and slugfests that are part of the atmosphere of the Church of the Holy Sepulchre. Archaeologist, author, and contributor to National Geographic, Kristin Romey, traveled to the Holy Land and spoke to numerous other archaeologists and scholars about Jesus' tomb. She was present at the opening of Christ's tomb at the Church of the Holy Sepulchre. There, she experienced an epiphany.

"At this moment, I realized that to sincere believers, the scholars' quest for the historical, non-supernatural Jesus is of little consequence," Romey wrote. "That quest will be endless, full of shifting theories, unanswerable questions, irreconcilable facts. But for true believers, their faith in the life, death, and resurrection of the Son of God will be evidence enough" (*National Geographic*, 2016).

That being the case, you may wish to visit both locations on your pilgrimage to the Holy City. Go to the Church of the Holy Sepulchre for information; go to the Garden Tomb for inspiration. Go to the Church of the Holy Sepulchre for facts; go to the Garden Tomb for feeling. Go to the Church of the Holy Sepulchre for the evidence; go to the Garden Tomb for the experience.

There is, however, one thing both sites have in common, one fact they share. In both the Garden Tomb and the Church of the Holy Sepulchre, the tombs are empty. There is no one there.

"Do not be afraid, for I know that you seek Jesus who was crucified. He is not here, for he has risen, as he said. Come, see the place where he lay. Then go quickly and tell his disciples that he has risen from the dead" (Matt 28:5–7).

The call of the angel is with us still today. "Come and see; go and tell."

Chapter 10

An Inventory of Jesus' Suffering Between Gethsemane and Golgotha

I do not wish to sensationalize the crucifixion as a Hollywood producer would, but I do think Christians should be a little less cavalier about saying "Christ died for my sins." Do we have the slightest concept of what that meant physically, emotionally, and spiritually for the Savior?

LIKE A DIAMOND SPARKLING in the sun, the crucifixion of the Savior has many facets to it. There are also many features to his suffering. The historical accounts we have of the life of Jesus of Nazareth indicate he endured a lifetime of suffering, which began as a newborn when his father had to whisk his wife and the baby away to Egypt to keep Herod the King from killing him (Matt 2:13–18). In this chapter, however, we will limit exploring his suffering during the last day of his life, the hours between Gethsemane and Golgotha. We'll consider the Savior's suffering by taking an inventory of it and viewing it from several facets to capture its meaning and agony more fully.

THE PHYSICAL SUFFERING OF JESUS

It's far too easy to gloss over the words "Jesus suffered and died" without stopping to consider the extent of his suffering. Our salvation does not come as a result of Jesus' suffering. It comes as a result of his death. But the suffering he endured before he handed over his spirit to his Heavenly Father was powerful, it was protracted, it was punishing, and it was painful. It revealed the worst in those inflicting the suffering and the best in the One who suffered for us.

Table 1: A Snapshot of Jesus' Suffering in Gethsemane

Cause of Suffering	Scriptures
Jesus struggles with the will of God	Matt 26:33–35; Mark 14:29–31; Luke 22:31–34
Jesus sweats large drops of blood	Luke 22:44
Jesus finds three disciples sleeping	Matt 26:40–45; Mark14:37–39
Jesus submits to the Father's will	Matt 26:44
Judas betrays Jesus with a kiss	Matt 26:49; Mark 14:45; Luke 22:48
The Temple police arrest Jesus	Matt 26:50; Luke 22;54; John 18:12
Peter slices off Malchus' ear	Matt 26:51–54; Lk 22:49–51; Jn 18:10–11
Jesus' disciples abandon him	Matt 26:56; Mk 14:50

I do not wish to sensationalize the crucifixion as a Hollywood producer would, but I do think Christians should be a little less cavalier about saying "Christ died for my sins." Do we have the slightest concept of what that meant physically, emotionally, and spiritually for the Savior?

We know best of the physical suffering our Lord endured at the cross and before. It will be easy for you to identify his physical in the lists below. In more or less chronological order, Tables 1–4 represent the locations in Jerusalem where Jesus of Nazareth was taunted and tortured before he yielded his life to the Heavenly Father. This list, representative of a much larger list, is painful, especially if you do not simply read through it. At each entry, stop and think of the location, the people involved in Jesus' suffering, and the pain of the suffering itself.

Jesus struggled when his human nature, wishing to avoid the pain ahead and then the cross itself, does battle with his divine nature that knows it is for this hour he was born, and in this hour, he must die. Thus, we begin with his suffering in the garden.

From the garden, Jesus was led by the Temple police, the religious leaders, and a mob of others to the house of Annas. It appears Annas continued to hold significant influence since he was the first to question Jesus. After this initial interrogation to get the facts upon which Jesus would be tried, Annas sent him across the High Priest's courtyard to the house of Caiaphas.

An Inventory of Jesus' Suffering Between Gethsemane and Golgotha   239

Here a miscarriage of justice like never seen before or since was conducted by a handful of Sanhedrin and Caiaphas. Jesus was physically and mentally abused before and after he was found guilty.

Table 2: A Snapshot of Jesus' Suffering at the High Priest's Palace

Location	Cause of Suffering	Scriptures
Annas' house	Jesus is interrogated	John 18:13
Annas' house	Jesus is slapped in the face	John 18:22–23
Caiaphas' house	Jesus accused of blasphemy	Matt 26:65; Mark 14:63;Luke 22:71
Caiaphas' house	Sanhedrin spit in Jesus' face	Matt 26:67; Mark 14:65;
Caiaphas' house	Sanhedrin strike Jesus	Matt 26:67; Mark 14:65; Luke 22:63
Caiaphas' house	Jesus is slapped by a servant	Matt 26:67; Mark 14:65; Luke 22:63
Caiaphas' house	Sanhedrin mock Jesus	Matt 26:68; Mark 14:65; Luke 22:64
Caiaphas' courtyard	Peter denies Jesus three times	Matt 26:69–75; John 18:15–18

Just when it seemed things could not get worse, Jesus was hustled from the High Priest's compound to the Jerusalem palace of Herod the Great. This palatial compound was the residence of Pontius Pilate whenever the prefect was in Jerusalem. Since the crucifixion weekend was also Passover, this was the busiest time of the year for Jerusalem. Hundreds of thousands of Jewish pilgrims from all over the land and the diaspora were in the city for the most important festival of the year—the *Pesach*.

Nonetheless, early on Friday morning, Caiaphas and the Jewish religious leaders whisked Jesus to Pilate's residence for sentencing. This was because these religious leaders did not have the legal authority to crucify anyone they condemned. Caiaphas and his religious cohorts did not just want Jesus dead; they wanted him crucified. Since only the Roman governor could do that, off to Pilate Jesus went for even greater suffering.

"Spitting upon another person, especially onto the face, is a global sign of anger, hatred, disrespect or contempt. It can represent a 'symbolical regurgitation' or an act of intentional contamination."[299] As bad as twice being spit in the face was, as bad as being pummeled with Roman fists and slapped with Jewish hands was, as bad as being mocked, scorned, and manhandled was, and as bad as being scourged with Roman whips was, the worst physical suffering for Jesus was yet to come. At a place called Golgotha, the killing field for the city of Jerusalem, Jesus accepted the ultimate suffering, the anguish of being nailed to a Roman cross and hanging there nearly lifeless for six hours. Don't let the pain of these hours slip by you too easily. Let them penetrate your mind and soften your heart.

Although Jesus' physical suffering is the easiest to identify and understand because it is the most graphically portrayed, it was not the only form of suffering Jesus had to endure that final Passover weekend. The physical is the kind of suffering people think about when they think of the cross.

Table 3: A Snapshot of Jesus' Suffering at Pilate's Praetorium

Location	Cause of Suffering	Scriptures
Jerusalem street	Jesus is shuffled to Pilate	Matt 27:2; Mark 15:1; Luke 23:1; John 18:28
Outside Pilate's Headquarters	Jewish leaders accuse Jesus	Luke 23:1; John 18:29–30
Outside Pilate's Headquarters	Pilate interrogates Jesus	Matt 27:11–14; Mark 15:2–5; Luke 23:3
Inside Pilate's Headquarters	Pilate continues his interrogation of Jesus	John 18:33–38; 19:9–11
Outside Pilate's Headquarters	Jewish leaders accuse Jesus	Mark 15:3; Luke 23:5
Antipas's palace	Pilate sends Jesus to Antipas	Luke 23:7
Antipas's palace	Antipas interrogates Jesus	Luke 23:9
Antipas's palace	Jewish leaders accuse Jesus	Luke 23:10
Outside Pilate's Headquarters	Jews ask for Barabbas' release	Matt 27:15–21; Mark 15:6–11; Luke 23:18–19
Outside Pilate's Headquarters	Jews call for Jesus' crucifixion	Matt 27:22; Mark 15:14; Luke 23:23; John 19:15
Inside Pilate's Headquarters	Roman soldiers scourge Jesus	Matt 27:26; Mark 15:15; John19:1
Inside Pilate's Headquarters	Roman soldiers mock Jesus	Matt 27:28; Mark 15:17; John 19:5
Inside Pilate's Headquarters	Soldiers dishonor Jesus with a crown of thorns	Matt 27:29; Mark 15:17; John 19:2,5
Inside Pilate's Headquarters	Soldiers strike Jesus and spit on him	Matt 27:30; Mark 15:19; John 19:3

An Inventory of Jesus' Suffering Between Gethsemane and Golgotha

The suffering of Jesus was important enough to the early church to make mention of it in their creeds. There are three major credos adopted by members of the earliest centuries of the Christian Church. They are:

- The important Nicene Creed (325 AD) states in part, "For our sake he was crucified under Pontius Pilate, he suffered death and was buried, and rose again on the third day in accordance with the Scriptures."
- The Apostle's Creed (ca. 340 AD) notes, "He suffered under Pontius Pilate, was crucified, died, and was buried."
- The Athanasian Creed (ca. 500 AD) unequivocally states: "God and Man is one Christ; Who suffered for our salvation; descended into hell; rose again the third day from the dead. He ascended into heaven, he sitteth on the right hand of God the Father Almighty."

In each of the three important creeds of Christianity, the suffering of Jesus is highlighted. But when the Apostle's Creed, for example, says "He suffered under Pontius Pilate," it means much more than physical suffering. To understand the fullest extent of Jesus' suffering we must also consider his emotional and spiritual suffering.

THE EMOTIONAL SUFFERING OF JESUS

First, a definition. What is emotional suffering? In cases of the law, "Emotional pain and suffering is a measure of the amount of suffering you experience from nonphysical injuries." This is how a well-known Chicago personal injury law firm describes how they fight for compensation for their clients who have been emotionally troubled by another person. "You can often receive compensation for emotional pain and suffering as part of your compensation for a physical personal injury . . . But sometimes you can also get compensation for emotional pain and suffering even if there is no physical injury."[300]

> "Far worse than the breaking of his body
> is the shredding of his heart."
> —Max Lucado

My point in beginning with how the term is used in the courtroom is that there is a clear delineation in law between physical suffering and emotional suffering. Physical pain is the pain of the body; emotional pain is pain at the seat of the emotions.

In writing the Old Testament, when the author wanted to express the deepest seat of one's emotions, he used the word that the King James Version translated as "reins" (Hebrew: כִּלְיָה; English: *kilyâh*). Many newer translations render this with the word "heart" as in Job 19:27, "Whom I shall see on my side, and my eyes shall behold, and not another. My heart faints within me!" (ESV, RSV, HCSB, NASB, etc. Interestingly, the Good News Translation uses the word "courage" for *kilyâh*). But I don't see "heart" as the best rendering, certainly not the strongest.

In each of the versions just mentioned, when they come to a verse that uses the word *kilyâh* (literally the Hebrew word means the kidneys), each one translates it with the word "minds." This is because the same verse already contains the word for "heart" (Hebrew: לֵב; English: *lêb*), (see Pss 7:9; 26:2; Jer 11:20; 17:10; 20:12), and they couldn't use the translation "heart" twice. So, for example, Psalm 26:2 in the ESV reads, "Prove me, O Lord, and try me; test my heart and my mind," but a footnote admits that this verse literally reads, "Test my heart and my kidneys."

So, why the kidneys? The Hebrew language did not have a word for the innermost emotions, the innermost being, so they substituted a word for a physical organ that was deep within the body, i.e., the kidneys.[301] It doesn't make a lot of sense in English, but it made perfect sense to the ancient Hebrews. When speaking of their heart, they were not talking about some mystical quality as in "that woman has a lot of heart." No, they were talking about their physical heart, the organ that pumps blood, the seat of their physical being. And when they wanted to talk about the seat of their emotional being, they spoke of their kidneys, located deep within the body and equidistant from the crown of the head and the sole of the feet.

Jesus' emotional suffering was different from his physical suffering. Emotional suffering was the suffering of the spirit, not the suffering of the body. Jesus suffered both internally (emotional suffering) and externally (physical suffering).

In his classic work William Stroud, MD says, "That the seat of his sufferings at this time was his soul . . . The words set forth the greatness of his soul-sufferings. His soul was not only sorrowful but exceeding sorrowful. The word signifies to be beset with sorrow roundabout and is well expressed in the Psalms, 'The sorrows of death compassed me, and the pains of hell got hold upon me' (Ps 18:5–6; Ps 116:3)."[302]

Table 4: A Snapshot of Jesus' Suffering at Golgotha

Location	Cause of Suffering	Scriptures
Via Dolorosa	Jesus' Journey to Golgotha	Matt 27:31; Mark 15:20
Via Dolorosa	Soldiers conscript Simon	Matt 27:32; Mark 15:21; Luke 23:26
Via Dolorosa	Jesus speaks to the women	Luke 23:28–31
Golgotha	Jesus refuses a numbing drink	Matt 27:33–34; Mark 15:23
Golgotha	Soldiers nail Jesus to the cross	Matt 27:35; Mark 15:24; Luke 23:33; John 19:18
Golgotha	Soldiers divvy up Jesus' clothes	Matt 27:35; Mark 15:24; Luke 23:34; John 19:23
Golgotha	Jesus speaks forgiving words	Luke 23:34
Golgotha	Jesus is crucified with violent criminals	Matt. 27:38; Mark 15:27; Luke 23:32; John 19:18
Golgotha	Jesus speaks hope to one of the criminals	Luke 23:42–44
Golgotha	The passers-by mock Jesus	Matt 27:39; Mark 15:29
Golgotha	The elders and chief priests mock Jesus	Matt 27:41–42; Mark 15:31; Luke 23:35
Golgotha	The criminals mock Jesus	Matt 27:44; Mark 15:32
Golgotha	Jesus cries out to his Father	Matt 27:46; Mark 15:34
Golgotha	The soldiers mock Jesus	Luke 23:36–37
Golgotha	Jesus speaks to his mother	John 19:25–27
Golgotha	Jesus sighs, "I thirst."	Matt 27:48; Mark 15:36; John 19:29
Golgotha	Jesus cries, "It is finished."	John 19:30
Golgotha	Jesus commits his human spirit to God the Father	Matt 27:50; Mark 15:37; Luke 23:46; John 19:30
Golgotha	Jesus' body pierced with a lance	John 19:31–35

Here are some of the emotional sufferings experienced by Jesus.

- Jesus was abandoned by his closest friends, disciples whom he had chosen personally, and who traveled with him throughout his ministry.

- Jesus was ridiculed and mocked in Caiaphas' palace, the whole time knowing how corrupt the High Priesthood's office had become.

- Jesus was ridiculed and mocked in Pilate's palace, the entire time knowing Pilate had no authority except that which came from God.

- Jesus was ridiculed and mocked in Herod's palace, the whole time knowing "that fox" didn't deserve his kingdom.
- Jesus was ridiculed by soldiers kneeling in feigned worship, the whole time knowing one day they would bow their knees to him in reality.
- Jesus was forced to march before the taunts of the crowd along the Via Dolorosa, the whole time knowing those taunts had been prophesied.
- Jesus was crucified in a public place, where everyone who wanted could see him, the whole time knowing he was about to die in place of those who mocked him.
- Jesus was crucified naked, the common practice of the Romans, the whole time knowing that a royal robe awaited him in heaven.
- Jesus was ridiculed and mocked by two criminals while hanging on their crosses, the whole time knowing he was there in innocence, and they were there in guilt.

"Grief of mind is harder to bear than pain of body. You can pluck up courage and endure the pang of sickness and pain, so long as the spirit is hale and brave; but if the soul itself be touched, and the mind becomes diseased with anguish, then every pain is increased in severity."[303]

> "The crucifixion of God's Son is no senseless tragedy. . . The insistent reference to the Old Testament and the will of the Father shows that Jesus' death, far from being devoid of all rhyme or reason, corresponds with the highest purposes of all: The plan of God."
> —Peter G. Bolt

Today it is called bullying (often cyberbullying). In Jesus' day, it was just called taunting or mocking. "Now the men who were holding Jesus in custody were mocking (Greek: ἐνέπαιζον ; English: *enepaizon*) him as they beat him" (Luke 22:63). The word the Greeks used for this comes from the root word (Greek παίζω; English: *paizo*) which means "to make sport of" as children having fun by taunting and terrorizing another child.

The kind of mockery Jesus had to endure was not unlike the occasion of King Agrippa's visit to Alexandria when he encountered a poor man from the streets whom Agrippa described as "a certain madman named Carabbas." Carabbas was being taunted and derided by the crowd. Philo describes the despicable treatment of Carabbas. "This man spent all his days and nights naked in the roads, minding neither cold nor heat, the sport of idle children and wanton youths."[304] Jesus was the victim of the same kind of childish taunting and torture.

Observations:

- Although Jesus was from Galilee, both of these series of temptations occurred in or near Jerusalem.
- From the failure of these temptations, it is apparent Jesus didn't need to prove to anyone who he was.
- In each temptation, the conditional "if" clause was used because none of the temptations were true.
- In each temptation, Satan or his minions tried to interject doubt in Jesus' mind; it didn't work.
- Each temptation was directed at Jesus' very essence: Son of God, Christ of God, and King of the Jews.
- Each temptation was in the form of mockery, but mockery only works if you give in to it. Jesus never did.
- When you do not fall for temptation, you do not foil the plan of God.

While remembering that Jesus was fully divine, we must also remember he was fully human as well. He had feelings the same as we do. He experienced the same temptations we do (Heb 4:15). He was susceptible to the same emotional attacks as we are. Jesus was not unfamiliar with "the place of the skull." Every time he headed north on the road out of Jerusalem, he passed by it, likely arrayed each time with criminals being punished. He looked at Golgotha with eyes of sympathy, awaiting his day, his turn, his date with destiny. Calvary was as much an emotional challenge as it was a physical one.

Yet when all the insults were being thrown at him, when all the taunts and emotional barbs were aimed at his inner being, Jesus still forgave his attackers, still offered hope to a repentant criminal, and still took care of his mother. He must have had remarkable emotional strength.

> He permitted these emotions to produce their painful effects to the fullest extent upon his will and, through the will, upon the other faculties of his soul. But at the same time, he presented to his soul counter-motives, which encouraged him to patiently undergo the sufferings, and, for our example, he simultaneously addressed himself in earnest prayer to his Heavenly Father. Thus he suffered and still always retained perfect control over these inner emotions.[305]

THE SPIRITUAL SUFFERING OF JESUS

Like the rest of us, Jesus had a body, soul, and spirit. His body is what connected him to the physical world around him. His soul is what made his body live; it animated the body. Genesis 2:7, "The Lord God formed the man of dust from the ground and breathed into his nostrils the breath of life, and the man became a living creature" (Hebrew: נֶפֶשׁ; English: *nephesh*). Everyone and everything of God's creation that breathes the air has a soul. It's that breathing process that keeps our soul alive. When we stop breathing, we stop living, and no longer have a soul.

But like the rest of us, Jesus had a spirit as well as a body and soul. His body connected him with the world. His soul connected him with life. But it was his spirit that connected him with God. This is true for every human being. In any Trinitarian belief, Jesus' deity was demonstrated by his eternality and equality with the Father and Holy Spirit. Jesus' humanity was demonstrated by his connection with the Father and Holy Spirit through his human spirit.

This spiritual connection with the Father and Holy Spirit is seen throughout the life of Jesus on Earth. At the beginning of his ministry, at his baptism by John the Baptist, Matthew 3:16-17 declares those who were present saw, "the Spirit of God descending like a dove and coming to rest on him; and behold, a voice from heaven said, 'This is my beloved Son, with whom I am well pleased.'" The Father identified his Son with a term of deity but remarked about his obedience to the Father in terms of being pleased with his humanity.

This is further evidenced by Jesus' statement in John 10:17-18, "For this reason the Father loves me, because I lay down my life that I may take it up again. No one takes it from me, but I lay it down of my own accord. I have authority to lay it down, and I have authority to take it up again. This charge I have received from my Father." Jesus would voluntarily lay down his life at the time determined by his Father, and in doing so, his obedience would demonstrate his spiritual connection with the Father.

Also, when Jesus left the site of his baptism, Luke 4:1-2 tells us, "And Jesus, full of the Holy Spirit, returned from the Jordan and was led by the Spirit in the wilderness for forty days, being tempted by the devil." In each of these instances, Jesus' spiritual connection with the Father and Spirit is evident, and it is demonstrated in his obedience.

Matthew 20:28, "The Son of Man came not to be served but to serve, and to give his life as a ransom for many." Here Jesus speaks both of his connection with the Heavenly Father, "The Son of Man came . . ." and with his fellow man "to give his life as a ransom for many." These connections are not so much physical or emotional as they are spiritual.

The Apostle Peter preached a mighty sermon at the house of Cornelius in Caesarea. Acts 10:37–39 records his words.

> You yourselves know what happened throughout all Judea, beginning from Galilee after the baptism that John proclaimed: how God anointed Jesus of Nazareth with the Holy Spirit and with power. He went about doing good and healing all who were oppressed by the devil, for God was with him. And we are witnesses of all that he did both in the country of the Jews and in Jerusalem.

Here again, Peter demonstrates he understood the spiritual connection between Jesus of Nazareth and the Father and Holy Spirit. He claimed the good Jesus did was the result of that connection, being directed by the Father and empowered by the Spirit. Peter also reminded his audience that he was an eyewitness to the results of that spiritual connection.

Table 5: Parallels Between Jesus' Temptations at the Beginning and End of His Earthly Ministry

The Beginning of Jesus' Earthly Ministry	The End of Jesus' Earthly Ministry
Satan Mocking: Son of God Matthew 4:3, "If you are the Son of God, command these stones to become loaves of bread."	*Passersby Mocking: Son of God* Matthew 27:39–40, "And those who passed by derided him, saying, 'If you are the Son of God, come down from the cross.'"
Satan Mocking: Son of God Matthew 4:6–10, "If you are the Son of God, throw yourself down, for it is written, 'He will command his angels concerning you'"	*Jewish Rulers Mocking: Christ of God* Luke 23:35, "The rulers scoffed at him, saying, 'He saved others; let him save himself, if he is the Christ of God, his Chosen One!'"
Satan Mocking: Fall down and worship Matthew 4:9, "And he said to him, 'All these I will give you, if you will fall down and worship me.'"	*Roman Soldiers Mocking: King of the Jews* Luke 23:36–37, "The soldiers also mocked him saying, 'If you are the King of the Jews, save yourself!'"

Nowhere is the spiritual element of Jesus' make-up more evident, however, than at that crucifixion weekend. Examples come easily to mind. His spiritual struggle with maintaining obedience in doing the will of the Father is juxtaposed with the possibility of giving in to the physical and emotional components of his life and abandoning the cross. The struggle in the Garden of Gethsemane was not primarily physical or even emotional. It was a spiritual struggle that Jesus won by obedience to the Father. His spiritual connection remained intact.

Another example of Jesus' spiritual struggle is evident while he was hanging on the cross. Jesus' cry, "'Eli, Eli, lema sabachthani?'" that is, "'My God, my God, why have you forsaken me?'" was not the cry of deity, but the cry of humanity. At Golgotha, Jesus' spiritual pain was most dominant at that dark moment when his spiritual connection with the Father was challenged. While we often don't see evidence of it because it is so overshadowed by the horrendously cruel physical aspect of his crucifixion, the spiritual pain Jesus endured was real.

Here are some of the spiritual sufferings experienced by Jesus. Jesus knew he had to die on the cross, but even the prospect of it caused a spiritual challenge to his will in Gethsemane.

- Jesus knew he was innocent and didn't deserve the cross, but he had to go anyway to accomplish the eternal plan of God for our salvation.
- Jesus knew he could end his suffering anytime he chose, but that would commit him to a path of disobedience to the Father and the Holy Spirit.
- Jesus willingly absorbed all the sin, of all the world, of all time knowing how heavy the weight of that sin would be on his spiritual connection to the Father and Holy Spirit.
- Jesus had to be separated from his Father, and that had never occurred before in his experience as a human.
- Jesus agonized at the separation from God the Father; it was the point of his deepest spiritual struggle.
- Jesus saw few tangible results from his ministry on earth other than people fed, and a few others healed, but he knew the results of his death would accomplish more spiritual good than all the results of his life.

We can never know how deeply Jesus' separation from the Father while on the cross was a struggle for him spiritually. We can never know what it felt like to bear the weight of the sin of the world (Isa 53:6; 1 Pet 2:24). We will never know what the wrath of God feels like (Rom 5:9). This was all a new experience for Jesus. Up to this point, Jesus had never experienced sin (Heb 4:15; 7:26; 9:14; 1 Pet 2:22; John 8:46; 2 Cor 5:21). However, at the cross, Jesus didn't just experience sin; he *became* sin for the first and last time in history when God judged him for our sin.

An Inventory of Jesus' Suffering Between Gethsemane and Golgotha

> "The sorrows of David over the injustices of the chosen people, the grief and indignation of Elias at the scandals and the idolatries of Israel, the tears of the prophet Jeremiah over the infidelities of Jerusalem were merely faint figures of the sadness of Jesus when he beheld the sins of the entire world."
> —James Groenings

The day Jesus died was the most important in history. That day things changed forever. Without his death, there would be no resurrection. Without his death, there would be no opportunity for forgiveness of our sin and guilt. The Apostle Paul wrote, "For our sake he [God the Father] made him [Jesus] to be sin who knew no sin, so that in him [Jesus] we might become the righteousness of God." It all happened during six hours that Friday. It's what makes this book important. Nobody likes to suffer. Nobody even likes to think about suffering. But the suffering of Jesus of Nazareth was unlike any before him or after him. His was cosmic suffering. His was maximum suffering. His was substitutionary suffering. His was necessary suffering. However, rejoice with me because . . .

> The strife is o'er, the battle done;
> The victory of life is won;
> The song of triumph has begun:
> Alleluia!
> The pow'rs of death have done their worst;
> But Christ their legions has dispersed;
> Let shouts of holy joy outburst:
> Alleluia!
> The three sad days are quickly sped;
> He rises glorious from the dead;
> All glory to our risen Head:
> Alleluia!
> Lord, by the stripes which wounded You,
> In us, You've won the vict'ry too,
> That we may live, and sing to You:
> Alleluia! Alleluia! Alleluia! Alleluia!
> Anonymous

Epilogue

We have probed Jesus of Nazareth's trials, death, burial, and more. Still, we mustn't lose sight of the One who died for us. He is the Messiah of Israel. He is the Lamb of God who takes away the sin of this world.

THOSE SCHOLARS AND NON-SCHOLARS alike who dismiss the Gospel narratives as myth or legend rob themselves unnecessarily of so much detail and so many interesting features of the crucifixion of Jesus. Failure to accept the Gospel accounts as history often gives rise to many implausible theories and presumptions that deprive a person of truth and the real impact of the gospel. This is much more than a shame. It is an eternal catastrophe, given that the Gospel narratives are the setting for the message of the gospel itself.

The Apostle Paul's declaration of faith in the gospel is the reason he trusted the veracity and historicity of the gospel. "For I am not ashamed of the gospel, for it is the power of God for salvation to everyone who believes, to the Jew first and also to the Greek. For in it the righteousness of God is revealed from faith for faith, as it is written, 'The righteous shall live by faith'" (Rom 1:16–17).

> "New Testament writers assume the historicity of the crucifixion of Jesus and focus their attention upon its significance."
> —J. J. Scott Jr.

The four Gospels—Matthew, Mark, Luke, and John—are not biographies of the life of Jesus of Nazareth. If that were the writers' intent, each failed miserably.

The four evangelists wrote historical narratives that included the reason God became a man. "For the Son of Man came to seek and to save the lost" (Luke 19:10).

The four evangelists wrote historical narratives that revealed the love of God for humankind. "And as Moses lifted up the serpent in the wilderness, so must the Son of Man be lifted up, that whoever believes in him may have eternal life. For God so loved the world, that he gave his only Son, that whoever believes in him should not perish but have eternal life. For God did not send his Son into the world to condemn the world, but in order that the world might be saved through him" (John 3:14–17).

The four evangelists wrote historical narratives that clearly revealed the purpose of their writing. The last two verses of the Gospel of John tell us why John undertook to document Jesus and his crucifixion. "Now Jesus did many other signs in the presence of the disciples, which are not written in this book; but these are written so that you may believe that Jesus is the Christ, the Son of God, and that by believing you may have life in his name" (John 20:30–31).

In the ten chapters of this book, we have mined the depths of the Gospel accounts related to Jesus' two trials, his sentence of death, his brutal and bloody crucifixion, and his burial in a borrowed tomb.

Along the way, we have opened the door just a crack to see the heart of God in sending his Son to die for our sins. We have followed the Savior to Calvary and then to the grave. We have seen his determination to carry out the plan for our salvation that the Father, the Holy Spirit, and he formulated before time began.

We have probed Jesus of Nazareth's trials, death, burial, and more. Still, we mustn't lose sight of the One who died for us. He is the Messiah of Israel. He is the Lamb of God who takes away the sin of this world. He is the Savior who died in our place. He is the Prince of Peace. He is the King of Kings. He is the difference maker in our lives and for that, we must both be vocal, 'Let the redeemed of the Lord say so" (Ps 107:2), and eternally grateful.

THE DIFFERENCE MAKER

Born in a Bethlehem stable and nestled in the straw of a borrowed manger, his first visitors were simple shepherds. His only journey from his tiny homeland came in response to an attempt on his infant life by a jealous monarch.

Raised a carpenter's son in a frontier town, his family lived in poverty and obscurity. As a child, he astounded intellectuals with his godly wisdom and understanding. His gentle spirit and compassion were reciprocated by hometown hatred.

As a man, he called rugged fishermen to leave their nets and in silent submission, they followed him. From a borrowed boat he promised his disciples little but deprivation and death. Still, multitudes came.

As his life neared an end, He borrowed a colt upon which to ride in victory. He borrowed a room where he ate with his disciples for the final time. He borrowed a garden in which to pray. When envy and hatred rose against him, mockers borrowed a robe to scorn him. When he was condemned to die, they borrowed a shoulder to carry his cross. Once he was dead, they borrowed a tomb in which to bury him. And when he was raised from the dead, his enemies borrowed a lie to deny his resurrection.

One who never wrote a book, never composed a song, or never received an award of any kind should likely have passed from the pages of history without notice. But if he had, we wouldn't know the only name that brings salvation, the only name at which every knee shall bow—Jesus, the only Savior the world will ever know.

Of all the prophets, monarchs, sages, or artists who ever graced this globe, none so changed it as Jesus of Nazareth. His life, death, and resurrection have become the focal point of history. He is not traced in our memories as much as he is plowed into the soil of our history. More than anyone else, he is the difference maker. He certainly made a difference in my life. He will in yours as well.

Blessings.
Woodrow Michael Kroll

Endnotes

1. Benoit, *Passion*, 81.
2. Brown, *Death*, 412.
3. Allen, "Why Pilate," 82.
4. Mansfield, *Killing Jesus*, 115–16.
5. Joseph M. Baumgarten indicates that while monetary cases only require two witnesses, capital cases require three. See "Judicial Procedures" in *Exegetical Dictionary*, 2:445–60.
6. Abrahams, *Studies in Pharisaism*, 132–33. Also see Barclay, *Crucified and Crowned*, 58.
7. Schnabel, *The Last Days*, 251.
8. ———, *The Last Days*, 260.
9. Benoit, *Passion*, 43–44.
10. In ancient Greek texts, this game is described under the name of *myinda*. One of the players puts his hand over his eyes and must guess what object has been presented to him or who had touched him. If he guesses right, he wins, and the other player must cover his eyes in his turn. If wrong, he must begin guessing again.
11. Juster, *Les Juifs*, 2:132–45.
12. Schürer, *History*, 2:261.
13. Lietzmann, *Der Prozess*, 251–63.
14. Chapman, *The Trial*, 2. For the plausibility of an ad hoc meeting of the Sanhedrin, see Kirner, Strafgewalt, 167–68, 259.
15. Yamauchi, "Historical Notes," *Christianity Today*, 9 April 1971, 9.
16. Ratzinger, Jesus of Nazareth, 175–76. Joseph Aloisius Ratzinger was elected the 265th pope, head of the Catholic Church, and sovereign of the Vatican City State from 2005 until his resignation in 2013. In my view, as an Evangelical Protestant, he was one of the keenest theologians produced by the Roman Catholic Church in generations.
17. Lane, *Mark*, 533.
18. Wilkinson, *Jerusalem*, 136–37.
19. Schnabel, *The Last Days*, 258–59.
20. These are not the only charges the Jews made against the Savior. Josef Blinzler lists others: blasphemy (Mark 2:7; John 5:18; 8:59; cf. Lev 24:16; Exod 22:27), profanation of the Sabbath (Mark 2:24; 3:2–6; John 5:16; 9:16; cf. Numbers 15:35; Exod 31:14–15; 35:2), sorcery/necromancy (Mark 3:22; John 8:48; 10:20; cf. Exod 22:17; Lev 19:26, 31; 20:27; Deut 18:10–11), false prophecy (Mark 6:15; Matt 21:11, 46; Luke 7:16, 39; 13:33; John 6:14; 7:40, 52; 9:17; cf. Deut 13:6; 18:20). Blinzler, *The Trial*, 86.

21. Evans, *The Final Days*, 41–42.
22. ———, *The Final Days*, 41–42.
23. Clarke, *Commentary*, 1967.
24. Bock, "Blasphemy," 635.
25. Kohler, "Blasphemy" in *The Jewish Encyclopedia*.
26. Brown, *Death*, 531.
27. Hooker, *Mark*, 173.
28. Bock, "Blasphemy," 247, 616.
29. Darrell L. Bock, "Blasphemy and the Jewish Examination of Jesus," in *Key Events in the Life of the Historical Jesus*, Darrell L. Bock and Robert L. Webb, eds. Grand Rapids, MI: Eerdmans, 2010, 661.
30. Wilkinson, *Jerusalem*, 137.
31. Sherwin-White, *Roman Society*, 3, 4–5, 8.
32. ———, *Roman Society*, 12.
33. Caesar, *Gallic Wars* 2.1.3; 5.41.5; 77.14–16; Velleius 2.37.5; 117.3–4.
34. Sherwin-White, *Roman Society*, 4,5,9, quoting *Digesta iuris Romani*, 1.16,6; i.18,8–9 in *Corpus Iuris Civilis*.
35. Jolowicz, *Roman Law*, 412.
36. See Garnsey, *Social Status*, 121.
37. Lyall, "*Roman law*," *The Evangelical Quarterly* 48 (January-March 1976):12.
38. Garnsey, "Governors," *JRS* 58 (1968), 51–59.
39. Brown, *Death*, 478.
40. Bammel, *The Trial*, 7.
41. Berger, *Encyclopedic Dictionary*,418. See also Cohn, *Trial*, 171–72.
42. *Digesta, The Digest of Justinian*, vol. 4, Watson, et al., 48.4.1, 11.
43. Hunter, *Introduction*, 58–59; Theodore Mommsen, *The History of Rome*, vols. 1–5. Oxford: Benediction Classics, 2011, 423.
44. Sherwin-White, *Roman Society*, 13.
45. Jolowicz, *Historical Introduction*, 413.
46. Barclay, *Mark*, 358–59.
47. See Chapman, *The Trial*, 243ff.
48. Egypt Exploration Fund, *The Oxyrhynchus Papyri*, Grenfell, et al.,1898.
49. Berger, *Encyclopedic Dictionary*, 648.
50. Mommsen, *History of Rome*, 149, 362.
51. Campbell, "Praetorium,"11:775.
52. William. *Dictionary*, 2013.
53. Powell, *The Trial*, 102; see also Steele, "The Pavement" *ExpTim* 34 (1922–23), 562–63.
54. Quiller-Couch, *Art of Writing*, 562–63.
55. Schnabel, *The Last Days*, 276.
56. Singer, *Cross Examination*, 23–24.
57. Schürer, *History*, 55.
58. ———, *History*, 48–49. See also *Ant.* 17.10.2–3; *Wars* 2.17.8.
59. Vincent, "Chronique," *RB* 42 1933, 83–113.
60. See de Sion, "La Forteresse Antonia," 1955.
61. Josephus, *Wars* 1.21.1
62. Shimon Gibson, "The Trial of Jesus at the Jerusalem Praetorium: New Archaeological Evidence," in Craig A. Evans, ed., *The World of Jesus and the Early Church* (Peabody, MA: Hendrickson Publishers, 2011), pp. 97–118.
63. Josephus, *Wars* 5.4.3.
64. Josephus, *Antiquities* 15.9.3.

65. Philo, vol. 10, *On the Embassy to Gaius*, 299–306.
66. See Brown, "John (13–21)," 845.
67. See Benoit, *Jesus and the Gospel*, 1168–182; see also Lane, *Mark*, 549; Blinzler, *The Trial*, 256–59; and Mackowski, *Jerusalem*, 104.
68. Magness, *Archaeology*, 158–59.
69. Gibson, "The Trial, 104.
70. Mommsen, *History of Rome*, 149, 362.
71. See Lattey, "The Praetorium of Pilate" *JTS* 11 (`1930) 180–82.
72. Berger, *Encyclopedic Dictionary*, 693; Symmachus, *Epistulae* 10.23.4.
73. MacElree, *The Trial*, 50.
74. For a running account of Jesus' trial before Pilate see Schnabel, *The Last Days*, Table 13, 272–73.
75. See Himmelfarb, *De-Moralization*, 1994.
76. Mansfield, *Killing Jesus.*, 144–45.
77. See Crook, *Consilium Principis*, , 21–30; see further, Bammel, *Theologische Literaturzeitung*, 77, 205–10.
78. Phillips, *The View*, 128–29.
79. Benoit, *The Passion*, 149–50.
80. Maier, *Fullness*, 156.
81. Groenings, *The Passion*, 235.
82. See Tacitus, *The Annals*, I. I c. 72, 73, 74; Suetonius, *Lives*, in Tiberius, c. 58.
83. Hoehner, *Chronological Aspects*, 111.
84. Schilder: *Christ on Trial*, 494–95.
85. Cary, "Lady Macbeth," *The New York Times*, September 12, 2006.
86. William Shakespeare used this image in his 1606 classic play, *The Tragedy of Macbeth*. In Act V, Scene 1, Lady Macbeth becomes racked with guilt from the crimes she and her husband have committed. She compulsively washes her hands, attempting to wash off imaginary bloodstains, and famously begs, "*Out, damned spot! out, I say!*" Shakespeare may have popularized the idea of washing your hands to relieve yourself of guilt, but it was Pontius Pilate who initiated the practice in literature.
87. McDowell, *Resurrection Factor*, 1981.
88. When Hieron II became king of Sicily in 215 BC, there was a *coup* attempting to replace him. When the *coup* failed, he had Thraso, the leader of the *coup* attempt, tortured. The verb torture (Latin: *torque*) means "to turn, twist, distort, or wrench." It is used when, as in the case of Thraso, the limbs of the body are twisted or wrenched to extract information or inflict cruel punishment.
89. Meister, *Adranodorus*, 153.
90. Davis, " Crucifixion," 183–87.
91. Hutton, *There*, 115–16.
92. The fact that the Jews have been a "wandering people" was not just a misfortune; it was the promise of God as a result of their disobedience. The Prophet Hosea knew that when he said, "My God will reject them because they have not listened to him; they shall be wanderers among the nations" (Hos 9:17).
93. See Cohn, *Trial*, 1971.
94. ———, *Trial*, 96.
95. Haim Cohn's book caused a lot of buzz when it was first published because he had served as an Attorney General and a Supreme Court justice in Israel. Nevertheless, his premises and theories in the book did not live up to his credentials. His hypothesis that the Sanhedrin was trying to protect Jesus and not kill him is ludicrous and has not been given serious acceptance by the academic community.

96. In 2013, Dola Indidis, a Kenyan lawyer, actually petitioned the International Court of Justice in The Hague asking it to declare the trial of Jesus invalid because it was conducted in a manner contrary to the principles of a fair trial. Lawyer Indidis said, "I want a declaratory judgment declaring that the trial judgment and sentence entered were badly done and therefore null and void." He did not get a judgment.

97. Jaubert, *La Date*, 1957.

98. Although there is some debate about the exact location of Caiaphas' palace, if you visit the Roman Catholic site of St. Peter in Gallicantu you will descend through three levels within the church. The lowest one is a dungeon presumably where the High Priest kept those awaiting trial or a sentence.

99. For more on the God who calls himself "the I Am," see Kroll, *The I AM God*, 1998.

100. The Mishnah tractate *Sanhedrin* records many disqualifying factors for a witness including: "A dice player, a usurer, pigeon racers, or traffickers in Seventh Year produce." Also, relatives are disqualified as witnesses. "A suitor's father, brother, father's brother, mother's brother, sister's husband, father's sister's husband, mother's sister's husband, mother's husband, father-in-law, or wife's sister's husband them and their sons and their sons-in-law; also the suitor's stepson only [but not the stepsons' sons]." It was a dizzying array of disqualifications. "A friend or an enemy [is disqualified]. 'A friend' is one's groomsman. 'An enemy' is anyone whom he has not spoken to in three days because of anger."

101. http://www.jewishencyclopedia.com/articles/3354-blasphemy

102. The most common, unfortunate expression of the twenty-first century—"Oh, my God"—violates explicitly the Third Commandment by speaking of God without a reason to do so.

103. The Tetragrammaton refers to the four Hebrew letters, read from right to left, - *yodh, he, waw,* and *he*—יהוה. "YHWH" (יהוה) which is the English transliteration of the covenant name of Israel's God. Jewish belief regards this name as too holy even to be pronounced. No one knows how to pronounce it correctly. Ancient Hebrew used only consonants, no vowels. Therefore, in translating "YHWH," both Jewish and Christian translators substituted a rough translation of the word "Lord" (אָדוֹן; English: 'âdôwn), which is another Hebrew name used for God. To indicate that "YHWH" was the original Hebrew word in the text, however, publishers of Bible translations in English printed "LORD" in all capitals, as opposed to "Lord." There is no consensus about the etymology or the pronunciation of the name.

104. http://www.jewishencyclopedia.com/articles/3354-blasphemy

105. Throughout the *Tanakh*, the Hebrew Old Testament, the Jewish people always recognized the right hand as the symbol of power, support, and privilege (see Exod 15:6, 12; Deut 33:2; Pss 16:8, 11; 18:35; 20:6; 44:1–3; 60:5; 63:8; 73:23; 78:54; 80:17; 89:13; 98:1; 108:6; 109:31; 118:15–16; 138:7, 10; Prov 3:16; Isa 48:13; 62:8; Lam 2:3; Hab 2:16; *et al*).

106. Edersheim, *Life and Times*, 309.

107. Moore, *Judaism*, vol. 2, 197, n. 5.

108. Danby, "Rabbinical Criminal Code," *JTS* 21 (1919–1920), 51–76.

109. Blinzler, Das Synedrium von Jerusalem, 1961.

110. Strobel, *Die Stunde*, 46–94.

111. https://www.namb.net/apologetics-blog/passion-problems/

112. See Brown, *Death*, vol. 1, 330.

113. ———, *Death*, 331.

114. See Neusner, *Mishnaic Law*, 5:101–3, 169–73.

115. Blinzler, *The Trial*, 157.

116. Halitzah is the process by which a childless widow and a brother of her deceased husband may avoid the duty to marry under the law of levirate marriage.

117. In historical Jewish practice, *kareth* was a form of punishment that may mean premature death, or perhaps exclusion from the people.

118. Chandler, *The Trial*, 187.

119. Lohse, Martyrer, 40. In Latin *jus gladii* literally means "the right of the sword" and refers to the legal authority of an individual or nation to execute someone for a capital offense.

120. Blinzler, *The Trial*, 223–24.

121. Neusner, *Mishnaic Law*, 105–10, 169–73.

122. Strobel, *Die Stunde*, 81–84.

123. The subject of being led astray is mentioned frequently in the scrolls (Cf. 1QM XIV, 9; 1Qha XII, 8, 9; 4Q200 Fragments 6, 8; 4Q504 Fragments 1–2 V, 12; 4Q509 Fragments 12 I–13, 1; 11Q5 XVIII, 6; 4Q491 Fragments 8–10 I, 7).

124. Powell, *The Trial*, 80.

125. Schnabel, *The Last Days*, 265.

126. Wilkinson, *Jerusalem*, 131–33.

127. https://www.namb.net/apologetics-blog/passion-problems/

128. Blinzler, *The Trial*, 1959; see also Jeremias, *Jerusalem*, 178.

129. ———, "Das Synedrium," 60.

130. Bammel, *The Trial*, 152.

131. Appel, *Judicial Monitor*, Jul/Aug 2007, vol. 2, is 2.

132. See the Statute of the Permanent Court of International Justice art. 38(1)(3) and the Statute of the International Court of Justice art. 38(1)(c).

133. MacArthur, *Murder*, 104–5.

134. Schilder, *Christ on Trial*, 370.

135. Brown, *Death*, 912.

136. Tacitus, *Annals*, 2, 32; 15, 60; 14, 33; Plutarch, *Galba*, 9; Plautus, *Pseudolus*, 12.5.98.

137. Horace, *Epodes*, V, 99, and the scholia of Crusius; Pliny, *Naturalis Historia*. 36. 107.

138. Justus Lipsius, *Iusti Lipsi*, 2018.

139. Johnson, "Medical" 70 (3):97–102.

140. Brown, *Death*, 912.

141. Murphy-O'Connor, *The Holy Land*, 50.

142. Kiehl, *The Passion*, 132.

143. For information about walking the Rampart Walk see https://www.touristisrael.com/ramparts-walk/7767/

144. For a complete discussion of the problems identifying the "third wall" see "The Jerusalem Wall That Shouldn't Be There," Hershel Shanks, *BAR* 13:03, May-June 1987.

145. The following Bible translations also use the noun "Calvary": Wycliffe 1395; Tyndale 1524; Coverdale 1535; The Great Bible 1540; Matthew's Bible 1549; the Bishops' Bible 1568; the Geneva Bible 1557 to 1599; The Beza N.T. 1599; the Mace NT. 1729; the Worsley N.T. 1770; the Haweis N.T. 1795; the Thomson Translation 1808; Webster Bible 1833;, The Revised English Bible 1877; The Clarke N.T. 1913; the New Life Version 1969; the NKJV 1982; the KJV 21st Century Version 1994; Worldwide English NT. 1998; The Third Millennium Bible 1998; The Revised Geneva Bible 2005; and others. Some versions, such as the Douay-Rheims 1582 and the Wycliffe Bible. translate this word as "Calvary" in all four of the Gospels.

146. The Worldwide English New Testament [WE] translates all four Gospel accounts as they do Matthew 27:33, "They came to a place called Golgotha. That means, `The place of a head bone.'"

147. Wilson, *Golgotha*, 24–29.
148. Jeremias, *Golgotha*, 2.
149. Evans, "The Holy Sepulchre," *PEQ* 100 (1968), 112.
150. Wilson, *Golgotha*, 24–29.
151. Phillips, *The View*, 203.
152. Chrysostom, *John*, 756.
153. For more information, see Napier, *History*, 2005.
154. Schmidt, *A Scandalous Beauty*, 34.
155. Thiering, *Secret*, 113–15.
156. Martin, *Secrets*, 10.
157. *Mishnah Parah* 3:6. "The red heifer, the goat for Azazel, and the red wool (used in the Yom Kippur service) are paid for by using communal funds from the Temple treasury. The ramp for the heifer, the ramp for the goat, the thread between the goat's horns, the channel of water in the Temple, the Jerusalem city wall and its towers, and all city needs were paid for using money left in the treasury after the sacrificial needs were met. Abba Shaul said the kohanim paid for the ramp for the heifer using their own funds" (*Shekalim* 4.2). Of the Talmudic books, Shekalim deals with the size and weight of the shekel. Thus, the discussion of paying for the ramp for the red heifer.
158. In Jewish thinking, the sages say, "Man was created from the very spot which atones for him" (*B'reishith Rabbah* 14:6). The exact location of the altar associated with the Holy of Holies has been established since eternity. King David and King Solomon built an altar on this site in the days of the First Temple. In the Second Temple, the altar was erected at the very same site. In Jewish belief, this is the very spot where Adam, the first man, was created. It was on this spot on Mount Moriah that Abraham, in a test of faith, built an altar and was prepared to sacrifice his only son Isaac.
159. Martin, *Secrets*, 15.
160. For the importance of the east, see Hutchinson, "Further Notes" in *PEQ* (July 1873): 113–15.
161. Martin, *Secrets*, 24; *Babylonian Talmud*, Yoma 68b.
162. ———, *Secrets*, 24.
163. ———, *Secrets*, 85.
164. The closest to using the word "thing" was found in the rather obscure Disciples' Literal New Testament, the Orthodox Jewish Bible, and the Wycliffe Bible.
165. Martin, *Secrets*, 82.
166. Charles George Gordon, the son of a Royal Artillery officer, entered the Royal Military Academy in 1848. In 1860, Gordon was posted to China as part of the Allied Expeditionary Force that was fighting the Second Opium War. Gordon became known as 'Chinese Gordon' back in England. In 1884 when the Mahdi, a Muslim fundamentalist leader, led a revolt in Sudan against Anglo-Egyptian rule, the British government appointed "Chinese" Gordon as Governor General of Sudan. He arrived in Khartoum in February 1884. When the Mahdi besieged Gordon in Khartoum, the government was implored by everyone, including the Queen, to send a relief mission. Parliament refused until October 1884. The relief column reached Khartoum 2 days after it fell to the Mahdi on January 26, 1885. Gordon was murdered at this battle or some point after it.
167. Gordon, *Reflections*, 2019.
168. Conder, *Tentwork*, 2019.
169. ———, *The City of Jerusalem*, 2005.
170. Chadwick, "Revisiting Golgotha" *Religious Educator* 4, no. 1 (2003): 13–48.
171. Eusebius, *Onomasticon*, 74.
172. Finegan, *Archeology*, 110.
173. "Description of the Holy Fire," holyfire.org.; Auxentios of Photiki, *The Paschal Fire*, 1999

174. For professional pictures of the Church of the Holy Sepulchre, see http://justfunfacts.com/interesting-facts-about-the-church-of-the-holy-sepulchre/
175. Dumper, *Cities*, 2007.
176. Fisher-Ilan, *"Punch-up" The Guardian. London. (September 28, 2004)*.
177. El Deeb. *"Christians Brawl" San Francisco Chronicle, (April 21, 2008)*.
178. See: "Riot Police," *The Times*, November 10, 2008, and Toni O'Laughlin November 10, 2008. "The monks," *The Guardian*.
179. According to tradition, the Nuseibeh family took its name from a woman named Nusayba, who complained to the Prophet Muhammad about the unfair treatment of women. Nusayba was an early example of women taking leadership roles in Islam. Since the Muslim conquest of Jerusalem in the seventh century, the Sunni Muslim family has held the key to the Church of the Holy Sepulchre. This arrangement emerged during the days of the second Muslim caliph, Umar Ibn al-Khattab. This caliph awarded the keys to the church to avoid clashes among rival Christian groups for control over it.
180. McMahon, "Holy Sepulchre" in *Catholic Encyclopedia*, 1913.
181. See Kroesen, *The Sepulchrum*, 11.
182. Fergusson, *Architecture*, 2010.
183. Gold, *The Fight*, 2007.
184. Savage, "Pilgrimages," 37.
185. Ágoston, "Suleyman I" in the *Encyclopedia of the Ottoman Empire*, 541–45.
186. Serr, "Golgotha" *BAR*. May/June 2016.
187. Kateregga, *Islam and Christianity*, 141.
188. "The Muslim World," J. Dudley Woodberry, 164.
189. Deedat, *Cruci-fiction?* 2011).
190. For additional biblical and historical proof that Jesus died and was raised from the dead, read these New Testament references. Matt 17:22–23; 20:17–18; Mark 8:31; Mark 9:9, 30–31; Luke 24:5; John 2:22; 20:8–9; 19:48–49; 21:14; Acts 4:10; 17:2–3, 31: 26:22–23; Rom 1:2–4; 6:10; 7:4; 8:11, 34; 14:9, 15; 1 Cor 8:11; 15:12–20; Gal 1:1; Col 1:18; 1 Thess 1:9–10.
191. *The Gospel of Barnabas*, of Ebionite origin, 202, or Diatessaronic origin, Joosten, *HTR* 95 (1) 2002: 73–96.
192. Anawati, "Īsā" in *Encyclopaedia of Islam*, 2005.
193. For an alternative view of the disciples, see Robyn Walsh, *The Origins of Early Christian Literature: Contextualizing the New Testament Within Greco-Roman Literary Culture*. Cambridge, UK: Cambridge University Press, 2023.
194. Zugibe, *Forensic Inquiry*, 145.
195. Flygt, *Notorious*, 1963.
196. Bahrdt, *Ausführung*, 2019.
197. Joyce, *The Jesus Scroll*. 1973.
198. Sklar, *King Arthur*, 214.
199. Miller, *The Da Vinci Con, New York Times*, February 22, 2004.
200. Thiering, *Jesus the Man*, 2006.
201. *The New York Review of Books*, Dec 1, 1994.
202. Wright, *Who was Jesus?* 23.
203. Kerston, *Jesus lebte in Indien*, 1998.
204. ———, *Jesus Lived in India*, 260.
205. Parmeshwaranand, "Bhavisya Purana," 278ff and Doniger, *Purāna Perennis*, 105.
206. Kaplan, "Life after 'The Da Vinci Code.'" *Parade*, September 13, 2009.
207. Mirsch, *The Open Tomb*, 2011.
208. Edwards, Physical Death, vol. 255, no. 11.

209. Zugibe, *Forensic Inquiry*, 161–62.
210. Strauss, *The Life of Jesus*, 412.
211. McDowell, *The New Evidence*, 223–25.
212. Craig, *On Guard*, 252.
213. Strobel, *The Case for Christ*, 200–201).
214. While these are scholars, it is important to remember that views such as these are mere speculation, pure guesswork. There is no written tradition or archaeological suggestion, let alone proof, that Jesus body was treated as a common criminal. On the other hand, the Bible clearly and repeatedly maintains that Jesus was buried in the tomb of Joseph of Arimathea.
215. Guignebert, *Jesus*, 1956.
216. Loisy, *The Birth*, 1962.
217. Crossan, *The Birth of Christianity*, 542.
218. ———, *Who Killed Jesus?* ch 6; *The Historical Jesus*, 392–93.
219. Kee, "Quests," *Theology Today*, 52 (1995): 22; 24.
220. Wright, *Victory of God*, 44; Crossan, *The Historical Jesus*, 1992.
221. Meyer, *The Historical Jesus*, CBQ 55 [1993], 576.
222. Philo, *In Flaccum*, 83; Josephus, *Life*, 420–421; Plutarch, *Antonius*, 2; Cicero, *Orationes Phillippicae*, 2.7.17–18.
223. Magness, "Jesus' Tomb, *BAR*, 2006, 212–26.
224. *The Digest of Justinian*, vol. 4. bk. 48, 863.
225. The Jewish Encyclopedia says, "According to R. Jose b. Ḥalafta, the members of the Great Bet Din were required to possess the following qualifications: scholarship, modesty, and popularity among their fellow men (Tosefta, *Ḥagigah* 2.9; Sanhedrin 88b) . . . R. Johanan, a Palestinian amora of the third century, enumerates the qualifications of the members of the Sanhedrin as follows: they must be tall, of imposing appearance, and of advanced age" (*Sanhedrin*. 19a).
226. A *kokh* (Hebrew: כוך; English: *kokh*; plural: *kokhim* or *kokîm*) is a complex in which the enshrouded bodies of the dead are placed in niches cut into the rock wall that are just slightly larger than the body. These niches could be cut lengthwise or widthwise. An arcosolium, from the Latin *arco*- (a derivative of the Latin *arcus* meaning "bow") plus *solium* meaning "seat" (derived from *sedere*, "to sit") is an arched recess cut into the rock face of a tomb with a shelf that is used as a place of entombment.
227. See https://ofm.org/blog/know-tomb-jesus-since-opened/
228. Wilson, *The Evidence*, 137.
229. Egypt unveils biggest ancient coffin find in over a century. Archaeology World Team, October 20, 2019.
230. Stevenson, *Verdict*, 41.
231. For a comparison of these differing Greek words, see Arndt, *A Greek-English Lexicon*, 177, 264, 270.
232. Stevenson, *Verdict*, 41.
233. *Code of Jewish Law*, 'Laws of Mourning,' chs 351–52.
234. "Aloe," *World Checklist*.
235. See Sylva, "Nicodemus" *NTS* 34 (1988): 148–51.
236. Nazianzus, *Epistle* 18, Tome 1, 781.
237. Henry, Commentary, 2014. https://www.christianity.com/bible/commentary.php?com=mh&b=40&c=27
238. Benoit, *The Passion*, 226.
239. Baring-Gould, *The Death*, 45–46.
240. See Edersheim, *The Life and Times*, ch 15.
241. Baring-Gould, *The Death*, 46.

242. For a full description, see McBirnie, *Search*, 1975, and Barkay, "The Garden Tomb," *BAR*, March/April 1986.

243. Pappe, *Modern Palestine*, 2006.

244. For a complete discussion of the problems in identifying the "third wall" see "The Jerusalem Wall That Shouldn't Be There," Hershel Shanks, *BAR* 13:03, May-June 1987.

245. Conder, *Tentwork*, 372.

246. ———, *Tentwork*, 372–73.

247. ———, *Tentwork*, 373.

248. Kloner, "Sobah," *Hadashot Archaelogiot* 78–79 (1982), 71–71 (in Hebrew).

249. McRay, *Archaeology*, 207.

250. Conder, PEF Quarterly Statement, April 1890, 69–70.

251. Hanauer, PEF Quarterly Statement, July 1892, 199.

252. See Murphy-O'Connor, "The Holy Land, 21.

253. Adrian J. Boas, *Crusades*, 53.

254. Barkay, "The Garden Tomb," *BAR* March/April 1986, 50.

255. See Mazar, "Damascus Gate Jerusalem," *IEJ* 26, 1976, 1–8.

256. These suppositions were made by Ron Wyatt, a former nurse anesthetist who became an enthusiast of archaeology. Known for his "discoveries" (more than 100 of them) of Bible-related locations, including Noah's ark and the ark of the covenant, Wyatt's work has been dismissed by scientists, historians, biblical scholars, and the entire academic community in general.

257. Hachlili, *Jewish Funerary Customs*, 2004.

258. Kloner, "Rolling Stone" *BAR* 25, no. 5 (September/October 1999:28).

259. ———, "Rolling Stone" *BAR* 25, no. 5 (September/October 1999:28.

260. Barkay, "The Garden Tomb," *BAR*, March/April 1986.

261. McRay, *Archaeology*, 212.

262. Murphy-O'Connor, "The Garden Tomb" *BAR* 12:2, March/April 1986.

263. There is a beautiful website created by Galyn Wiemers that provides pictures, diagrams, and explanations of nearly every feature of the Church of the Holy Sepulchre: http://www.generationword.com/jerusalem101/52-holy-sepulcher.html.

264. Murphy-O'Connor, *The Holy Land*, 56, 59.

265. See Romey, "Jesus Burial Tomb," October 31, 2016.

266. Goldman, "Tomb of Jesus," The New York Times, March 22, 2017. Additional funding was provided by three denominations and a personal contribution made by King Abdullah II of Jordan.

267. See McMahon, "Holy Sepulchre" in the *Catholic Encyclopedia*; Eusebius, *Life of Constantine*, 1999; Renner, "Tomb of Christ?," 1996.

268. Stephenson, *Constantine*, 206.

269. Bahat, "Holy Sepulchre," *BAR* 12 (1986), 26–45.

270. Wilkinson, *Jerusalem*, 146.

271. For the history of the site of Golgotha, see Gibson, *Beneath*, 1994.

272. The *nomen gentilicium* or "gentile name" designated a Roman citizen as a member of a particular *gens*—a "family" or "clan"—which constituted an extended Roman family, all of whom claimed descent from a common ancestor and shared the same *nomen*.

273. Speller, *Following Hadrian*, 218.

274. Wilkinson, *Jerusalem*, 146–47.

275. For more information, see Serr, Archaeological Views, *BAR* 42:03.

276. For additional information, see Serr, Archaeological Views, *BAR* 42:03.

Endnotes

277. Major cities in which there are cathedrals dedicated to Alexander Nevsky include Warsaw and Łódź (Poland), Belgrade (Serbia), Yalta (Crimea), Tbilisi, (Georgia), and half a dozen Russian cities including St. Petersburg and Moscow.

278. See Drijvers, *Helena Augusta*, 1991, and Thiede, *The Quest*, 2000.

279. On the Sessorian palace and Santa Croce, see Affanni, ed., *La Basilica di S. Croce*, 1997.

280. Eusebius's obvious appreciation for the emperor is evident in the way he wrote about Constantine. "Thus, like a faithful and good servant, did he act and testify, openly declaring and confessing himself the obedient minister of the supreme King" (*Life of Constantine*, 1.6); "Constantine, the friend of God" (*Life of Constantine*, 1.52); "God himself, whom Constantine worshiped" (*Life of Constantine* 1.4).

281. Drijvers, *Helena Augusta*, 1991.

282. The Greek and Latin versions of the Helena legend can be explored in Rufinus (*Historia Ecclesiastica*, 10.7–8), Socrates (*Historia Ecclesiastica* 1.17 *PG* 67, 117ff), Sozomen (*Historia Ecclesiastica* 2.1–2) Theodoretus (*Historia Ecclesiastica* 1.18), Ambrose (*De Obitu Theodosii* 40–49), Paulinus of Nola (*Epistulae*, 31.4–5), and Sulpicius Severus (*Chronica* 2.22–34).

283. Jeffery, A *Brief Description*, 2.

284. González, "14—Official Theology, 129.

285. The first words of the Introduction to *The Pilgrimage of Etheria* by M. L. McClure are: "This book was discovered by Signor Gamurrini in an MS. Of the eleventh century at Arezzo, and he published it first in 1887." McClure, *The Pilgrimage of Etheria*, 7.

286. Jeffery, *A Brief Description*, 4.

287. ———, *A Brief Description*, 4.

288. Jerusalem, and the Church of the Holy Sepulchre, in particular, was mentioned as the center of the Earth by Arculf, the seventh-century bishop who toured the Holy Land in around 680 AD and is called "the place called Compass" by Sæwulf.

289. Rhodes "Optically, 461–488.

290. See Dalton, *Franks Bequest*, 27, note 174.

291. An ampulla or ampullae in the plural, in Ancient Rome, was a small round glass vessel, usually made with two handles. It was used for sacred purposes such as containing holy water or holy oil in the Middle Ages. Ampullae were often purchased in Jerusalem as souvenirs and taken back to Europe.

292. See Grabar, *Les Ampoules des Terre Sainte*, 1958.

293. Meshorer, "Ancient Gold Ring," *BAR* 12.3 (1986): 46–48.

294. Rousseau, *Jesus and His World*, 169.

295. ———, *Jesus and His World*, 167–68. The singular presence of the so-called "Herod family tomb" to the west of Jerusalem's Old City, on the grounds of the present-day King David Hotel, is explained by its distance from the Temple Mount—over 2,000 cubits, or 3,000 feet.

296. ———, *Jesus and His World*, 169.

297. Yaakov Meshorer, "Ancient Gold Ring Depicts the Holy Sepulchre," *BAR* 12.3 (1986): 46–48).

298. Eusebius, *Life of Constantine* 3.46. For modern stories about Helena, see, e.g., Waugh's *Helena*, 1950, and the recently published *Priestess of Avalon* by Bradley, 2001.

299. Prakash Pillappa, *Civic Sense*. New Delhi, India: Excel Books India, 2012, 116.

300. Willens & Baez, Personal Injury Lawyers, P.C. What Is Emotional Pain and Suffering? | Willens & Baez (willenslaw.com)

301. The kidneys are a pair of bean-shaped organs located below the rib cage behind your belly, one on each side of the spine. The kidneys help remove waste products from the body, maintain balanced electrolyte levels, and regulate blood pressure. Each kidney is approximately 4 or 5 inches long, around the size of a fist. (*Medical News Today*, January 05, 2023). Kidneys: Location, function, anatomy, pictures, and related diseases (medicalnewstoday.com)

302. Stroud, *A Treatise*, 102–3.

303. Spurgeon, *Christ's Words*, 52.

304. Philo, *In Flaccum*, vol. 4 of the *Works of Philo Judaeus*, 36–38. See also Cassius Dio 64.20–21 for a similar treatment of the deposed Emperor Vitellius (69 AD).

305. Groenings, *Hidden Meaning*, 3–4.

Bibliography

Abrahams, Israel. *Studies in Pharisaism and the Gospels*, 2nd series. New York: Ktav, 1967.

Allen, J. E. "Why Pilate," in Ernst Bammel, *The Trial of Jesus*. London: SCM, 1970.

Appel, James G., co-editor. *The International Judicial Monitor*, American Society of International Law and the International Judicial Academy Jul/Aug 2007, vol. 2, issue 2.

Bammel, Ernst, ed. *The Trial of Jesus*. London: SCM, 1970.

Barclay, William. *Crucified and Crowned*. London: SCM, 1961.

William Barclay, *William Barclay's Daily Study Bible, The Gospel of Mark*. Louisville, KY: WJK, rev ed, 1975.

Baring-Gould, Sabine. *The Death and Resurrection of Jesus*. New York: James Pott, 1888.

Barton, George A. "A Bone of Him Shall Not be Broken," *JBL* 49 (1930), 207–9.

Baumgarten, Joseph M., "Judicial Procedures" in *Exegetical Dictionary of the New Testament*, 3 vols. Edited by Horst Balz and Gerhard Schneider. Grand Rapids, MI: Eerdmans, 1990–993.

Benoit, Pierre. *The Passion and Resurrection of Jesus Christ*. New York: Herder and Herder, 1970.

Berger, Adolph. *Encyclopedic Dictionary of Roman Law*. Clark, NJ: The Lawbook Exchange, Ltd., 2014.

Blinzler, Josef. Das Synedrium von Jerusalem und die Strafprozeßordung der Mischna, *Zeitschrift für die neustetamentliche Wissenschaft* 52 (1961).

———. *The Trial of Jesus*. Westminster, MD: Newman, 1959.

Bock, Darrell L. "Blasphemy and the Jewish Examination of Jesus" in *Key Events in the Life of the Historical Jesus: A Collaborative Exploration of Context and Coherence*. Edited by Darrell L Bock and Robert L. Webb. Grand Rapids, MI: Eerdmans, 2010.

Brown, Raymond E. "The Gospel According to John (13–21)" in the *Anchor Bible* 29A. Garden City, NY: Doubleday 1970.

Campbell, J. B. "Praetorium," *Brill's New Pauly: Encyclopedia of the Ancient World*, Hubert Cancik, et al., eds., 22 vols, 11:775. Leiden: E. J. Brill, 2002–2012.

Cary, Benedict. "Lady Macbeth Not Alone in Her Quest for Spotlessness," *The New York Times*, September 12, 2006.

Chapman, David W. *Ancient Jewish and Christian Perceptions of Crucifixion*. Tübingen: Mohr Siebeck, 2008.

Chapman, David W. and Eckhard J. Schnabel, *The Trial and Crucifixion of Jesus: Texts and Commentary*. Peabody, MA: Hendrickson Publishers, 2019.
Chandler, Walter Marion. *The Trial of Jesus from a Lawyer's Standpoint*. vol. 1: *The Hebrew Trial*. New York: Empire, 1980.
Clarke, Adam. *Adam Clarke's Commentary on the Bible*, Ralph Earle, adaptor. Grand Rapids, MI: Baker, 1967.
Cohn, Haim. *The Trial and Death of Jesus*. New York: Harper & Row, 1971.
Conder, Claude Reignier. *Tent Work in Palestine: A Record of Discovery and Adventure*. New York: Wentworth, 2019.
Craig, William Lane. *On Guard*. Colorado Springs, CO: David C. Cook, 2010.
Crook, John. *Consilium Principis, Imperial Councils and Counsellors from Augustus to Diocletian*. Cambridge: University Press, 1955.
Crossan, John Dominic. *The Historical Jesus*. New York: HarperCollins, 1992.
Danby, Herbert. "The Bearing of the Rabbinical Criminal Code on the Jewish Trial Narratives in the Gospels." *JTS* 21 (1919–1920), 51–76.
Davis, C. T. "The Crucifixion of Jesus: The Passion of Christ from a Medical Point of View." *Arizona Medicine* 22:183–87, 1965.
Drijvers, Jan Willem. *Helena Augusta: The Mother of Constantine the Great and the Legend of Her Finding of the True Cross*. Leiden, Netherlands, Brill, 1991.
Edersheim, Alfred. *Life and Times of Jesus the Messiah*. 5 vols. Grand Rapids, MI: Eerdmans, 1962.
Evans, Craig A. and N. T. Wright, *Jesus, The Final Days*. Louisville, KY: WJK, 2009.
Finegan, Jack. *The Archeology of the New Testament*. Princeton, NJ: Princeton University Press, 1992.
Garnsey, Peter. "The Criminal Jurisdiction of Governors," *JRS* 58 (1968).
———. *Social Status and Legal Privilege in the Roman Empire*. London: Oxford University Press, 1970.
Gibson, Shimon and Joan E. Taylor. *Beneath the Church of the Holy Sepulchre, Jerusalem: The Archaeology and Early History of Traditional Golgotha*. London: PEF, 1994.
Gibson, Shimon. "The Trial of Jesus at the Jerusalem Praetorium: New Archaeological Evidence," in *The World of Jesus and the Early Church*. Edited by Craig A. Evans. Peabody, MA: Hendrickson, 2011.
Gordon, Charles G. *Reflections on Palestine*. New York: Wentworth, 2019.
Grenfell, Bernard P. et al., eds. *The Oxyrhynchus Papyri*, London: Egypt Exploration Fund/Society,1898.
Groenings, James. *The Passion of Jesus and Its Hidden Meaning*. Rockford, IL: Tan, 1987.
Hachlili, Rachel. *Jewish Funerary Customs, Practices and Rites in the Second Temple Period*. Leiden, Netherlands: Brill, 2004.
Himmelfarb, Gertrude. *The De-Moralization of Society*. New York: Knopf, 1994.
Hoehner, Harold W. *Chronological Aspects of the Life of Christ*. Grand Rapids: Zondervan, 1977.
Hooker, Morna D. *The Son of Man in Mark: A Study of the Background of the Term "Son of Man" and Its Use in St. Mark's Gospel*. London: SPCK, 1967.
Humphreys, Colin J. *The Mystery of the Last Supper*. Cambridge: Cambridge University Press, 2011.
Hunter, W. A. *Introduction to Roman Law*, 9th ed. London: Sweet & Maxwell, 1934.
Hutton, John A. *There They Crucified Him*. New York: Doran, nd.
Jaubert, Anne. *La Date de la Cène: Calendrier Biblique et Liturgie Chrétienne*. Paris: Gabalda, 1957.

Jeremias, Joachim. *Golgotha*. Leipzig: Pfeiffer, 1926.
———. *Jerusalem in the Time of Jesus: An Investigation into Economic and Social Conditions during the New Testament Period*. Philadelphia: Fortress, 1969.
Jeffery, George. *A Brief Description of the Holy Sepulchre in Jerusalem and other Christian Churches in the Holy City*. Cambridge: Cambridge University Press, 1919.
Jolowicz, H. F. *Historical Introduction to the Study of Roman Law*. Cambridge: University Press, 2009.
Josephus, Flavius. *The Works of Josephus, Complete and Unabridged*. Translated by William Whiston. Peabody, MA: Hendrickson, 1987.
Juster, Jean. *Les Juifs dans l'empire romain. Leur condition juridique*, économique et social. 2 vols. Paris: Geuthner, 1914.
Kidger, Mark. *The Star of Bethlehem: An Astronomer's View*. Princeton, NJ: Princeton University Press, 1999.
Kiehl, Erich H. *The Passion of Our Lord*. Grand Rapids, MI: Baker, 1990.
Kirner, Guido O. *Strafgewalt und Provinzialherrschaft, Eine Untersuchung zur Strafgewaltspraxis der romischen Statthalter in Judea (6–66 AD)* Berlin: Duncker & Humblot, 2004.
Kohler, Kaufmann and David Werner Amram. "Blasphemy" in *The Jewish Encyclopedia*.
Kroll, Woodrow. *The I AM God*. Lincoln, NE: Back to the Bible, 1998.
Lane, William L. *The Gospel According to Mark*. Grand Rapids, MI: Eerdmans, 1974.
Lattey, Cuthbert. "The Praetorium of Pilate" *JTS* 11 (`1930) 180–82.
Lietzmann, Hans. *Der Prozess Jesu, in Kleine Schriften II, Text un Untersuchungen* 68. Berlin: Akademie-Verlag, 1958.
Lohse, Eduard. *Martyrer und Gottesknecht. Untersuchungen zur unchristlichen Verkündigung vom Sühntod Jesu Christi*, 2. Durchgesehene und erweiterte Auflage. Göttingen: Vanderhoeck & Ruprecht, 1963.
Lyall, Francis. *"Roman law in the Writings of Paul—Aliens and Citizens,"* *EQ* 48 (January-March 1976):12.
MacArthur, John. *The Murder of Jesus*. Nashville: Word, 2000.
MacElree, Wilmer W. *The Trial of Jesus*. West Chester, PA: D. Edwards Biehn, 1940.
Mackowski, Richard M. *Jerusalem, City of Jesus: An Exploration of the Traditions, Writing, and Remains of the Holy City from the Time of Christ*. Grand Rapids, MI: Eerdmans, 1980.
Macleod, Donald. *Christ Crucified. Understanding the Atonement*. Downers Grove, IL: IVP Academic, 2014.
Magness, Jodi. *The Archaeology of the Holy Land*. New York: Cambridge University Press, 2012.
Maier, Paul L. *In The Fullness of Time*. Grand Rapids, MI: Kregel, 1997.
———. *Pontius Pilate*. Grand Rapids, MI: Kregel, 1968.
Mansfield, Stephen. *Killing Jesus*. Brentwood, TN: Worthy, 2013.
Martin, Ernest L. *Secrets of Golgotha*. Portland, OR: Associates for Scripture Knowledge, 1996.
McDowell, Josh. *The Resurrection Factor*. Nashville, TN: Campus Crusade, 1981.
McRay, John. *Archaeology and the New Testament* Grand Rapids: Baker Academic, 1991.
Meister, Klaus. Adranodorus in *Brill's New Pauly*, vol. 1, 22 vols. Hubert Cancik, et al., eds. Leiden: E. J. Brill, 2001.
Mommsen, Theodore. *The History of Rome*, vols. 1–5. Oxford: Benediction Classics, 2011.

Moore, George F. *Judaism in the First Centuries of the Christian Era*. Cambridge, MA: Harvard University Press, 1958.

Murphy-O'Connor, Jerome. *The Holy Land: An Oxford Archaeological Guide*. New York: Oxford University Press, 2008.

Neusner, Jacob. *A History of the Mishnaic Law of Damages*, 5 vols. Studies in Judaism in Late Antiquity 35. Leiden: E. J. Brill, 1982–1985.

Nicholson, William R. *The Six Miracles of Calvary*. Grand Rapids, MI: Discovery House, 2001.

Phillips, John. *The View from Mount Calvary*. Grand Rapids, MI: Kregel, 2006.

Philo, vol. 10, *On the Embassy to Gaius*. Translated by Francis Henry Colson. Cambridge, MA: Harvard University Press, 1962.

Powell, Frank J. *The Trial of Jesus Christ*, 3 vols. Grand Rapids, MI: Eerdmans, 1949.

Quiller-Couch, Arthur. *On the Art of Writing*. Mineola, NY: Dover, 2006.

Ratzinger, Joseph. *Jesus of Nazareth. Holy Week: From the Entrance into Jerusalem to the Resurrection*. San Francisco: Ignatius, 2011.

Rousseau, John J. and Rami Arav. *Jesus and His World: An Archaeological and Cultural Dictionary*. Minneapolis, MN: Fortress, 1995.

Schilder, Klaas. *Christ on Trial*. Minneapolis: Klock & Klock, 1978.

Schnabel, Eckhard J. *Jesus in Jerusalem. The Last Days*. Grand Rapids, MI: Eerdmans, 2018.

Schürer, Emil. *The History of the Jewish People in the Age of Christ* (175 BC–AD 135). Revised by Geza Vermes, et al. Edinburgh: T & T Clark, 1973–1987.

Sherwin-White, A. N. *Roman Society and Roman Law in the New Testament*. New York: Oxford University Press, 1963.

Singer, Randy. *The Cross Examination of Jesus Christ*. Colorado Springs, CO: Waterbrook, 2006.

Sion de, M. Aline. "*La Forteresse Antonia et la question du prétoire à Jérusalem.*" Jerusalem: Ex typis PP. Fransiscalium, 1955.

Smith, William. *Dictionary of Greek and Roman Antiquities*, 2nd ed. Cambridge: Cambridge University Press, 2013.

Spurgeon, Charles Haddon. *Christ's Words from the Cross*. Grand Rapids, MI: Baker, 1981.

———. *The Power of Christ's Tears*, edited by Lance Wubbels. Lynwood, WA: Emerald, 1996.

Steele, John Aulay. "The Pavement" *ET*, 34 (1922–23), 562–63.

Stephenson, Paul. *Constantine: Roman Emperor, Christian Victor*. New York: Overlook, 2010.

Stevenson, Kenneth E. and Gary R. Habermas, *Verdict on the Shroud*. Ann Arbor, MI: Servant, 1981

Strobel, August. *Die Stunde der Wahrheit: Untersuchungen zum Strafverfahren gegen Jesus*. Tübingen, Germany, Mohr Siebeck, 1980.

Stroud, William. *A Treatise on The Physical Cause of the Death of Christ*. London: Hamilton and Adams, 1847.

Suetonius. *The Lives of the Caesars*, vol. 1, *Julius. Augustus. Tiberius. Gaius. Caligula*. Translated by J. C. Rolfe. Cambridge, MA: Harvard University Press, 1914.

Taylor, Vincent. *The Cross of Christ* London: Macmillan, 1956.

Thiede, Carsten Peter and Matthew d'Ancona. *The Quest for the True Cross*. New York: Palgrave, 2000.

Tacitus. *The Annals of Imperial Rome*, Translated by John Jackson. Cambridge, MA: Harvard University Press, 1937.
Thiering, Barbara. *Jesus and the Secret of the Dead Sea Scrolls*. San Francisco: Harper, 1992.
Trocmé, Étienne. *The Childhood of Christianity*. London, SCM, 1997.
Vermes, Geza. *The Passion*. London: Penguin, 2005.
Vincent, L. H. "Chronique: L'Antonia et la Prétoire," *RB* 42 1933, 83–113.
Watson, Alan, et al., eds. *Digesta, The Digest of Justinian*, vol. 4, Philadelphia, PA: University of Pennsylvania Press, 1985.
Wilkinson, John. *Jerusalem as Jesus Knew It*. London: Thames and Hudson, 1978.
Wilson, Sir Charles William. *Golgotha and the Holy Sepulchre*. London: PEF, 1906.
Wilson, Ian. *Jesus: The Evidence*. San Francisco, CA: Harper San Francisco, 1997.
Witherington, Ben. "Biblical Views: The Turn of the Christian Era: The Tale of Dionysius Exiguus," *BAR* 43.6 (2017): 26.
Wright, N. T. *Who was Jesus?* Grand Rapids, MI: Eerdmans, 1993.
———. *Jesus and the Victory of God*. Minneapolis: Fortress, 1996, 44.
Yamauchi, Edwin M. "Historical Notes on the Trial and Crucifixion of Jesus Christ," *Christianity Today*, 9 April 1971.
Zugibe, Frederick T. *The Crucifixion of Jesus: A Forensic Inquiry*. Lanham, MD; M. Evans, 2005.

Author/Person Index

Abrahams, Israel, 5, 19
Africanus, Julius, 145
Ahmad, Hazrat Mirza Ghulam, 154,
    158, 189
Aristotle, 47, 52
Alexander, Cecil Frances, 102, 217
Alliata, Eugenio, 146, 173
Ambrose, 104
Arnobius of Sicca, 146
Augustine, 104

Bahrdt, Karl Friedrich, 153
Bammel, Ernst, 35
Barclay, William, 56
Barkay, Gabriel, 116, 191, 203, 204
Biagent, Michael, 109
Bishop, Jim, 34
Bishop of,
    Antioch, 147
    Caesarea, 215
    Constantinople, 34
    Durham, 157
    Ephesus, 165
    Jerusalem, 117, 124, 215, 234, 235
Bishops,
    Arculf, 264
    Basil the Great, 104
    Cyril, 234, 235
    Eusebius, 97, 120, 129, 130, 145,
        215, 218, 221, 222, 223, 225,
        226, 233, 234, 262
    Hypatius, 165
    Ignatius of Antioch, 144, 147

John Chrysostom, 84, 104
Macarius, 124, 215, 234
Samuel Gobat, 117
N. T. Wright, 157
Blake, William, 103
Blinzler, Josef, 11, 81, 86, 90
Blomberg, Craig, 81, 89
Bock, Darrell L., 22, 24, 33
Bolen, Ted, 119
Brown, Dan, 98, 135, 158
Brown, Raymond C., 11, 23, 81, 96, 128
Bunting, Henrich, 114, 128, 129, 130
Bunyan, John, 103

Cassiodorus, 145
Celsus, ix
Chandler, Walter, 80
Chapman, David W., 11, 23
Churchill, Winston, 28
Clarke, Adam, 21
Clephane, Elizabeth, xiii
Cohn, Haim, 59, 60, 61, 63, 64, 67, 69,
    71, 80, 255
Coke, Thomas, 49
Conder, Claude, 105, 117, 195, 202
Cook, Frederick Charles, 160
Corleone, Michael, 50
Craig, William Lane, 160
Crossan, John Dominic, 5, 165, 166

Danby, Herbert, 80
Deedat, Ahmad, 133
Defoe, Daniel, 103

Author/Person Index

Donne, John, 104, 105
Douglas, J. Archibald, 155

Edersheim, Alfred, 76, 172
Edwards, W. D., 159
El-Enany, Khaled, 174
Eliot, T. S., 155
Epiphanies of Salamis, 104
Evans, Craig, 20, 164
Ewen, Pamela Binnings, 71

Finegan, Jack, 120
Fox, George, 103

Gabel, W. J., 159
Gantry, Elmer, 28
Geike, Cunningham, 51
Gibson, Shimon, 43, 45
Gordon, General Charles "Chinese," ix, xxv, 116, 117, 118, 119, 120, 190, 192, 193, 216, 258
Graves, Robert, 155
Grenfell, Bernard Pyne, 37
Guignebert, Charles, 165

Heusler, Erika, 11
Hooker, Morna D., 24
Horace, 169
Hosmer, F. E., 159
Hull, Edward, 117
Hunt, Arthur Surridge, 37
Hutchinson, R. F., 113
Hutton, John A., 55

Ignatius of Antioch, 125, 127
Irenaeus, 144

Jerome, 94, 202, 234
Johnson, Charles Duane, 96
Jones, Jim, 28
Josephus, Flavius, ix
    Antiquities xxiv, 20, 37, 41, 43, 44, 144, 166
    Wars of the Jews, 20, 37, 41, 43, 44, 99, 100, 127, 166, 193
    Against Apion, 166
Joyce, Donovan Maxwell, 155, 156
Juster, Jean, 9

Justin, 144
Justinian, 170

Kerston, Holger, 157
Kee, Howard Clark, 165
Kiehl, Erich, 97
Kortens, Jonas, 117
Kroll, Woodrow Michael, ix, xiii, 80, 189, 252

Leigh, Richard, 156, 158
Lietzmann, Hans, 9
Lincoln, Henry, 156
Lipsius, Justus, 96
Lohse, Eduard, 86
Loisy, Alfred, 165

Macleod, George F., 95
Magness, Jodi, 44, 166
Martin, Ernest L., 110, 111, 113, 114, 115, 116, 118
Mattox, F. W., xii
McDowell, Josh, 160
McIntyre, John, 105
Meyer, Ben, 165
Mirsch, David, 159
Montgomery, James, 103
Mommsen, Theodor, 45
Moore, George Foot, 80
Müller, Max, 155
Murphy, Peter, 78
Murphy-O'Conner, Jerome, 210, 220

Notovitch, Nikolai Aleksandrovich, 154, 155

Origen, 104, 145

Paulus, Heinrich, 154
Peppard, Michael, 16
Philo, ix, 43, 166, 244
Philophonos, Johannes, 145
Plautus, 95
Podro, Joshua, 155
Porphyry, ix
Powell, Frank J., 86
Prince, Clive, 158

Quiller-Couch, Arthur, 38
Quintilian, 93

Re'em, Amit, 44
Rippon, John, 103

Sandys, George, 119
Schick, Conrad, 117, 127, 191, 192
Schilder, Klaas, 94
Schmidt, Thomas, 105
Schnabel, Eckhard J., 6, 11, 13, 39, 89
Schonfield, Hugh Joseph, 156
Schürer, Emil, 9, 41
Shalivahana, 158
Serr, Marcel, 127
Sherwin-White, E. N., 36
Starbird, Margaret, 158
Stevens, J. Clay, 96
Strauss, David, 160
Strobel, August, 81
Strobel, Lee, 160

Tacitus, 95
Taylor, Vincent, xii
Tertullian, 144, 153, 202
Thenius, Otto, 117, 193

Thiering, Barbara, 107, 108, 109, 110, 157
Tristram, Henry Baker, 117
Trueblood, Elton, 161

Ulpian, 165

Venerable Bede, 103
Venturini, Karl, 153
Vermes, Géza, 109, 157
Vieweger, Dieter, 127
Vincent, Père L. H., 42, 113

Wagner-Lux, Ute, 127
Warren, Sir Charles, 116
Watts, Isaac, 103
Wesley, Susanna, 103
Wilkinson, John, 13, 89, 216, 218
Wilson, Sir Charles, 12, 116, 104
Witherington III, Ben, 32
Wright, N. T., 20, 53, 157, 224

Yadin, Yigael, 156
Yamauchi, Edwin M., x, 11

Zugibe, Frederick T., 152, 159

Subject Index

Abraham, 28, 65, 175, 258
Achan, 82
Acts of Pilate, 152
Adam, 104, 105, 161, 175
Adam's skull, 104
Aelia Capitolina, 218, 220
Age of the Enlightenment, ix
Ahmadiyyas, 154
Al-Hakim bi-Amr Allah, 124
Ali az-Zahir, 124
Allah, 132, 133
Altar of the Cross, 220
Amicus Caesaris, 52, 53
Angel(s), 105, 133, 152, 184, 200, 201,
    223, 231, 236
Annas, xi, xxiii, xxiv, 1, 2, 3, 4, 5, 6, 11,
    16, 27, 55, 62, 63, 72, 87, 152,
    180, 238, 239
Antonia Fortress, ix, 41, 42, 44, 100, 194
Apostle's Creed, The, 169, 241
Archaeology, 107, 116, 127, 128, 174,
    191, 204, 229, 261
Athaliah, 7
Athens, 187, 214
Ayyubid Dynasty, 125

Babylonia(n), 40, 87
Babylonian Captivity, 164
Babylonian Talmud, 61, 62, 95
Bahri Mamluk Dynasty, 125
Barabbas, 29, 31, 68, 240
Barnabas, 7, 146
Barnabas, Gospel of, 133, 146, 147
Basil the Great, 104

Basilica of St. John Lateran, 39
Battle of Hattin, 125
Bēma, Bēmatos, 36, 37
Beth ha-Deshen, 113
Bethlehem, 94, 110, 222, 251
Bhavishya Purāna, 158
Biblical Archaeology Review, 203, 208, 209
Blasphemy, 6, 7, 10, 17, 22, 23, 60, 69,
    75, 76, 88, 96, 169, 239, 253
"Boneyard," 103
"Broad Wall," 99
Bunhill Fields, 103, 104
Burji Mamluk Dynasty, 125

Caesar, 19, 28, 29, 35, 51, 52, 53, 145,
    166, 179, 181, 218
Caesarea,
    Maritima, 37, 46, 225
    Philippi, 14, 94
Caiaphas, xi, xv, xxiii, xxiv, 2, 3, 4, 5, 6, 7,
    8, 9, 10, 11, 12, 13, 15, 18, 19, 22,
    24, 27, 32, 34, 35, 47, 48, 50, 51,
    52, 53, 54, 55, 56, 57, 58, 59, 60,
    61, 62, 63, 64, 65, 66, 70, 71, 72,
    73, 74, 75, 76, 77, 79, 80, 85, 86,
    87, 88, 89, 90, 91, 147, 148, 152,
    178, 184, 238, 239, 243, 256
Calvaria, 101, 102; see Calvary
Calvary, ix, 56, 63, 93, 101, 102, 103,
    104, 116, 118, 119, 120, 130, 131,
    132, 135, 136, 137, 138, 139, 140,
    141, 142, 143, 144, 146, 154, 161,
    162, 187, 190, 193, 195, 216, 221,
    227, 235, 245, 251, 257

275

Subject Index

Calvary's Cross, 135, 136, 137, 138, 139, 140, 141, 142, 143, 144
Campus Esqulinus, 95, 105
Campus Martius, 187
Cana of Galilee, 94
Capernaum, 94
Catholic(s), ix, x, 11, 39, 40, 81, 102, 116, 121, 159, 165, 211, 212, 221, 253, 256
Centurion, The, 23, 36, 114, 115, 116, 137, 138, 152, 179
Cephas, 141, 168; see Peter
Chamber of Hewn Stone, The, 3, 11, 12, 13, 16, 61, 62, 74, 84, 87, 88, 89, 112
Chief Priests, 2, 3, 8, 9, 10, 11, 12, 26, 27, 28, 29, 32, 56, 68, 76, 87, 135, 138, 152, 243
Christ xxiv, 5, 6, 9, 10, 12, 14, 15, 16, 22, 26, 29, 30, 34, 48, 55, 64, 68, 70, 71, 86, 88, 91, 94, 103, 105, 108, 110, 112, 115, 132, 133, 134, 139–45, 147, 150, 158, 161, 168, 171, 179, 195, 201, 206, 210, 218, 237, 238, 241, 245, 247, 249, 251
Christ Crucified, 148
Christendom, 169, 170
Christian Quarter, 121, 216, 234
Chrysostom, 84, 104
Church of,
    The Anastasis, 121
    Armenian Apostolic Church, 121, 122
    Coptic Church of Egypt, 121
    England, 103
    Ethiopian Orthodox Tewahedo Church, 121, 211
    The Last Supper, 120
    The Redeemer, 26, 127, 216, 217, 219, 220
    The Resurrection, 126
    Saint-Étienne, 203
    St. John the Baptist, 126
    Saint Stephen, 203
    Syrian Orthodox Church of Antioch, 121
    The Witness of the Resurrection, 203
    Worldwide Church of God, 10

Church of the Holy Sepulchre, xxv, 98, 100, 103, 105, 107, 115, 120, 121, 122, 123, 124, 125, 126, 127, 128, 130, 185, 190, 191, 194, 195, 211, 212, 213, 215, 216, 217, 218, 219, 220, 221, 222, 223, 225, 226, 227, 228, 230, 231, 232, 233, 236, 259, 262
Citadel of Jerusalem, ix, 99
"Clouds of heaven, The," 24, 64, 65, 70, 71, 88
Code of Hammurabi, 58
Cross, The, xiii, xxv, xxvi, 1, 15, 18, 28, 32, 35, 36, 68, 96, 104, 105, 109, 120, 131, 133, 134, 135, 136, 138, 140, 144, 145, 146, 147, 150, 151, 152, 154, 159, 160, 161, 162, 163, 165, 167, 168, 169, 171, 178, 189, 192, 217, 221, 223, 227, 234, 235, 238, 240, 243, 247, 248
Crucifixion, ix, xi, xv, xxiii, xxv, 1, 2, 3, 15, 20, 37, 53, 55, 56, 60, 81, 93, 95, 105, 107, 109, 110, 116, 117, 120, 123, 127, 128, 129, 130, 131, 132, 133, 134, 135, 140, 145, 148, 149, 150, 153, 154, 156, 159, 160, 165, 166, 169, 171, 179, 181, 185, 208, 210, 211, 212, 227, 230, 233, 237, 238, 239, 244, 247, 250
Crusade(s), 124, 125, 227, 228
Crusader(s), 99, 124, 125, 126, 203, 210, 219, 227, 228, 229, 230
Cyrus Cylinder, The, 58

Damascus, 73, 120
Damascus Gate, 120, 193, 204
The Da Vinci Code, 155, 159
Day of Atonement, 112, 113
Day of Preparation, 1, 2, 5, 27, 87, 144, 167, 178, 180, 187
Day of Resurrection, 132
Dead Sea Scrolls, 108, 166
Delphi, Greece, 129, 130
Demons, 13, 21, 23, 27, 68, 224
Denarius, Denarii, 13, 28

Subject Index   277

David, 7, 14, 15, 16, 70, 98, 99, 104, 113, 120, 142, 180, 208, 219, 249. 258, 262
Disciples, xxv, 1, 4, 5, 13, 14, 15, 20, 21, 22, 23, 25, 26, 30, 63, 68, 71, 72, 73, 88, 109, 133, 134, 135, 137,138, 139, 144, 148, 149, 150, 151, 154, 159, 160, 167, 168, 170, 178, 180, 181, 183, 186, 200, 202, 236, 238, 243, 251, 252
   Andrew, 15
   John, 4, 5, 14, 16, 20, 23, 30, 44, 64, 72, 97, 102, 139, 148, 149, 151, 161, 164, 165, 167, 170, 175, 176, 178, 181, 184, 187, 206, 251
   Judas, 13, 133, 147, 186, 238
   Matthew, 8, 9, 11, 15, 49, 56, 64, 67, 76, 115, 138, 165, 178, 180, 190, 200, 208
   Nathaniel, 23
   Peter,14, 23, 63, 140, 143, 148, 168, 169, 176, 184, 238, 239, 247
   James, 137, 168, 169, 184
   Thomas, 30
Docetism, 147

Earthquake(s), 114, 115, 124, 137, 145, 146, 154, 200
Easter, 121, 122, 177
Eastern (Greek) Orthodox Church, 121, 211, 212
Ecce Homo Arch, ix, 5, 49, 220
Edict of Milan, 124, 215
ἐγώ εἰμι, 65
Egypt, 2, 5, 36, 37, 119, 121, 124, 125, 164, 174, 187, 226, 237, 243
Elders, 2, 5, 8, 10, 11, 12, 27, 45, 62, 68, 84, 87, 135, 138, 152, 179, 243
Empires,
   Byzantine, 124
   Holy Roman, 148
   Ottoman, 98, 193
   Persian, 124
   Roman, 33, 58, 95, 123, 158, 170, 186, 195, 218, 224
   Sasanid, 124
Epicurean(s), 147
Essenes, 108, 153, 154

Evangelical(s), x, 11, 81, 253
Ezekiel, 113, 130

Fatimids, 124, 125
Florus, Gessius, 44

Gabbatha, 40, 41, 51
Galilean(s), 2, 50
Galilee, 19, 30, 94, 109, 137, 138, 150, 152, 154, 160, 217, 245, 247
Garden Tomb, ix, xxv, 100, 102, 107, 115, 118, 119, 120, 128, 173, 185, 190, 191, 192, 193, 194, 195, 196, 197, 198, 199, 200, 202, 203, 204, 205, 206, 207, 208, 209, 210, 211, 216, 230, 235, 236
Garden Tomb Association, The, 118, 193, 205
Gate, 95, 97, 100, 152, 191, 203, 220
Gates,
   Damascus, 120, 193, 204
   Eastern, 111, 112, 203
   Essenes, 100, 193
   Gennath, 100, 194
   Jaffa, 42, 219
   Lion's, 203,
   Nicanor, 112
   St. Stephen's, 203
   Triple 229
German Evangelical Institute for Ancient Studies, 81
German Protestant Institute of Archaeology, 127
Gethsemane, xxiv, 1, 10, 63, 68, 147, 179, 180, 187, 206, 237, 238, 248
Gnostic(ism), 147
God, xii, xiii, 3, 4, 13, 15, 17, 18, 22, 23, 24, 28, 48, 52, 55, 60, 63, 64, 65, 69, 70, 71, 77, 79, 81, 83, 84, 86, 94, 96, 98, 104, 105, 114, 116, 130, 132, 136, 139, 140, 141, 142, 143, 144, 146, 161, 162, 164, 169, 170, 177, 179, 187, 201, 222, 224, 225, 238, 241, 243, 245, 246, 247, 248, 249, 255, 256, 262
Godfather of Israel, The, 72

Subject Index

Golgotha, 20, 42, 53, 54, 55, 93, 96, 97, 98, 100, 101, 102, 103, 104, 105, 106, 107, 110, 111, 114, 116, 117, 118, 120, 121, 122, 124, 127, 128, 129, 130, 131, 133, 135, 139, 146, 153, 161, 163, 166, 169, 172, 186, 187, 189, 191, 192, 193. 208, 212, 215, 216, 217, 218, 220, 221, 223, 225, 227, 233, 237, 240, 243, 245, 248, 257

Golgotha's Cross, 15, 95, 131, 135, 155

Good Friday, xi, xxiii, 109

Gordon's Calvary, ix, 116, 118, 119, 120, 190, 193, 216

Gospel, The (message), 13, 71, 78, 140, 161, 162, 190, 250

Gospel (historical accounts), xxv, 2, 8, 36, 41, 44, 48, 59, 63, 64, 65, 67, 90, 91, 97, 103, 109, 110, 115, 131, 133, 135, 146, 147, 149, 153, 160, 167, 168, 177, 180, 185, 201, 250, 251

Gospel of Barnabas, 133, 146, 147

Gospel of Peter, 145, 179

Giv'at ha-Mivtar, 167

Gratus, Valerius, xxiv

Great Earthquake, 120, 145, 200, 201

Ha Mashiach, 16

Hadith, 134

Hallucinations, 149

Hamlet, 89

Hasmonean Dynasty, 99

Hebrews, book of, 23, 66, 95, 110, 111, 113, 142

Helena, Mother of Constantine, 39, 97, 100, 124, 215, 221, 222, 223, 225, 226, 227, 228, 234, 235

Helena, Queen of Adiabene, 195

Hemis Monastery, 154, 155

Herods, 5
    Agrippa, 166, 244
    Antipas, 3, 34, 48, 51, 52, 94, 99, 151, 186, 240
    Great, The, 20, 25, 37, 38, 41, 43, 44, 46, 237, 239, 262

Hezekiah, 7, 99, 193

High Priest, xxiv, 1, 2, 4, 5, 6, 7, 9, 11, 15, 16, 22, 23, 24, 29, 48, 50, 51, 55, 56, 60, 64, 65, 68, 70, 71, 72, 73, 75, 77, 78, 82, 87, 88, 89, 90, 95, 110, 113, 147, 148, 180, 183, 201, 256

High Priesthood, The, 72, 243

Holy City, 2, 43, 93, 96, 98, 101, 107, 123, 125, 128, 186, 223, 236

Holy Fire, 121

Holy One, The, 18, 69

Holy Spirit, xii, 162, 246, 247, 248, 251

Holy Week, 121, 226

House of the Ashes, 113

India, 133, 154, 155, 157, 158, 189,

Irregularity, Irregularities, xi, xxiii, xxiv, 71, 72, 72, 73, 74, 75, 76, 77, 78, 79, 80, 91

Īsä, Son of a Virgin, 158

Isaac, 28, 52, 258

Israel Antiquities Authority, 44, 190, 213

Israel Law Review Association, 59

Italy, 119, 226, 228

Itinerarium Sacrae Scripturae, 128

Jacob, 7, 28, 52

Jehovah, 22, 69; see YHWH

Jeremiah, 64, 182, 183, 202, 203, 249

Jeremiah's Grotto, 117, 118, 119, 196

Jericho, 94

Jerusalem, ix, 2, 3, 4, 6, 9, 13, 14, 15, 16, 17, 19, 20, 24, 28, 29, 30, 31, 38, 41, 42, 43, 44, 45, 46, 49, 56, 70, 72, 73, 81, 86, 90, 95, 96, 97, 98, 99, 100, 102, 104, 105, 106, 110, 111, 112, 113, 114, 115, 116, 117, 118, 119, 120, 121, 123, 124, 125, 126, 127, 128, 129, 130, 135, 140, 145, 149, 150, 153, 154, 156, 160, 163, 164, 167, 168, 169, 170, 173, 180, 186, 187, 188, 190, 191, 192, 193, 195, 197, 198, 201, 203, 204, 205, 206, 207, 208, 211, 212, 215, 216, 217, 218, 219, 220, 221, 222, 223, 225, 226, 227, 228, 229, 230, 231, 232, 234, 235, 238, 239, 240, 245, 247, 249, 258, 259, 262

Subject Index 279

Jerusalem Talmud, 144
Jesus, ix, x, xi, xiii, xv, xxiii, xxiv, xxv, xxvi, 1–42, 44–68, 70–81, 85–91, 93–101, 103, 104, 105–12, 114, 115, 116, 118, 120, 121, 123, 124, 125, 127–73, 175–95, 200, 201, 203, 204, 205, 206, 208, 210, 211, 212, 215–21, 224, 227–31, 233–52, 256, 259, 260
Jesus,
    The Good Shepherd, 14, 65
    "I AM" God, The, 30, 48, 65
    King of the Jews, 13, 19, 24, 25, 34, 35, 54, 56, 70, 245, 247
    Lord of Glory, xxiv
    Messiah, xii, 2, 6, 13, 14, 15, 16, 19, 21, 22, 35, 70, 113, 132, 153, 158, 159, 160, 172, 181, 189, 250, 251
    Nazarene, The, xxv, 12, 16 48, 51
    Savior, xii, xiv, 3, 6, 9, 16, 31, 33, 55, 70, 72, 73, 90, 107, 131, 133, 134, 140, 147, 181, 184, 201, 208, 213, 237, 238, 251, 252, 253
    Son of the Blessed, 10, 70, 88
    Son of David, 14, 15
    Son of God, xii, 5, 6, 10, 13, 14, 15, 18, 22, 23, 32, 50, 64, 70, 88, 115, 134, 137, 141, 142, 181, 201, 236, 245, 257, 251
    Son of the Living God, 14
    Son of Man, 24, 27, 56, 64, 65, 70, 88, 135, 137, 138, 208, 246, 251
    Suffering Savior, The, 16, 55
Jewish Encyclopedia, 69, 260
Jewish, ix, x, xi, xxiii, xxiv, xxv, 1, 2, 3, 4, 5, 10, 12, 14, 15, 16, 19, 22, 23, 24, 25, 26, 27, 29, 30, 31, 32, 34, 41, 45, 46, 48, 50, 51, 52, 53, 54, 55, 58, 59, 60, 61, 62, 63, 64, 65, 66, 67, 69, 70, 72, 73, 75, 76, 77, 79, 81, 83, 86, 87, 89, 90, 94, 96, 102, 109, 118, 124, 127, 132, 148, 150, 151, 153, 154, 155, 159, 160, 163, 164, 166, 167, 169, 170, 175, 176, 177, 178, 179, 180, 181, 187, 192, 195, 196, 202, 208, 210, 218, 232, 233, 239, 240, 247, 256, 258

John the Baptist, 126, 246
Jordan,
    Desert, 227
    Nation, 126, 177, 206, 261
    River, 94, 246
    Valley, 207
Joseph of Arimathea, xi, xxiii, 21, 121, 147, 148, 153, 165, 166, 167, 170, 171, 173, 176, 178, 181, 185, 187, 188, 190, 195, 204, 205, 211, 212, 221, 223, 260
Joudeh al-Goudia (al-Ghodayya) Family, 22, 123
Judea, xxiv, 11, 17, 19, 30, 32, 37, 40, 42, 43, 44, 52, 72, 93, 94, 109, 120, 154, 166, 218, 247
Judaism, 30, 64, 67, 129, 130, 132, 174

Kangaroo Court, 63, 90, 91
Kashmir, 158, 189
Killing Field, 93, 96, 103, 104, 106, 146, 169, 240
Killing Squad, 133, 163
Kishle, 44
Knights Templar, 156
Kranion, 101; see Calvary

Lazarus, 13, 201
Law,
    Civil, 17, 35, 36, 86, 144
    Halakha, 62, 63
    International, 80, 90, 91
    Jewish, 5, 23, 50, 58, 61, 62, 63, 64, 67, 73, 86, 170, 175, 176, 202
    Levirate marriage, 82, 257
    Levitical, 58, 97
    Mishnaic, 64, 73, 74, 75, 76, 78, 79, 81, 83, 84, 85, 86, 90
    Mosaic, 4, 5, 7, 12, 21, 27, 30, 58, 59, 61, 64, 66, 67, 74, 75, 77, 81, 84, 86, 113, 141, 142
    Modern, 32, 35, 36, 58, 241, 256
    Roman, 33, 34, 35, 36, 37, 48, 54, 93, 94, 97, 151, 164, 170
    Sadducean, 81, 90
    Two or Three Witnesses, 66, 142
Lithostrotos, 38, 39, 40, 41, 44, 46
London, xxiv, 55, 103, 196

Subject Index

Mamluks, 99, 125
Man of a Lie, 108
Martha, sister of Mary, 13, 23
Martin Luther, 125
Mary,
    the Egyptian, 227
    Magdalene, 109, 137, 147, 148, 157, 158, 159, 184, 189, 231
    mother of James and Joseph, 137, 184
    mother of Jesus, 116, 132, 147
    sister of Martha, 13
    of the Talpiot Tomb, 190
Masada, 155, 156
Merciful One, The, 69, 144
Messianic Psalm, 70
Middle East, 6, 116, 188,
Miles Gloriosus, 95
Mishnah, ix, 5, 8, 12, 60, 61, 66, 69, 71, 72, 73, 74, 75, 76, 77, 81, 82, 83, 84, 85, 86, 90, 91, 111, 114, 118, 160, 166, 176, 232, 256, 258
Molech, 82
Monument of the Fuller, 100
Moses, 30, 58, 66, 77, 81, 96, 111, 113, 142, 186, 208, 251
Mount,
    Calvary, 102, 103
    Carmel, 208
    Hor, 208
    Moab, 207
    Moriah, 258
    Nebo, 208
    Olives, 11, 38, 113, 114, 116, 121, 154, 208, 222, 232, 233, 262
    Samaritan, 120
    Sion, 120
    Temple, 12, 13, 20, 61, 62, 99, 111, 114, 130, 229, 233
    Transfiguration, 186
Muhammad, 132, 134, 158, 254
Muristan, 126, 216, 219
Muslim(s), ix, 99, 118, 123, 124, 125, 132, 133, 134, 189, 192, 258, 259

Nablus Road, 120, 192, 197
"Navel of the World, The," 129
New Jerusalem, 130, 225
New Testament, ix, xii, xiii, 14, 15, 16, 26, 29, 38, 44, 46, 61, 81, 101, 108, 109, 128, 133, 141, 143, 156, 157, 159, 162, 164, 182, 190, 201, 206, 210, 220, 250
Nicene Creed, The, 169, 241
Nicodemus, xi, xxiii, 170, 171, 172, 175, 176, 177, 178, 184
"No Friend of Caesar," 51, 52, 179, 181
Nuseibeh Family, The, 122, 123, 259

Old City, 97, 98, 100, 127, 187, 192, 216, 219, 234, 262
Old Jerusalem, 46, 121, 127, 130
Old Street Underground Station, 103
Old Testament, xxvi, 16, 82, 83, 105, 108, 113, 156, 244, 246, 256
Omphalos, 129
Ottoman Empire/Period, 44, 98, 125, 193
Oxyrhynchus Papyri, 36, 37

Palestine, 116, 124, 125, 144, 167, 192, 195, 222, 225, 226, 228
Palestine Exploration Society, 116, 117
Palm Sunday, 122
Patibulum, 172
Passion, 13, 25, 50, 51, 55, 93, 101, 144, 186, 224, 234,
Passover, 1, 2, 5, 13, 18, 32, 64, 93, 144, 156, 170, 180, 212, 232, 239, 240
The Passover Plot, 156
Patricians, 35
Paul, The Apostle, 7, 23, 37, 66, 139, 140, 141, 148, 149, 153, 161, 168, 269, 249
Pavement, The Stone, 37, 38, 39, 40, 51
Pentateuch, 81, 95
Period,
    Ayyubid, 125
    Byzantine, 124, 204, 229
    Crusader, 124, 203, 229
    First Muslim, 124
    First Temple, 197
    Heriodian, 196, 231
    Iron Age, 205
    Iron Age B, 205
    Julio-Claudian, 34
    Mamluk 125

Subject Index   281

Ottoman, 44, 125
Roman, 123, 233
Second Temple, 12, 61, 99, 190, 196, 205
Usha, 86
Pesher, 108, 109
Pharisees, 2, 26, 27, 68, 80, 90, 96, 147, 178
Pilate, Pontius, ix, xi, xv, xxiii, xxiv, xxv, 3, 4, 11, 12, 13, 15, 16, 17, 18, 21, 25, 26, 27. 29, 30, 31, 32, 33, 34, 35, 36, 38, 39, 40, 41, 43, 44, 45, 46, 47, 48, 49, 50, 51, 52. 53, 54, 55, 56, 57, 68, 89. 94, 131, 138, 139, 144, 147, 151, 152, 166, 167, 169, 170, 178, 179, 180, 186, 188, 239, 240, 241, 243, 255
"Place of the Skull," 93, 96, 97, 102,103, 103, 104, 245
Plebians, 35
Poland, Ghettos of, 58, 262
Pool of,
  Bethesda, 22
  Siloam, 100, 193
Pope,
  Benedict, 253
  Nicholas IV, 125
  Urban II, 111
"Power, the right hand of," 10, 24, 64, 65, 70, 71, 88, 142, 241, 256
Praetorian Guard, 37
Praetorium, 16, 31, 37, 38, 39, 40, 41, 44, 45, 46, 51, 56, 57, 80, 240
Prefect, xxiv, xxv, 12, 15, 33, 34, 37, 43, 44, 46, 48, 50, 51, 52, 94, 96, 179, 239
Priory of Sion, 157
Procula, 46
Protestant(s), ix, x, 116, 117, 127, 128, 235, 253

Quaker Movement, 103
Quorum, 8, 11, 62, 89
Qur'an, 133, 134

Rabbi,
  Akiva, 234
  Ashi, 181
  Ben Zakkai, 75
  Ishmael ben Jose, 72
  Joshua ben Korcha, 69
  Judah Ha-Nasi, 84, 86
  Yehuda, 161,
  Samuel bar Naḥmani, 84
  Shimon, 84
  Yosei, 61
Ramparts Wall, 98, 257
Red Heifer, 111, 113, 114, 258
Reflections on Palestine, 116
Roman,
  Cohort, 34, 37, 41, 42, 43, 44
  Empire, 33, 58, 95, 123, 158, 170, 187, 195, 215, 224
  Flagrum, 49
  Governor, xxiv, 12, 26, 28, 33, 34, 36, 37, 38, 39, 41, 47, 56, 94, 170, 180, 239
  Imperial Guard, 38
  Legion, 41
  Senate, 94
  Soldiers, 4, 8, 9, 17, 25, 36, 37, 41, 42. 44, 45, 47, 54, 55, 70, 95, 97, 131, 133, 137, 147, 151, 161, 163, 179, 180, 182, 183, 184, 240, 243, 244, 247
Roman Catholic Church, 121, 159, 165, 221, 253
Roman Emperor(s), 51
  Augustus, 35, 43, 218
  Tiberius, 43
  Titus Flavius, 123, 168, 205
  Hadrian, 123, 126
  Constantine the Great, 129
  Constantine IX Monomachos, 125
  Julian, 223
  Justinian, 170
  Theodosius II, 203
Roman & Greek Gods,
  Aphrodite, Greek Goddess of Love, 97
  Jupiter (Venus), Rome's supreme god, 97, 124, 215, 218, 233
  Jupiter Capitolinus, Aelia Capitolina named after him, 124
  Apollo, Greek God of the Sun, 129

Subject Index

Roman Temples,
    Aphrodite, 97
    Jupiter (Venus, Juno, Minerva), 97, 124, 215, 218
    Jupiter Capitolinus, 110
Rome, xxiv, 5, 16, 17, 35, 37, 39, 51, 52, 94, 95, 105, 106, 147, 173, 187, 218, 222, 235, 262
Russian Orthodox Church, 220

Sabbath, 13, 21, 22, 26, 27, 63, 64, 68, 82, 96, 140, 172, 178, 180, 184, 191, 205
Sadducees, Saduccean, 26, 68, 80, 81, 90
Samaria, 14, 15, 94, 166
Saladin, 122, 125
Satan, 23, 245, 247
Sanhedrin, xi, xiv, xxiii, xxiv, 1, 2, 3, 4, 5, 6, 8, 9, 10, 11, 12, 13, 16, 17, 19, 21, 24, 26, 27, 29, 32, 47, 55, 59, 60, 61, 62, 63, 64, 66, 68, 69, 70, 71, 72, 73, 74, 75, 76, 77, 78, 79, 80, 81, 82, 85,86,87, 89, 90, 91, 92, 112, 144, 148, 163, 166, 169, 170, 171, 172, 181, 196, 239, 255, 256, 260
    Council, The, 2, 4, 9, 10, 11, 12, 15, 21, 22, 31, 32, 37, 59, 64, 68, 71, 74, 76, 78, 87, 88, 90, 166, 169
Supreme Court of Israel, 59
Saul of Tarsus, 73; see Paul
Scala Sancta, 39
Scribes, 5, 8, 10, 11, 12, 26, 27, 28, 29, 68, 87, 135, 179
Sea of Galilee, 94, 125
Secrets of Golgotha, 110, 114
Sedition, 28, 32
Seljuk Turks, 125
Solomon, 16, 99, 258
Sidon, 94
Simeon, 163
Simon of Cyrene, 133
Simon the Just, 195
Simon the Leper, 13
Simon Peter, 15, 168; see Peter
Six-Day War, 126
"Skull," The, 102, 118, 119, 138
"Skull Hill," 102, 117

Srinagar, India, 154, 189
Status Quo Agreement, 121, 122, 211
Stephen, 96, 187, 203, 210
Stipes, 172
Stoic Philosophers, 147
Suleiman the Magnificent, 98, 99, 125, 126, 193
Summa Theologica, 58
Supreme Court of Israel, 59
Sweat, 105, 175
Sweat, Bloody, 1
Swoon Theory, 133, 151, 152, 153, 159
Sychar of Samaria, 94
Synoptics, The, 12, 26, 176, 208
Syria, 119, 125, 218, 226

Tamar, 7
Teacher of Righteousness, 108
Temple,
    Ceremonies and Rituals, 111
    Chamber of Hewn Stone, 11, 12, 88, 89
    Coffers/Treasury, 3, 258
    Corruption, 3, 16, 20, 31
    Court of the Gentiles, 61, 62
    Curtain, 104, 115, 145
    Rebuilding Herod's Temple took 46 years, 20
    Jesus teaching in, 5, 55, 68, 88
    Magnificence, 20, 21, 43
    Officials, 37
    Outer Altar, 112, 113, 114
    Police, 10, 52, 149, 152, 179, 180, 181, 182, 183, 184, 238
    Precincts, 42, 60, 61, 87, 100, 111, 179
    Rebuild in Three Days, 10, 13, 16, 19, 20, 21, 79, 88
Ten Commandments, 52
Tent Work in Palestine, 117
Tesserae, 38, 39
Tetragrammaton, The, 22, 69, 256
Texts,
    Biblical, ix, 144
    Christian, ix
    Greek, 253
    Jewish, ix
    Roman, ix

The DaVinci Code, 109
"The Immovable Ladder," 122
Third Day, The, 15, 21, 57, 131, 135, 137, 140, 141, 145, 150, 151, 168, 169, 178, 180, 181, 183, 184, 241
Titulus, 25
Tomb,
    Kokhim-type, 172, 173, 190, 196, 230, 231
    Arcosolium-type, 172, 173, 188
Tomb of David, 120
Torah, 83
Tosefta, 81, 260
Towers,
    David, 44, 45
    Hippicus, 100, 193, 194
Trial and Death of Jesus, The, 71, 90
Tribe of Judah, The, 113
Tribute to Caesar, 19, 28, 29
Triumphal Entry, 13, 68
"True Cross," The, 124, 223, 226, 227, 234, 235
Twelve Tablets, 35
Tyropoean Valley, 12, 100

UNESCO World Heritage Site, 98

Valleys,
    Cheesemongers, 99
    Hinnom, 208
    Jezreel, 208
    Jordan, 207
    Kashmir, 189
    Kidron, 100, 111, 114, 194, 208
    Tyropoean, 12, 100
Via Dolorosa, ix, 42, 46, 55, 121, 133, 186, 219, 220, 243, 244

Walls of Jerusalem, The, 98, 115, 125, 187, 193
Warren's Shaft, 116
Week Days,
    Sunday, 142, 147, 176, 177, 178, 200
    Wednesday, 109
    Thursday, 4, 6, 11, 87
    Friday, xi, xxiii, xxv, 4, 6, 11, 87, 89, 109, 204, 239, 249
    Shabbat, 122, 147, 176, 177, 178
Western World, xii, 36
Wicked Priest, 108, 109, 157
Wilson's Arch, 12, 116
Witnesses, False or Disqualified, 3, 5, 6, 10, 12, 19, 21, 60, 64, 66, 67, 68, 74, 75, 76, 77, 78, 79, 84, 85, 88, 91, 256
Word of God, 142, 144
World Religions,
    Buddhism, 134
    Christianity, ix, xii, 124, 129, 130, 132, 134, 212, 215, 221, 225, 241
    Confucianism, 134
    Hinduism, 134
    Islam, 129, 130, 132, 134, 154, 259
    Jainism, 134
    Judaism, 30, 64, 67, 129, 130, 132, 175
    Shintoism, 134
    Sikhism, 134
    Taoism, 134

Xystos, 12

Yahweh, 22, 52, 60, 69; see YHWH
Yehohanan, 166, 167
Yeshua ben Ya'akob ben Gennesareth, 156
YHWH, 7, 22, 27, 52, 69, 70, 256
Yuz Asaf, 154

Zion, 40, 98

www.ingramcontent.com/pod-product-compliance
Lightning Source LLC
Chambersburg PA
CBHW050337230426
43663CB00010B/1891